Napoleon Hill was born in 1883 in Wise Country, Virginia and died in 1970 after a long and successful career as a consultant to business leaders, lecturer and author. *Think and Grow Rich* is the all-time bestseller in its field whose success made Hill a millionaire in his own right. Hill established the Napoleon Hill Foundation, a non-profit educational institution whose mission is to promote his philosophy of leadership, self-motivation and individual achievement.

Dr Arthur R. Pell holds B.A., M.A. and Ph.D. degrees and a professional diploma in Personnel Psychology and is a nationally known author, lecturer and consultant in human resources management. He has worked with companies, government agencies, universities and not-for-profit organisations in the areas of employment, training, employee counselling, motivation and communication.

Dr Pell is the author of numerous articles, audiocassette training programmes and 50 books on management, personnel, career planning and human relations, including *The Supervisor's Infobank: 1000 Quick Answers to Your Toughest Problems* and *The Complete Idiot's Guide to Managing People*, which has sold over 125,000 copies. He is a frequent commentator on radio and television and has conducted seminars and workshops on various aspects of human resources management that have been attended by over 250,000 people throughout the United States and Canada.

THINK AND GROW RICH

NAPOLEON HILL

Revised and expanded by

Dr Arthur R. Pell

Vermilion

LONDON

10

First published in the United Kingdom in 2004 by Vermilion,
an imprint of Ebury Press
Random House UK Ltd
Random House
20 Vauxhall Bridge Road
London SW1V 2SA

Random House Australia (Pty) Limited
20 Alfred Street, Milsons Point, Sydney
New South Wales 2061, Australia

Random House New Zealand Limited
18 Poland Road, Glenfield
Auckland 10, New Zealand

Random House (Pty) Limited
Isle of Houghton, Corner of Boundary Road & Carse O'Gowrie,
Houghton 2198, South Africa

Random House Publishers India Private Limited
301 World Trade Tower, Hotel Intercontinental Grand Complex,
Barakhamba Lane, New Delhi 110 001, India

Random House UK Limited Reg.No. 9 54009
www.randomhouse.co.uk

Papers used by Vermilion are natural, recyclable products
made from wood grown in sustainable forests.

Mixed Sources
Product group from well-managed
forests and other controlled sources
www.fsc.org   Cert no. TT-COC-2139
© 1996 Forest Stewardship Council
FSC

A CIP catalogue record for this book is available from the British Library.

ISBN: 9780091900212

Typeset by SX Composing DTP, Rayleigh, Essex

Printed and bound in Great Britain by
Cox & Wyman Ltd, Reading, Berkshire

CONTENTS

AUTHOR'S PREFACE TO ORIGINAL EDITION

Every chapter of this book mentions the money-making secret that has made fortunes for more than 500 exceedingly wealthy people whom I have carefully analysed over a long period of years.

The secret was brought to my attention more than a quarter of a century ago by Andrew Carnegie. The canny, lovable old Scotsman carelessly tossed it into my mind when I was but a boy. Then he sat back in his chair, with a merry twinkle in his eyes, and watched carefully to see if I had brains enough to understand the full significance of what he had said to me.

When he saw that I had grasped the idea, he asked if I would be willing to spend 20 years or more preparing myself to take it to the world, to men and women who, without the secret, might go through life as failures. I said I would, and with Mr Carnegie's cooperation, I have kept my promise.

This book contains the secret, which has been put to a practical test by thousands of people from almost every walk of life. It was Mr Carnegie's idea that the magic formula, which gave him a stupendous fortune, ought to be placed within reach of people who do not have time to investigate how people make money. He hoped that I might test and demonstrate the soundness of the formula through the experience of men and women in every calling. He believed the formula should be taught in all schools and colleges, and expressed the opinion that if it were properly taught it would so revolutionise the entire educational system that the time spent in school could be reduced to less than half.

His experience with Charles M. Schwab (see page 58), and other young men of Mr Schwab's type, convinced Mr Carnegie that much of what is taught in schools is of no value whatsoever in connection with the business of earning a living or accumulating riches. He arrived at this decision having taken into his business one young man after another, many with little schooling, and developed in them rare leadership by coaching them in the use of this formula. Moreover, his coaching made fortunes for every one of them who followed his instructions.

In the chapter on Faith, you will read the astounding story of how the formula was applied to the organisation of the giant United States Steel Corporation. It was conceived and carried out by one of the young men through whom Mr Carnegie proved that his formula will work for all who are ready for it. This single application of the secret by that young man – Charles M. Schwab – made him a huge fortune in both money and *opportunity*. Roughly speaking, this particular application of the formula was worth 600 million dollars.

These facts – and they are facts well known to almost everyone who knew Mr Carnegie – give you a fair idea of what the reading of this book may bring to you, provided you *know what you want*.

Even before it had undergone 20 years of practical testing, the secret was passed on to more than 100,000 men and women who have used it for their personal benefit, as Mr Carnegie planned that they should. Some have made fortunes with it. Others have used it successfully in creating harmony in their homes.

The secret to which I refer has been mentioned no fewer than a hundred times throughout this book. It has not been directly named, for it seems to work more successfully when it is merely uncovered and left in sight, where *those who are ready* and *searching for it* may pick it up. That is why Mr Carnegie tossed it to me so quietly, without giving me its specific name.

If you are *ready* to put it to use, you will recognise this secret at least once in every chapter. I wish I could tell you how you will know if you are ready, but that would deprive you of much of the benefit you will receive when you make the discovery in your own way.

While this book was being written, my own son, who was then finishing the last year of his college work, picked up the manuscript of Chapter 2, read it, and discovered the secret for himself. He used the information so effectively that he went directly into a responsible position at a starting salary greater than the average man ever earns. His story has been briefly described in Chapter 2. When you read it, perhaps you will dismiss any feeling you may have had, at the beginning of the book, that it promised too much. And, too, if you have ever been discouraged, if you have had difficulties to surmount which took the very soul out of you, if you have tried and failed, if you were ever handicapped by illness or physical affliction, this story of my son's discovery and use of the Carnegie formula may prove to be the oasis in the Desert of Lost Hope, for which you have been searching.

This secret was extensively used by President Woodrow Wilson, during World War I. It was passed on to every soldier who fought in the war, carefully wrapped in the training received before going to the front. President Wilson told me it was a strong factor in raising the funds needed for the war.

Early in the 20th century, Manuel L. Quezon (then Resident Commissioner of the Philippine Islands), was inspired by the secret to gain freedom for his people, and went on to lead them as its first president.

A peculiar thing about this secret is that those who acquire it and use it find themselves literally swept on to success with but little effort, and they never again submit to failure! If you doubt this, study the names and records of those who have used it, wherever they have been mentioned, and be convinced.

There is no such thing as SOMETHING FOR NOTHING!

The secret to which I refer cannot be had without a price, although the price is far less than its value. Those who are not intentionally searching for it cannot have it at any price. It cannot be given away; it cannot be purchased for money because it comes in two parts. One part is already in possession of those who are ready for it.

The secret serves equally well all who are ready for it. Education has nothing to do with it. Long before I was born, the secret had found its way into the possession of Thomas A. Edison, and he used it so intelligently that he became the world's leading inventor, although he had but three months of schooling.

The secret was passed on to a business associate of Mr Edison. He used it so effectively that, although he was then making only $12,000 a year, he accumulated a great fortune, and retired from active business while still a young man. You will find his story at the beginning of the first chapter. It should convince you that riches are not beyond your reach, that you can still be what you wish to be, that money, fame, recognition and happiness can be had by all who are ready and determined to have these blessings.

How do I know these things? You should have the answer

before you finish this book. You may find it in the very first chapter, or on the last page.

While I was performing the 20-year task of research, which I had undertaken at Mr Carnegie's request, I analysed hundreds of well-known men, many of whom admitted that they had accumulated their vast fortunes through the aid of the Carnegie secret. Among these men were:

Henry Ford
Theodore Roosevelt
William Wrigley
John Wanamaker
James J. Hill
Wilbur Wright
William Jennings Bryan
Woodrow Wilson
William Howard Taft
Elbert H. Gary
King Gillette
Alexander Graham Bell
John D. Rockefeller
Thomas A. Edison
F. W. Woolworth
Clarence Darrow

These names represent but a small fraction of the hundreds of well-known Americans whose achievements, financially and otherwise, prove that those who understand and apply the Carnegie secret reach high stations in life. All the people I have known who have been inspired to use the secret have achieved noteworthy success in their chosen calling. I have never known any person to distinguish himself, or to accumulate riches of any consequence, without possession of the secret. From these two facts I draw the conclusion that the secret is more important, as a part of the knowledge essential for self-determination, than anything one receives through what is popularly known as 'education'.

What is *education*, anyway? As far as schooling is concerned, many of these men had very little. John Wanamaker once told me that what little schooling he had he acquired in very much the same manner as a locomotive takes on water, by 'scooping it up as it runs'. Henry Ford never reached high school, let alone college. I am not attempting to minimise the value of schooling, but I am trying to express my earnest belief that those who master and apply the secret will reach high stations, accumulate riches, and bargain with life on their own terms, even if their schooling has been meagre.

Somewhere, as you read, the secret to which I refer will jump from the page and stand boldly before you, *if you are ready for it*! When it appears, you will recognise it. Whether you receive the sign in the first or the last chapter, stop for a moment when it presents itself and raise your glass to toast your epiphany.

Chapter 1 tells the story of my very dear friend who has generously acknowledged having seen the mystic sign, and whose business achievements are evidence enough that he turned down a glass. As you read his story, and the others, remember that they deal with the important problems of life, such as all people experience, the problems arising from one's endeavour to earn a living, to find hope, courage, contentment and peace of mind; to accumulate riches and to enjoy freedom of body and spirit.

Remember, too, as you go through the book that it deals with facts and not with fiction. Its purpose is to convey a great universal truth through which all who are *ready* may learn, not only *what to do* but also *how to do it*! and receive *the needed stimulus to make a start*.

As a final word of preparation, may I offer one brief suggestion that may provide a clue to recognising the Carnegie secret. It is this – *all achievement, all earned riches, have their beginning in an idea*! If you are ready for the secret, you already possess one half of it; therefore you will readily recognise the other half the moment it reaches your mind.

Napoleon Hill, 1937

PREFACE TO
CURRENT EDITION

When *Think and Grow Rich* was published in 1937, it was acclaimed as one of the great inspirational books of its time. Together with Dale Carnegie's *How to Win Friends and Influence People* and Norman Vincent Peale's *The Power of Positive Thinking,* it became essential reading for men and women who pursued success in their lives and careers.

Over 15 million copies of this book have been sold. It became a roadmap for many millions of people to escape the poverty of the Depression era and gain prosperity for themselves, their families and, in many cases, their employees.

Who was Napoleon Hill and what was the source of his philosophy? Napoleon Hill was born into a poor family in 1883 in a one-room cabin in rural Virginia. He was orphaned at the age of 12 and brought up by relatives. Overcoming poverty and his rebellious nature, he struggled to obtain an education and developed into one of the pragmatic geniuses of his time.

Aged 13, he started his writing career as a stringer for small-town newspapers – a reporter who wrote items and stories about happenings in his area for pennies a line. Perhaps because of his own struggle to overcome poverty, he became obsessed with why people fail to achieve true financial success and happiness in their lives.

To earn a living he chose to pursue careers in both law and journalism. His early career as a reporter helped finance his way through law school. His big break came when he was given an assignment to write a series of success stories of famous men.

One of the men he interviewed for this series was Andrew Carnegie, the world-renowned steel magnate. Mr Carnegie was so impressed by the young journalist that he gave him a commission that would dominate the next 25 years of Hill's life. The project was to interview over 500 millionaires to find a success formula that could be used by the average person.

The interviewees included the greatest and wealthiest men of the era. Among them were Thomas Edison, Alexander Graham Bell, Henry Ford, Charles M. Schwab, Theodore Roosevelt, William Wrigley Jr, John Wanamaker, William Jennings Bryan, George Eastman, Woodrow Wilson, William H. Taft, John D. Rockefeller, F. W. Woolworth, and many others who are not as well known today. During this period Andrew Carnegie became Hill's mentor, helping Hill formulate a philosophy of success, drawing on the thoughts and experience of the people who were interviewed.

The success of *Think and Grow Rich* led to a long career as consultant to business leaders, lecturer and writer of several more books, and made Hill a millionaire in his own right.

Napoleon Hill died in November 1970 after a long and successful career. His work stands as a guidepost to individual achievement and has influenced readers for almost 70 years.

Updating a classic work is a monumental task. The basic philosophy of the writer cannot be changed. It must always be Napoleon Hill's book, not mine. I approached it in the same way an art restorer looks at a classic painting that is being refurbished. I carefully studied the text and deleted stories and anecdotes that, although meaningful to the reader of the 1930s, have little significance to the reader of the 21st century. I replaced them with examples and illustrations of men and women who, in their careers in recent times, exemplify the principles Napoleon Hill promulgated.

In the following chapters you will learn these principles. In addition to reading the success stories of the people Hill studied for the original book, you will meet some of the top achievers of our time, such as Bill Gates, Mary Kay Ash, Arnold Schwarzenegger, Ray Kroc, Michael Jordan and others.

Napoleon Hill's proven steps to riches are as valid for today's reader as they were for his contemporaries. All who read, understand and apply this philosophy will be better prepared to attract and enjoy these higher standards of living that always have been and always will be denied to all except those who are ready for them.

Be prepared, therefore, when you actively follow Napoleon Hill's precepts to make major changes in your approach to life. It will pay off in enabling you to enjoy a life of harmony and understanding, as well as setting the stage for you to join the ranks of wealthy people.

Dr Arthur R. Pell, 2004

CHAPTER 1

THE POWER OF THOUGHT

The Man Who 'Thought' his Way into Partnership with Thomas A. Edison

Truly, 'thoughts are things', and powerful things at that, when mixed with purpose, persistence and a *burning desire* for their translation into riches or other material objects.

Edwin C. Barnes discovered how true it is that men really do *think and grow rich*. His discovery did not come about at one sitting. It came little by little, beginning with a *burning desire* to become a business associate of the great Thomas Edison.

One of the chief characteristics of Barnes' desire was that it was definite. He wanted to work *with* Edison, not *for* him. Observe, carefully, the description of how he went about translating his *desire* into reality, and you will have a better understanding of the 13 principles which lead to riches.

When this desire, or impulse of thought, first flashed into his mind he was in no position to act upon it. Two difficulties stood in his way. He did not know Mr Edison, and he did not have enough money to pay his rail fare to Orange, New Jersey. These difficulties were sufficient to have discouraged the majority of people from making any attempt to carry out the desire. But his was no ordinary desire! He was so determined to find a way to carry out his desire that he finally decided to travel by 'blind baggage', rather than be defeated. (To the uninitiated, this means that he went to East Orange on a freight train.)

He presented himself at Mr Edison's laboratory, and announced he had come to go into business with the inventor. In speaking of the first meeting between them, years later, Mr Edison said, 'He stood there before me, looking like an ordinary tramp, but there was something in the expression of his face which conveyed the impression that he was determined to get what he had come after. I had learned, from years of experience with men, that when a man really *desires* a thing so deeply that he is willing to stake his entire future on a single turn of the wheel in order to get it, he is sure to win. I gave him the opportunity he asked for, because I saw he had made up his mind to stand by until he succeeded. Subsequent events proved that no mistake was made.'

Just what young Barnes said to Mr Edison on that occasion was far less important than what he thought. Edison himself said so! It could not have been the young man's appearance that got him his start in the Edison office, for that was definitely against him. It was what he *thought* that counted.

If the significance of this statement could be conveyed to every person who reads it, there would be no need for the remainder of this book.

Barnes did not get his partnership with Edison on his first interview. He did get a chance to work in the Edison offices, at a very nominal wage, doing work that was unimportant to Edison, but most important to Barnes. It gave him an opportunity to display his 'merchandise' where his intended 'partner' could see it.

Months went by. Apparently nothing happened to bring the coveted goal, which Barnes had set up in his mind as his *definite major purpose*. But something important was happening in Barnes' mind. He was constantly intensifying his desire to become the business associate of Edison.

Psychologists have correctly said, 'When one is truly ready for a thing, it puts in its appearance.' Barnes was ready for a business association with Edison; moreover, he was determined to remain ready until he got that which he was seeking.

He did not say to himself, 'Ah well, what's the use? I guess I'll change my mind and try for a salesman's job.' But he did say, 'I came here to go into business with Edison, and I'll accomplish this end if it takes the remainder of my life.' He meant it! What a different story people would have to tell if only they would adopt a *definite purpose*, and stand by that purpose until it had time to become an all-consuming obsession!

Maybe young Barnes did not know it at the time, but his bulldog determination, his persistence with a single *desire*, was destined to mow down all opposition and bring him the opportunity he was seeking.

When the opportunity came, it appeared in a different form, and from a different direction than Barnes had expected. That is one of the tricks of opportunity. It has a sly habit of slipping in by the back door, and often comes disguised in the form of misfortune or temporary defeat. Perhaps this is why so many fail to recognise opportunity.

Mr Edison had just perfected a new office device, known at that time as the Edison Dictating Machine (later called the Ediphone). His salesmen were not enthusiastic over the machine. They did not believe it could be sold without great effort. Barnes saw his opportunity. It had crawled in quietly, hidden in a queer-looking machine that interested no one but Barnes and the inventor.

Barnes knew he could sell the Edison Dictating Machine. He suggested this to Edison and promptly got his chance. He did sell the machine. In fact, he sold it so successfully that Edison gave him a contract to distribute and market it all over the nation. Out of that business association grew the slogan, 'Made by Edison and installed by Barnes'. This business alliance made Barnes rich in money, but he accomplished something infinitely greater: he proved that one really may 'Think and Grow Rich'.

How much actual cash that original *desire* of Barnes was worth to him, I have no way of knowing. Perhaps it brought him two or three million dollars. Whatever the amount, it becomes insignificant when compared with the greater asset he acquired, the definite knowledge that an intangible impulse of thought can be transmuted into its physical counterpart by the application of known principles.

Barnes literally thought himself into a partnership with the great Edison! He thought himself into a fortune. He had nothing to start with, except the capacity to know what he wanted, and the determination to stand by that desire until he realised it.

He had no money to begin with. He had but little education. He had no influence. But he did have initiative, faith and the will to win. With these intangible forces he made himself number one man with the greatest inventor who ever lived.

Now, let us look at a different situation, and study a man who had plenty of tangible evidence of riches, but lost it because he stopped three feet short of the goal he was seeking.

Three Feet from Gold

One of the most common causes of failure is the habit of quitting when one is overtaken by temporary defeat. Every person is guilty of this mistake at one time or another.

R. U. Darby, who later became one of the most successful insurance salesmen in the country, tells the story of his uncle, who was caught by the 'gold fever' in the gold-rush days, and went west to dig and grow rich. He had never heard the saying that more gold has been mined from the brains of men than has ever been taken from the earth. He staked a claim and went to work with pick and shovel. The going was hard, but his lust for gold was definite.

After weeks of labour, he was rewarded by the discovery of the shining ore. He needed machinery to bring the ore to the surface. Quietly, he covered up the mine, retraced his footsteps to his home in Williamsburg, Maryland, and told his relatives and a few neighbours of the 'strike'. They got together money for the needed machinery and had it shipped. The uncle and Darby went back to work the mine.

The first car of ore was mined and shipped to a smelter. The returns proved they had one of the richest mines in Colorado! A few more cars of that ore would clear the debts. Then would come the big killing in profits.

Down went the drills! Up went the hopes of Darby and Uncle! Then something happened – the vein of gold ore disappeared. They had come to the end of the rainbow, and the pot of gold was no longer there. They drilled on, desperately trying to pick up the vein again, all to no avail.

Finally, they decided to quit. They sold the machinery to a junk man for a few hundred dollars, and took the train back home. Some 'junk' men are dumb, but not this one! He called in a mining engineer to look at the mine and do a little calculating. The engineer advised that the project had failed because the owners were not familiar with 'fault lines'. His calculations showed that the vein would be found *just three feet from where the Darbys had stopped drilling*! That is exactly where it was found.

The junk man took millions of dollars in ore from the mine because he knew enough to seek expert counsel before giving up. Most of the money which went into the machinery was procured through the efforts of R. U. Darby, who was then a very young man. The money came from his relatives and neighbours, because of their faith in him. He paid back every dollar of it, although he was years in doing so.

Long afterwards, Mr Darby recouped his loss many times over when he made the discovery that desire can be transmuted into gold. The discovery came after he went into the business of selling life insurance.

Remembering that he lost a huge fortune because he stopped three feet from gold, Darby profited by the experience in his chosen work. His simple method was to say to himself, 'I stopped three feet from gold, but I will never stop because men say "no" when I ask them to buy insurance.' He owes his 'stickability' to the lesson he learned from his 'quitability' in the gold mining business.

Before success comes to most people, they are sure to meet with much temporary defeat, and perhaps some failure. When faced with defeat the easiest and most logical thing to do is to *quit*. That is exactly what the majority of people do.

More than 500 of the most successful people America has ever known told the author their greatest success came just one step beyond the point at which defeat had overtaken them.

Failure is a trickster with a keen sense of irony and cunning. It takes great delight in tripping one up when success is almost within reach.

A Fifty Cent Lesson in Persistence

Shortly after Mr Darby received his degree from the 'University of Hard Knocks', and had decided to profit by his experience in the gold-mining business, he had the good fortune to be present on an occasion that proved to him that 'No' does not necessarily mean no.

One afternoon he was helping his uncle grind wheat in an old-fashioned mill. The uncle operated a large farm on which a number of sharecrop farmers lived. Quietly, the door was opened, and a small child, the daughter of a tenant, walked in and took her place near the door.

The uncle looked up, saw the child, and barked at her roughly, 'What do you want?'

Meekly, the child replied, 'My mammy says send her fifty cents.'

'I'll not do it,' the uncle retorted, 'Now you run on home.'

'Yes, sir,' the child replied. But she did not move.

The uncle went ahead with his work, so busily engaged he did not notice that the child had not left. When he looked up and saw her still standing there, he yelled at her, 'I told you to go on home! Now go, or I'll take a switch to you.'

The little girl said, 'Yes, sir,' but she did not budge an inch.

The uncle dropped a sack of grain he was about to pour into the mill hopper, picked up a barrel stave and started towards the child with an expression on his face that indicated trouble.

Darby held his breath. He was certain he was about to witness a murder. He knew his uncle had a fierce temper. When the uncle reached the spot where the child was standing, she quickly stepped forward one step, looked up into his eyes and screamed at the top of her shrill voice, 'MY MAMMY'S GOTTA HAVE THAT FIFTY CENTS!'

The uncle stopped, looked at her for a minute, then slowly laid the barrel stave on the floor, put his hand in his pocket, took out half a dollar and gave it to her.

The child took the money and slowly backed towards the door, never taking her eyes off the man whom she had just conquered. After she had gone, the uncle sat down on a box and looked out the window into space for more than 10 minutes. He was pondering, with awe, on the whipping he had just taken.

Mr Darby, too, was doing some thinking. That was the first time in all his experience that he had seen the child of a sharecropper deliberately master an adult authority figure. How did she do it? What happened to his uncle that caused him to lose his fierceness and become as docile as a lamb? What strange power did this child use that made her master over her superior? These and other similar questions flashed into Darby's mind, but he did not find the answer until years later, when he told me the story.

Strangely, the story of this unusual experience was told to the author in the old mill, on the very spot where the uncle took his whipping. As we stood there in that musty old mill, Mr Darby repeated the story of the unusual conquest, and finished by asking, 'What can you make of it? What strange power did that child use that so completely whipped my uncle?'

The answer to his question will be found in the principles described in this book. The answer is full and complete. It contains details and instructions sufficient to enable anyone to understand and apply the same force that the little child accidentally stumbled upon.

Keep your mind alert and you will observe exactly what strange power came to the rescue of the child. You will catch a glimpse of this power in the next chapter. Somewhere in the book you will find an idea that will quicken your receptive powers and place at your command, for your own benefit, this same irresistible power. The awareness of this power may come to you in the first chapter, or it may flash into your mind in some subsequent chapter. It may come in the form of a single idea. Or it may come in the nature of a plan, or a purpose. Again, it may cause you to go back into your past experiences of failure or defeat, and bring to the surface some lesson by which you can regain all that you lost through defeat.

After I had described to Mr Darby the power unwittingly used by the little child, he quickly retraced his 30 years of experience as a life insurance salesman. He frankly acknowledged that his success in that field was due, in no small degree, to the lesson he had learned from the child.

Mr Darby pointed out: 'Every time a prospect tried to bow me out, without buying, I saw that child standing there in the old mill, her big eyes glaring in defiance, and I said to myself, "I've gotta make this sale." The better portion of all sales I have made were made after people had said "NO".'

He recalled, too, his mistake in having stopped only three feet from gold. 'But,' he said, 'that experience was a blessing in disguise. It taught me to keep on keeping on, no matter how hard the going may be, a lesson I needed to learn before I could succeed in anything.'

This story of Mr Darby and his uncle, the sharecropper's child and the gold mine will doubtless be read by hundreds of people who make their living by selling life insurance. To all of these, the author wishes to offer the suggestion that Darby owes to these two experiences his ability to sell more than a million dollars of life insurance every year.

Life is strange, and often imponderable! Both the successes and the failures have their roots in simple experiences. Mr Darby's experiences were commonplace and simple enough, yet as they held the answer to his destiny in life, they were as important (to him) as life itself. He profited by these two dramatic experiences because he analysed them and found the lesson they taught. But what of the person who has neither the time nor the inclination to study failure in search of knowledge that may lead to success? Where and how are they to learn the art of converting defeat into stepping stones to opportunity?

In answer to these questions, this book was written.

The answer called for a description of 13 principles. However, remember as you read that the answer you may be seeking to the questions which have caused you to ponder over the strangeness of life may be found in your own mind. Some idea, plan or purpose may spring into your mind as you read.

One sound idea is all you need to achieve success. The principles described in this book contain the best and most practical ways and means of creating useful ideas.

Before we go any further in our approach to the description of these principles, we believe you are entitled to receive this important suggestion: WHEN RICHES BEGIN TO COME, THEY COME SO QUICKLY, IN SUCH GREAT ABUN-DANCE, THAT ONE WONDERS WHERE THEY HAVE BEEN HIDING DURING ALL THOSE LEAN YEARS. This is an astounding statement, and all the more so when we take into consideration the popular belief that riches come only to those who work hard and long.

When you begin to think and grow rich, you will observe

that riches begin with a state of mind, with definiteness of purpose, with little or no hard work. You, and every other person, ought to be interested in knowing how to acquire a state of mind that will attract riches. I spent 25 years in research, analysing more than 25,000 people, because I, too, wanted to know 'how wealthy men become that way'.

Without that research, this book could not have been written.

Here take notice of a very significant truth: the business Depression started in 1929, and continued on an all-time record of destruction until sometime after President Roosevelt entered office. Then the Depression began to fade into nothingness. Just as an electrician in a theatre raises the lights so gradually that darkness is transmuted into light before you realise it, so did the spell of fear in the minds of the people gradually fade away and become faith.

As soon as you master the principles of this philosophy and begin to follow the instructions for applying those principles, your financial status will begin to improve. Everything you touch will begin to transmute itself into an asset for your benefit. Impossible? Not at all!

One of the main weaknesses of mankind is the average person's familiarity with the word 'impossible'. He knows all the rules that will *not* work. He knows all the things that *cannot* be done. This book was written for those who seek the rules that have made others successful, and are willing to stake everything on those rules.

A great many years ago I purchased a fine dictionary. The first thing I did was turn to the word 'impossible', and neatly clip it out of the book. That would not be an unwise thing for you to do.

Success comes to those who become *success conscious*.

Failure comes to those who indifferently allow themselves to become *failure conscious*.

The object of this book is to help all who seek it learn the art of changing their minds from *failure consciousness* to *success consciousness*.

Another weakness found in altogether too many people is the habit of measuring everything, and everyone, by their own impressions and beliefs. Some who read this will believe that no one can think and grow rich. They cannot think in terms of riches because their thought habits have been steeped in poverty, want, misery, failure and defeat.

Millions of people look at the achievements of Henry Ford and envy him his good fortune, or luck, or genius or whatever it is they credit for Ford's fortune. Perhaps one person in every hundred thousand knows the secret of Ford's success, and those who do know are too modest, or too reluctant, to speak of it, because of its simplicity. A single transaction will illustrate the 'secret' perfectly.

When Ford decided to produce his now famous V-8 motor, he chose to build an engine with the entire eight cylinders cast in one block, and instructed his engineers to produce a design for the engine. The design was placed on paper, but the engineers believed it was simply impossible to cast an eight-cylinder gas engine block in one piece.

Ford said, 'Produce it anyway.'

'But,' they replied, 'it's impossible!'

'Go ahead,' Ford commanded, 'and stay on the job until you succeed, no matter how much time is required.'

The engineers went ahead. There was no other option if they were to remain on the Ford staff. Six months went by and nothing happened. Another six months passed, and still nothing happened. The engineers tried every conceivable plan to carry out the orders, but the thing seemed out of the question; 'Impossible!'

At the end of the year Ford checked with his engineers, and again they informed him they had found no way to carry out his orders.

'Go right ahead,' said Ford, 'I want it, and I'll have it.'

They went ahead, and then, as if by a stroke of magic, the secret was discovered. The Ford *determination* had won once more!

This story may not be described with minute accuracy, but the sum and substance of it is correct. Deduce from it, you who wish to think and grow rich, the secret of the Ford millions, if you can. You'll not have to look very far.

Henry Ford is a success because he understands and applies the principles of success. One of these is desire: knowing what one wants. Remember this Ford story as you read, and pick out the lines in which the secret of his stupendous achievement has been described. If you can do this, if you can lay your finger on the particular group of principles that made Henry Ford rich, you can equal his achievements in almost any calling for which you are suited.

The Henry Ford of the late 20th century was Bill Gates. Just as Ford revolutionised the transportation industry by creating a car that almost anyone could afford and drive, Bill Gates transformed the computer industry by designing software that enabled everybody – not just the specialised technocrats – to be able to use computers, and later making the personal computer a virtual necessity in every office, school and home. This resulted in Bill Gates accruing billions of dollars and becoming the richest man in America.

He first became entranced with computers and began programming them at the age of 13. In 1973, he entered Harvard University, where he lived down the hall from Steve Ballmer, now Microsoft's chief executive officer. While at Harvard, Gates developed a version of the programming language BASIC for the first microcomputer.

Gates was so absorbed in his dream of building a software company that he left Harvard to devote his energies to fulfilling it. A few years earlier, he and his childhood friend Paul Allen had formed a company, Microsoft, as the vehicle for this endeavour. Guided by a belief that the computer would be a valuable tool on every office desktop and in every home, they began developing software for personal computers. Gates' foresight and his vision for personal computing have been central to the success of Microsoft and the software industry.

Having achieved his major goal, Bill Gates continues to pursue new goals both in the business of creating ever-improving computer programs and in his philanthropic work, having founded with his wife, Melinda, the largest charitable foundation in the world.

You are 'The Master of your Fate, the Captain of your Soul'

When the English poet W.C. Henley wrote the prophetic lines, 'I am the Master of my Fate, I am the Captain of my Soul', he should have informed us that the reason we are the Masters of our Fate, the Captains of our Souls is because we have the power to control our thoughts.

He should have told us that the ether in which this little planet floats, in which we move and have our being, is a form of energy moving at an inconceivably high rate of vibration, and that the ether is filled with a form of universal power which *adapts* itself to the nature of the thoughts we hold in our minds; and *influences* us, in natural ways, to transmute our thoughts into their physical equivalent.

If the poet had told us of this great truth, we would know why it is that we are the Masters of our Fate, the Captains of our Souls. He should have told us, with great emphasis, that this power makes no attempt to discriminate between destructive and constructive thoughts, that it will urge us to translate into physical reality thoughts of poverty just as quickly as it will influence us to act upon thoughts of riches.

He should have told us, too, that our brains become magnetised with the dominating thoughts we hold in our minds. By means with which no one is familiar, these 'magnets' attract to us the forces, the people, the circumstances of life which harmonise with the nature of our dominating thoughts.

He should have told us that before we can accumulate riches in great abundance, we must magnetise our minds with intense desire for riches, that we must become 'money conscious' until the desire for money drives us to create definite plans for acquiring it.

But, being a poet, and not a philosopher, Henley contented himself by stating a great truth in poetic form, leaving those who followed him to interpret the philosophical meaning of his lines. Little by little, the truth has unfolded itself, until it now appears certain that the principles described in this book hold the secret of mastery over our economic fate.

Another man who exemplifies being 'master of his fate' is Steven Spielberg, one of the all-time great motion picture directors. He dreamed of being a movie director from childhood. He began making amateur films with a primitive camera when he was still a child, and the dream never subsided.

How Spielberg broke into Universal Studios is a legend in the movie industry. He took the Universal Studios Tour, an attraction that enables visitors to get an inside look at the movie business. Visitors ride around the studio lots on a tram. Steven sneaked off the tram and hid between two sound stages until the tour ended. When he left at the end of the day, he made a point of saying a few words to the gate guard.

Day after day, he went back to the studio for three months. He walked past the guard, waved at him, and he waved back. He always wore a suit and carried a briefcase, letting the guard assume he was one of the students with a summer job in the studio. He made a point of speaking to and befriending directors, writers and editors. He even found a vacant office, took it over and listed his name in the building directory.

He made it his business to get to know Sid Sheinberg, then head of production for the studio's television arm. He showed him his college film project, which so impressed Sheinberg that he put the young man under contract with the studio.

His first full-length film, The Sugarland Express, received critical acclaim and won a best screenplay award at the 1974 Cannes Film Festival. Unfortunately, it did not do very well at the box office.

His big break came a year later when he discovered the book Jaws. The studio had already decided to produce Jaws and had chosen a well-known director to film it.

Spielberg desperately wanted to make this movie. Despite the financial failure of The Sugarland Express, his self-confidence had not diminished and he persuaded the producers to dismiss the chosen director and give the film to him.

It was not an easy assignment. From the beginning trouble beset the production. It ran into technical and budget problems. However, when Jaws was released in June 1975, it enjoyed twofold success: it broke box-office records, and the critics loved it. Within a month of its release, the film had taken in 60 million dollars at the box office, an unheard-of amount at the time.

Over the next few years Spielberg directed several movies, including the popular Indiana Jones series, the award-winning The Color Purple, Empire of the Sun and E.T.

He later directed Jurassic Park, *which would also become — at its time — the most successful movie in history, the third Spielberg film to break the record. It also brought in over one billion dollars in gross receipts, toys and other merchandise.*

Spielberg continues to pursue his dreams. When he and two other Hollywood moguls created their own production company, they called it 'Dreamworks'.

We are now ready to examine the first of these principles. Maintain a spirit of open-mindedness. Remember as you read that they are the invention of no single person. The principles were gathered from the life experiences of more than 500 men who actually accumulated riches in huge amounts; men who began in poverty, with little education or influence. The principles worked for these men. You can put them to work for your own enduring benefit.

You will find it easy, not hard, to do.

Before you read the next chapter, I want you to know that it conveys factual information that might easily change your entire financial destiny, as it has so definitely brought changes of stupendous proportions to two people described.

I want you to know, also, that the relationship between these two men and myself is such that I could have taken no liberties with the facts, even if I had wished to do so. One of them has been my closest personal friend for almost 25 years; the other is my own son. The unusual success of these two men, success that they generously accredit to the principle described in the next chapter, more than justifies this personal reference as a means of emphasising the far-flung power of this principle.

CHAPTER 2

DESIRE:
the Starting Point
of All Achievement

(The First Step to Riches)

When Edwin C. Barnes climbed down from the freight train in Orange, N. J., he may have resembled a tramp, but his thoughts were those of a king! As he made his way to Thomas A. Edison's office, his mind was at work. He saw himself *standing in Edison's presence*. He heard himself asking Mr Edison for an opportunity to carry out the one *consuming obsession of his life*, a *burning desire* to become the business associate of the great inventor.

Barnes' desire was not a hope. It was not a wish. It was a keen, pulsating *desire*, which transcended everything else. It was *definite*.

The desire was not new when he approached Edison. It had been Barnes' dominating desire for a long time. In the beginning, when the desire first appeared in his mind, it may have been – probably was – only a wish, but it was no mere wish when he appeared before Edison with it.

A few years later, Edwin C. Barnes again stood before Edison, in the same office where he first met the inventor. This time his desire had been translated into reality. He was in business with Edison. The dominating dream of his life had become a reality. Today, people who know Barnes envy him because of the 'break' life yielded him. They see him in the days of his triumph, without taking the trouble to investigate the cause of his success.

Barnes succeeded because he chose a definite goal, and placed all his energy, all his willpower and all his effort into achieving that goal. He did not become the partner of Edison the day he arrived. He was content to start in the most menial work, as long as it provided an opportunity to take even one step towards his cherished goal.

Five years passed before the chance he had been seeking made its appearance. During all those years not one ray of hope, not one promise of attainment of his desire had been held out to him. To everyone, except himself, he appeared only another cog in the Edison business wheel, but in his own mind *he was the partner of Edison every minute of the time*, from the very day he first went to work there.

It is a remarkable illustration of the power of a definite desire. Barnes won his goal because he wanted to be a business associate of Mr Edison more than he wanted anything else. He created a plan by which to attain that purpose. But he burned all bridges behind him. He stood by his desire until it became the dominating obsession of his life and, finally, a fact.

When he went to Orange, he did not say to himself, 'I will try to induce Edison to give me a job of some sort.' He said, 'I will see Edison and put him on notice that I have come to go into business with him.'

He did not say, 'I will work there for a few months, and if I get no encouragement, I will quit and get a job somewhere else.' He did say, 'I will start anywhere. I will do anything Edison tells me to do, but before I am through, I will be his associate.' He did not say, 'I will keep my eyes open for another opportunity, in case I fail to get what I want in the Edison organisation.' He said, 'There is but *one* thing in this world I am determined to have, and that is a business association with Thomas A. Edison. I will burn all bridges behind me, and stake my *entire future* on my ability to get what I want.'

He left himself no possible way of retreat. He had to win or perish! That is all there is to the Barnes story of success.

A long while ago, a great warrior had to make a decision which ensured his success on the battlefield. He was about to send his armies against a powerful foe, whose men outnumbered his own. He loaded his soldiers into boats, sailed to the enemy's country, unloaded soldiers and equipment, then gave the order to burn the ships that had carried them. Addressing his men before the first battle, he said, 'You see the boats going up in smoke. That means that we cannot leave these shores alive unless we win! We now have no choice – we win or we perish!' They won. Every person who wins in any undertaking must be willing to burn his ships and cut all sources of retreat. Only by so doing can one be sure of maintaining that state of mind known as a *burning desire to win*, essential to success.

The morning after the great Chicago fire, a group of merchants stood on State Street, looking at the smoking remains of what had been their stores. They went into a conference to decide if they would try to rebuild, or leave Chicago and start over in a more promising part of the country. They reached a decision – all except one – to leave Chicago.

The merchant who decided to stay and rebuild pointed a finger at the remains of his store, and said, 'Gentlemen, on that very spot I will build the world's greatest store, no matter how many times it may burn down.' The store was built. It stands there today, a towering monument to the power of that state of mind known as a *burning desire*. The easy thing for Marshal Field to have done would have been exactly what his fellow merchants did. When the going was hard and the future looked dismal, they pulled up and went where the going seemed easier.

Mark well this difference between Marshal Field and the other merchants, because it is the same difference that distinguishes Edwin C. Barnes from thousands of other young men who have worked in the Edison organisation. It is the same difference that distinguishes practically all who succeed from those who fail.

Every human being who understands the purpose of money wishes for it. Wishing will not bring riches. But desiring riches with a state of mind that becomes an obsession, then planning definite ways and means to acquire riches, and backing those plans with persistence which does not recognise failure, will bring riches.

The method by which *desire* for riches can be transmuted into its financial equivalent consists of six definite, practical steps:

1. Fix in your mind the exact amount of money you desire. It is not sufficient merely to say, 'I want plenty of money.' Be definite as to the amount. (There is a psychological reason for definiteness which will be described in a subsequent chapter.)

2. Determine exactly what you intend to give in return for the money you desire. (There is no such reality as 'something for nothing'.)

3. Establish a definite date when you intend to possess the money you desire.

4. Create a definite plan for carrying out your desire, and begin at once, whether you are ready or not, to put this plan into action.

5. Write out a clear, concise statement of the amount of money you intend to acquire. Name the time limit for its acquisition. State what you intend to give in return for the money, and describe clearly the plan through which you intend to accumulate it.

6. Read your written statement aloud, twice daily, once just before retiring at night, and once after rising in the morning. AS YOU READ, SEE AND FEEL AND BELIEVE YOURSELF ALREADY IN POSSESSION OF THE MONEY.

It is important that you follow the instructions described in these six steps. It is especially important that you observe and follow the instructions in the sixth paragraph.

You may complain that it is impossible for you to 'see yourself in possession of money' before you actually have it. Here is where a *burning desire* will come to your aid. If you truly *desire* money so keenly that your desire is an obsession, you will have no difficulty in convincing yourself that you will acquire it. The object is to want money, and to become so determined to have it that you *convince* yourself you will have it.

Only those who become 'money conscious' ever accumulate great riches. Money consciousness means that the mind has become so thoroughly saturated with the desire for money that one can see oneself already in possession of it.

To those who have not been schooled in the working principles of the human mind, these instructions may appear impractical. It may be helpful, to all who fail to recognise the soundness of the six steps, to know that the information they convey was received from Andrew Carnegie, who began as an ordinary labourer in the steel mills. Despite his humble beginning, Carnegie managed to make these principles yield him a fortune of considerably more than 100 million dollars.

It may be of further help to know that the six steps recommended here were carefully scrutinised by Thomas A. Edison. He placed his stamp of approval upon them as being not only the steps essential for the accumulation of money, but also for the attainment of any definite goal. The steps call for no 'hard labour'. They call for no sacrifice. They do not require one to become ridiculous, or credulous. To apply them calls for no great amount of education. But the successful application of these six steps does call for sufficient imagination to enable one to see, and to understand, that accumulation of money cannot be left to chance, good fortune and luck. One must realise that all who have accumulated great fortunes first did a certain amount of dreaming, hoping, wishing, *desiring* and *planning* before they acquired money.

You may as well know, also, that every great leader, from the dawn of civilisation down to the present, was a dreamer. If you do not see great riches in your imagination, you will never see them in your bank balance. Never has there been so great an opportunity for practical dreamers as now exists. We who are in this race for riches should be encouraged to know that this dynamic world in which we live is demanding new ideas, new ways of doing things, new leaders, new inventions, new methods of teaching, new methods of marketing, new books, new literature, new applications for computers, new cures for diseases and new approaches to every aspect of business and life. Behind this demand for new and better things there is one quality one must possess to win, and that is *definiteness of purpose*, the knowledge of what one wants, and a burning *desire* to possess it. To accomplish this requires practical dreamers who can, and will, put their dreams into action. The practical dreamers have always been, and always will be, the pattern-makers of civilisation. We who desire to accumulate riches should remember that the real leaders of the world have always been people who harnessed, and put into practical use, the intangible, unseen forces of unborn opportunity. They have converted those forces (or impulses of thought) into skyscrapers, cities, factories, aeroplanes, cars, better health care, and every form of convenience that makes life more pleasant.

Tolerance and an open mind are practical necessities for the dreamer of today. Those who are afraid of new ideas are doomed before they start. Never has there been a time more favourable to pioneers than the present. There is a vast business, financial and industrial world to be remoulded and redirected along new and better lines.

In planning to acquire your share of the riches, let no one influence you to scorn the dreamer. To win the big stakes in this ever-changing world, you must catch the spirit of the great pioneers of the past, whose dreams have given to civilisation all that it has of value, the spirit which serves as the life-blood of our society – your opportunity, and mine, to develop and market our talents. Let us not forget, Columbus dreamed of an unknown world, staked his life on the existence of such a world, and discovered it! Copernicus, the great astronomer, dreamed of a multiplicity of worlds, and revealed them! No one denounced him as 'impractical' after he had triumphed. Instead, the world worshipped at his shrine, thus proving once more that *success requires no apologies, failure permits no alibis.*

If the thing you wish to do is right, and you believe in it, go ahead and do it! Put your dream across, and never mind what 'they' say if you meet with temporary defeat, for 'they', perhaps, do not know that *every failure brings with it the seed of an equivalent success*.

Henry Ford, poor and uneducated, dreamed of a horseless carriage. He went to work with what tools he possessed, without waiting for opportunity to favour him, and now evidence of his dream belts the entire earth. He has put more wheels into operation than any man who ever lived because he was not afraid to back his dreams.

Thomas Edison dreamed of a lamp that could be operated by electricity. Despite more than 10,000 failures, he stood by that dream until he made it a physical reality. Practical dreamers *do not quit!*

Lincoln dreamed of freedom for the black slaves, put his dream into action, and barely missed living to see a united North and South translate his dream into reality. The Wright brothers dreamed of a machine that would fly through the air. Now one may see evidence all over the world that they dreamed soundly. Marconi dreamed of a system for harnessing the intangible forces of the ether. Evidence that he did not dream in vain may be found in every radio, TV and cell phone in the world. Moreover, Marconi's dream brought the humblest cabin and the most stately manor house side by side. It made the people of every nation on earth next-door neighbours by creating a medium where news, information and entertainment could instantly be disseminated throughout the world. It may interest you to know that Marconi's 'friends' had him taken into custody, and examined in a psychopathic hospital, when he announced he had discovered a principle through which he could send messages through the air, without the aid of wires or other direct physical means of communication.

The dreamers of today fare better. The world has become accustomed to new discoveries. Indeed, it has shown a willingness to reward the dreamer who gives the world a new idea.

Ray Kroc is another good example of someone who made his dream come true. Kroc was a salesman of milkshake mixers. Most of his customers — restaurants and diners — purchased one or two units. When he received an order for eight mixers from a small food outlet in San Bernadino, California, he decided to visit them and see how they could sell so many shakes. It was the busiest restaurant he had ever seen. The owners — the McDonald brothers — offered a very limited menu: hamburgers, cheeseburgers, French fries, shakes and soft drinks — all at the lowest prices in the area.

Kroc saw an opportunity. If he could open a chain of these restaurants, each as productive and profitable as this, money would flow in. He proposed the idea to the McDonald brothers and agreed to implement it. Within a few years, McDonald's not only became the top-selling food outlet in the country, but created the fast-food industry. Kroc later bought out the McDonald brothers and expanded the business into an international phenomenon, making him one of the richest men of his time.

The world is filled with an abundance of *opportunity* which the dreamers of the past never knew. *A burning desire to be and to do* is the starting point from which the dreamer must take off. Dreams are not born of indifference, laziness or lack of ambition. The world no longer scoffs at dreamers, nor calls them impractical. Remember, too, that all who succeed in life get off to a bad start, and pass through many heartbreaking struggles before they 'arrive'. The turning point in the lives of those who succeed usually comes at the moment of some crisis, through which they are introduced to their 'other selves'. John Bunyan wrote *The Pilgrim's Progress* after he had been confined in prison and sorely punished because of his religious views.

O. Henry discovered the genius that slept within his brain after he had met with great misfortune, and was confined in a prison cell in Columbus, Ohio. Being *forced*, through misfortune, to become acquainted with his 'other self' and to use his *imagination*, he discovered himself to be a great author instead of a miserable criminal and outcast. Strange and varied are the ways of life, and stranger still are the ways of infinite intelligence, through which people are sometimes forced to undergo all sorts of punishment before discovering their own brains, and their own capacity to create useful ideas through imagination.

Edison, the world's greatest inventor and scientist, was a part-time telegraph operator. He failed innumerable times before he was driven, finally, to the discovery of the genius that slept within his brain. Charles Dickens began by pasting labels on blacking pots. The tragedy of his first love penetrated the depths of his soul and converted him into one of the world's truly great authors.

Disappointment over love affairs generally has the effect of driving people to drink and ruin. This is because most people never learn the art of transmuting their strongest emotions into dreams of a constructive nature.

Helen Keller became deaf, dumb and blind shortly after birth. Despite her great misfortune, her name is written indelibly in the pages of the history of the great. Her entire life served as evidence that no one is ever defeated until defeat has been accepted as a reality. Robert Burns was an illiterate country lad. He was cursed by poverty and grew up to be a drunkard. The world was made better for his having lived because he clothed beautiful thoughts in poetry, thereby plucking a thorn and planting a rose in its place.

Booker T. Washington was born in slavery, handicapped by

race and colour. Because he was tolerant, had an open mind at all times, on all subjects, and was a *dreamer*, he left his impress for good on an entire race. Beethoven was deaf, Milton was blind, but their names will last as long as time endures because they dreamed and translated their dreams into organised thought.

Arnold Schwarzenegger is another person who converted his desire into action and achievement. He first came into the public eye as 'Mr Universe', a glorified weight-lifter.

But Schwarzenegger was not a typical 'muscle man'. He was a man with dreams and goals. He achieved them by becoming a wealthy businessman, one of the highest paid movie stars and, eventually, governor of California.

Born and raised in Austria, as a child he began training as a weight-lifter. At 18, he won his first body-building contest and the first of five consecutive Mr Universe titles. He emigrated to the United States and continued winning similar contests.

Although he had accomplished more than any other person in the art of body building, it was no longer a challenge. He sought other areas where he could use his talents. His training in physical development taught him that there was a need for knowledge about physical fitness. He had that knowledge and wanted to share it.

He wrote an autobiography, Arnold: The Education of a Body-builder, *which became a bestseller. He followed it with a book on body building for women, showing female readers how to use weight training to get in shape. This led to the creation of a mail-order exercise business, and a company to produce body-building events. These businesses started him on the road to business success.*

His next goal was to become a movie star. Even before he had secured his first movie role, he set himself a goal to be as big in movies as he was in body building. After turning down minor roles, his persistence paid off when he was cast as the lead in Conan the Barbarian. *This led to a series of action films that made him one of the highest paid actors in Hollywood.*

Success in the movies did not make Schwarzenegger complacent. He set new goals for himself, this time in the world of business. He invested in real estate, created a restaurant chain and became actively involved in other enterprises – and became a multi-millionaire.

As his successes mounted, however, he added what became his dream goal – to serve the community. He travelled around the country to promote health and fitness for youth. He went into the inner cities and inspired the kids to eschew violence and crime, to say 'no' to drugs, guns and gangs and 'yes' to education. He has taken an active leadership role in several organisations dedicated to physical fitness and heath.

In 2003, Schwarzenegger threw his hat into the ring and was overwhelmingly elected as the new governor of California.

You can learn much from this man. In setting goals you are not limited to any one area. Schwarzenegger could have limited his future to body building and become quite successful, but he dreamed of much more, set higher goals and strove to reach them. He learned from his successes and adapted this knowledge in other aspects of his life.

Like Schwarzenegger, do not be discouraged by criticism. Critics belittled his acting ability in his first films, but he was not dissuaded and pursued his goal to became one of the highest paid actors in Hollywood.

Before passing to the next chapter, kindle anew in your mind the fire of hope, faith, courage and tolerance. If you have these states of mind, and a working knowledge of the principles described, all else that you need will come to you when you are *ready* for it. Let Emerson state the thought in these words, 'Every proverb, every book, every byword that belongs to thee for aid and comfort shall surely come home through open or winding passages. Every friend whom not thy fantastic will, but the great and tender soul in thee craveth, shall lock thee in his embrace.'

There is a difference between *wishing* for a thing and being *ready* to receive it. No one is ready for a thing until he believes he can acquire it. The state of mind must be *belief*, not mere hope or wish. Open-mindedness is essential for belief. Closed minds do not inspire faith, courage or belief.

Remember, no more effort is required to aim high in life, to demand abundance and prosperity, than is required to accept misery and poverty. A great poet has correctly stated this universal truth through these lines:

> I bargained with Life for a penny
>> And Life would pay no more,
> However I begged at evening
>> When I counted my scanty store.

> For Life is a just employer,
>> He gives you what you ask,
> But once you have set the wages,
>> Why, you must bear the task.

> I worked for a menial's hire,
>> Only to learn, dismayed,
> That any wage I had asked of Life,
>> Life would have willingly paid.

Mary Kay Ash, the founder of Mary Kay Cosmetics, attributed her success to the development of self-confidence and faith in herself, and in all the people in her vast organisation, which now consists of more than 250,000 independent beauty consultants worldwide.

Her sales career began 25 years earlier when she joined Stanley Home Products. She often commented that she was not at all successful during her first year and was ready to give up. This changed when she attended her first Stanley sales seminar.

She reported: 'There I saw this tall, svelte, pretty, successful woman crowned queen as a reward for being the best in a company contest. I determined to be that queen the following year, which seemed impossible. However, I decided to go up and talk to the president and tell him that I intended to be queen next year.

'Mr Beveridge didn't laugh at me, but looked me in the eye, held my hand and said: "Somehow I think you will." Those five words drove me and the next year I was queen.'

Mary Kay preached and practised that the first step in achieving success is to firmly believe that you are an excellent person who deserves success. In an article in Personal Excellence, she suggested some exercises to help create your image of excellence and begin to establish an atmosphere of success in your life. Here are some of her suggestions:

IMAGINE YOURSELF SUCCESSFUL. *Always picture yourself successful. Visualise the person you desire to become. Set aside time each day to be alone and undisturbed. Get comfortable and relax. Close your eyes and concentrate on your desires and goals. See yourself in this new environment, capable and self-confident.*

REFLECT ON YOUR PAST SUCCESSES. *Every success, be it large or small, is proof that you are capable of achieving more successes. Celebrate each success. You can recall it when you begin to lose faith in yourself.*

SET DEFINITE GOALS. *Have a clear direction of where you want to go. Be aware when you begin to deviate from these goals and take immediate corrective action.*

RESPOND POSITIVELY TO LIFE. *Develop a positive self-image. Your image, your reactions to life and your decisions are completely within your control.*

Desire Outwits Mother Nature

As a fitting climax to this chapter, I wish to introduce one of the most unusual people I have ever known. I first saw him a few minutes after he was born. He came into the world without any physical sign of ears, and the doctor admitted, when pressed for an opinion, that the child might be deaf and mute for life.

I challenged the doctor's opinion. I had the right to do so; I was the child's father. I, too, reached a decision and rendered an opinion, but I expressed the opinion silently, in the secrecy of my own heart. I decided that my son would hear and speak. Nature could send me a child without ears, but Nature could not induce me to accept the reality of the affliction. In my own mind I knew that my son would hear and speak. How? I was sure there must be a way, and I knew I would find it. I thought of the words of the immortal Emerson, 'The whole course of things goes to teach us faith. We need only obey. There is guidance for each of us, and by lowly listening, we shall hear the right word.'

The right word? DESIRE! More than anything else, I *desired* that my son should not be a deaf mute. From that desire I never receded, not for a second. Many years previously, I had written, 'Our only limitations are those we set up in our own minds'. For the first time, I wondered if that statement were true. Lying on the bed in front of me was a newly born child, without the natural equipment of hearing. Even though he might hear and speak, he was obviously disfigured for life. Surely, this was a limitation which that child had not set up in his own mind. What could I do about it? Somehow I would find a way to transplant into that child's mind my own *burning desire* for ways and means of conveying sound to his brain without the aid of ears.

As soon as the child was old enough to cooperate, I would fill his mind so completely with a *burning desire* to hear that Nature would, by methods of her own, translate it into physical reality. All this thinking took place in my own mind, and I spoke of it to no one. Every day I renewed the pledge I had made to myself not to accept a deaf mute for a son.

As he grew older, and began to take notice of things around him, we observed that he had a slight degree of hearing. When he reached the age when children usually begin talking, he made no attempt to speak, but we could tell by his actions that he could hear certain sounds slightly. That was all I wanted to know! I was convinced that if he could hear, even slightly, he might develop still greater hearing capacity.

Then something happened which gave me hope. It came from an entirely unexpected source – we bought a record player. When the child heard the music for the first time, he went into ecstasies, and promptly appropriated the machine. He soon showed a preference for certain records, among them *It's a Long Way to Tipperary*. On one occasion, he played that piece over and over for almost two hours, standing in front of the record player with his teeth clamped on the edge of the case. The significance of this self-formed habit of his did not become clear to us until years later, for we had never heard of the principle of 'bone conduction' of sound at that time.

Shortly after he appropriated the record player, I discovered that he could hear me quite clearly when I spoke with my lips touching his mastoid bone behind the ear, or at the base of the brain. These discoveries placed in my possession the necessary

34

media by which I began to translate into reality my burning desire to help my son develop hearing and speech. By that time he was making stabs at speaking certain words. The outlook was far from encouraging, but *desire backed by faith* knows no such word as impossible.

Having determined that he could hear the sound of my voice plainly, I began, immediately, to transfer to his mind the desire to hear and speak. I soon discovered that the child enjoyed bedtime stories, so I went to work, creating stories designed to develop in him self-reliance, imagination and a keen desire to hear and to be normal.

There was one story in particular, which I emphasised by giving it some new and dramatic colouring each time it was told. It was designed to plant in his mind the thought that his affliction was not a liability, but an asset of great value.

Despite the fact that all the philosophy I had examined clearly indicated that *every adversity brings with it the seed of an equivalent advantage*, I must confess that I had not the slightest idea how this affliction could ever become an asset. However, I continued my practice of wrapping that philosophy in bedtime stories, hoping the time would come when he would find some plan by which his handicap could be made to serve some useful purpose.

Reason told me plainly that there was no adequate compensation for the lack of ears and natural hearing equipment. *Desire* backed by *faith* pushed reason aside, and inspired me to carry on.

As I analyse the experience in retrospect, I can see now that my son's faith in me had much to do with the astounding results. He did not question anything I told him. I sold him the idea that he had a distinct advantage over his older brother, and that this advantage would reflect itself in many ways. For example, the teachers in school would observe that he had no ears, and, because of this, they would show him special attention and treat him with extraordinary kindness. They always did. His mother saw to that by visiting the teachers and arranging with them to give the child the extra attention necessary. I sold him the idea, too, that when he became old enough to sell newspapers (his older brother had already become a newspaper merchant), he would have a big advantage over his brother as people would pay him extra money for his wares because they could see he was a bright, industrious boy, despite the fact he had no ears.

We noticed that, gradually, the child's hearing was improving. Moreover, he had not the slightest tendency to be self-conscious because of his affliction. When he was about seven, he showed the first evidence that our method of servicing his mind was bearing fruit. For several months he begged for the privilege of selling newspapers, but his mother would not give her consent. She was afraid that his deafness made it unsafe for him to go on the street alone. Finally, he took matters in his own hands. One afternoon, when he was left at home with the servants, he climbed through the kitchen window, shinned to the ground and set out on his own. He borrowed six cents in capital from the neighbourhood shoemaker, invested it in papers, sold out, reinvested, and kept repeating until late in the evening. After balancing his accounts, and paying back the six cents he had borrowed from his banker, he had a net profit of 42 cents. When we got home that night, we found him in bed asleep, with the money tightly clenched in his hand. His mother opened his hand, removed the coins and cried. Of all things! Crying over her son's first victory seemed so inappropriate. My reaction was the reverse. I laughed heartily, for I knew that my endeavour to plant in the child's mind an attitude of faith in himself had been successful. His mother saw, in his first business venture, a little deaf boy who had gone out in the streets and risked his life to earn money. I saw a brave, ambitious, self-reliant little business-man whose stock in himself had increased 100 per cent because he had gone into business on his own initiative, and had won. The transaction pleased me because I knew he had given evidence of a trait of resourcefulness that would go with him all through life.

Later events proved this to be true. When his older brother wanted something, he would lie down on the floor, kick his feet in the air, cry for it – and get it. When the 'little deaf boy' wanted something, he would plan a way to earn the money, then buy it for himself. He still follows that plan! Truly, my own son has taught me that handicaps can be converted into stepping stones on which one may climb towards some worthy goal, unless they are accepted as obstacles and used as alibis.

The little deaf boy went through the grades, high school and college without being able to hear his teachers, except when they shouted loudly, at close range. He did not go to a school for the deaf. We would not permit him to learn sign language. We were determined that he should live a normal life and associate with normal children, and we stood by that decision, although it cost us many heated debates with school officials.

While he was in high school, he tried an electrical hearing aid, but it was of no value to him. We believed this was due to a condition that was disclosed when the child was six. Dr J. Gordon Wilson of Chicago operated on one side of the boy's head and discovered that there was no sign of natural hearing equipment.

During his last week in college (18 years after the operation), something happened which marked the most important turning point of his life. Through what seemed to be mere chance, he came into possession of another electrical hearing device, which was sent to him on trial. He was slow about testing it, due to his disappointment with a similar device. Finally he picked the instrument up, and more or less carelessly placed it on his head, hooked up the battery, and lo! as if by a stroke of magic, his lifelong DESIRE FOR NORMAL HEARING BECAME A REALITY! For the first time in his life he heard practically as well as any person with normal hearing.

'God moves in mysterious ways, His wonders to perform.' Overjoyed because of the changed world that had been brought to him through his hearing device, he rushed to the telephone, called his mother, and heard her voice perfectly. The next day he plainly heard the voices of his professors in class for the first time in his life! He heard the radio. He heard the cinema. For the first time in his life, he could converse freely with other people without them having to speak loudly. Truly, he had come into possession of a changed world. We had refused to accept Nature's error, and, by *persistent desire*, we had induced Nature to correct that error, through the only practical means available.

Desire had commenced to pay dividends, but the victory was not yet complete. The boy still had to find a definite and practical way to convert his handicap into an equivalent asset.

Hardly realising the significance of what had already been accomplished, but intoxicated with the joy of his newly discovered world of sound, he wrote a letter to the manufacturer of the hearing aid, enthusiastically describing his experience. Something in his letter – something, perhaps, which was not written on the lines but between them – caused the company to invite him to New York. When he arrived, he was escorted through the factory. While talking with the Chief Engineer, telling him about his changed world, a hunch, an idea or an inspiration – call it what you wish – flashed into his mind. It was this impulse of thought which converted his affliction into an asset destined to pay dividends in both money and happiness to thousands for all time to come.

The sum and substance of that impulse of thought was this: it occurred to him that he might be of help to the millions of deaf people who go through life without the benefit of hearing devices, if he could find a way to tell them the story of his changed world. Then and there, he reached a decision to devote the remainder of his life to providing a useful service to the hard of hearing. For an entire month, he carried out intensive research. He analysed the entire marketing system of the manufacturer of the hearing device, and created ways and means of communicating with the hard of hearing all over the world for the purpose of sharing with them his newly discovered changed world. When this was done, he wrote a two-year plan based upon his findings. On presenting the plan to the company, he was instantly given a position for the purpose of carrying out his ambition. Little did he dream, when he went to work, that he was destined to bring hope and practical relief to thousands of deaf people who, without his help, would have been doomed forever to deaf mutism.

Shortly after he became associated with the manufacturer of his hearing aid, he invited me to attend a class conducted by his company for the purpose of teaching deaf mutes to hear and speak. I had never heard of such a form of education, therefore I visited the class sceptical but hopeful that my time would not be entirely wasted. Here I saw a demonstration that gave me a greatly enlarged vision of what I had done to arouse and keep alive in my son's mind the *desire* for normal hearing. I saw deaf mutes actually being taught to hear and speak through application of the self-same principle I had used, more than 20 years previously, in saving my son from deaf mutism.

Thus, through some strange turn of the wheel of fate, my son, Blair, and I were destined to aid in correcting deaf mutism for those as yet unborn. There is no doubt in my mind that Blair would have been a deaf mute all his life if his mother and I had not managed to shape his mind as we did.

When Blair was an adult, Dr Irving Voorhees, a noted specialist on such cases, examined him thoroughly. He was astounded when he learned how well my son hears and speaks, and said his examination indicated that 'theoretically, the boy should not be able to hear at all'. But the lad does hear, despite the fact that X-ray pictures show there is no opening in the skull, whatsoever, from where his ears should be to the brain.

When I planted in his mind the *desire* to hear and talk, and live as a normal person, there went with that impulse some strange influence which caused Nature to become bridge-builder, and span the gulf of silence between his brain and the outer world by some means which the keenest medical specialists have not been able to interpret. It would be sacrilege for me to even conjecture as to how Nature performed this miracle. It would be unforgivable if I neglected to tell the world as much as I know of the humble part I assumed in the strange experience. It is my duty and a privilege to say I believe, and not without reason, that nothing is impossible to the person who backs *desire* with enduring *faith*.

I have no doubt that a *burning desire* has devious ways of transmuting itself into its physical equivalent. Blair *desired* normal hearing; now he has it! He was born with a handicap, which might easily have sent one with a less defined *desire* to the street with a bundle of pencils and a tin cup. That handicap now promises to serve as the medium by which he will render useful service to many millions of hard of hearing, as well as to give him useful employment at adequate financial compensation for the remainder of his life. The little 'white lies' I planted in his mind when he was a child, leading him to *believe* his affliction would become a great asset on which he could capitalise, have been justified. There is nothing, right or wrong, which *belief* plus *burning desire* cannot make real. These qualities are free to everyone.

In all my experience in dealing with men and women who had personal problems, I never handled a single case which more definitely demonstrates the power of *desire*. Authors sometimes make the mistake of writing of subjects of which they have but superficial, or very elementary, knowledge. It has been my good fortune to have had the privilege of testing the soundness of the *power of desire* through the affliction of my own son. Perhaps it was providential that the experience came as it did, for surely no one is better prepared than he to serve as an example of what happens when desire is put to the test. If Mother Nature bends to the will of desire, is it logical that mere men can defeat a burning desire? Strange and imponderable is the power of the human mind! We do not understand the method by which it uses every circumstance, every individual, every physical thing within its reach as a means of transmuting desire into its physical counterpart. Perhaps science will uncover this secret. I planted in my son's mind the desire to hear and to speak as any normal person hears and speaks. That desire has now become a reality. I planted in his mind the desire to convert his greatest handicap into his greatest asset. That desire has been realised.

The modus operandi by which this astounding result was achieved is not hard to describe. It consisted of three very definite facts. First, I MIXED FAITH with the DESIRE for normal hearing, which I passed on to my son. Second, I communicated my desire to him in every conceivable way available, through persistent, continuous effort, over a period of years. Third, HE BELIEVED ME!

Several years ago, one of my business associates became ill. He became worse as time went on, and finally was taken to the hospital for an operation. Just before he was wheeled into the operating room, I took a look at him and wondered how anyone as thin and emaciated as he could possibly go through a major operation successfully. The doctor warned me that there was little, if any, chance of my ever seeing him alive again. But that was the *doctor's opinion*. It was not the opinion of the patient. Just before he was wheeled away, he whispered feebly, 'Do not be disturbed, Chief, I will be out of here in a few days.'

The attending nurse looked at me with pity. But the patient did come through safely. After it was all over, his physician said, 'Nothing but his own desire to live saved him. He never would have pulled through if he had not refused to accept the possibility of death.' I believe in the power of *desire* backed by *faith* because I have seen this power lift people from lowly beginnings to places of power and wealth; I have seen it rob the grave of its victims; I have seen it serve as the medium by which people staged a comeback after having been defeated in 100 different ways; I have seen it provide my own son with a normal, happy, successful life, despite Nature having sent him into the world without ears.

How can one harness and use the power of *desire*? This has been answered through this chapter, and the subsequent chapters of this book.

I wish to convey the thought that all achievement, no matter what its nature or purpose, must begin with an intense, *burning desire* for something definite. Through some strange and powerful principle of 'mental chemistry', Nature wraps up in the impulse of *strong desire* 'that something' which recognises no such word as impossible, and accepts no such reality as failure.

CHAPTER 3

FAITH:

Visualising and Believing in the Attainment of Desire

(The Second Step to Riches)

FAITH is the head chemist of the mind. When *faith* is blended with the vibration of thought, the subconscious mind instantly picks up the vibration, translates it into its spiritual equivalent, and transmits it to Infinite Intelligence, as in the case of prayer.

Faith, *love* and *sex* are the most powerful of all the major positive emotions. When the three are blended, they have the effect of 'colouring' the vibration of thought in such a way that it instantly reaches the subconscious mind, where it is changed into its spiritual equivalent, the only form that induces a response from Infinite Intelligence.

Love and faith are psychic; related to our spiritual side. Sex is purely biological, and related only to the physical. The mixing, or blending, of these three emotions has the effect of opening a direct line of communication between the finite, thinking mind and Infinite Intelligence.

How to Develop Faith

FAITH is a state of mind that may be induced, or created, by affirmation or repeated instructions to the subconscious mind, through the principle of autosuggestion. As an illustration, consider the purpose for which you are, presumably, reading this book. The object is, naturally, to acquire the ability to transmute the intangible thought impulse of *desire* into its physical counterpart, *money*. By following the instructions laid down in Chapter 3 on autosuggestion, and Chapter 11 on the subconscious mind, you may *convince* the subconscious mind that you believe you will receive what you ask for. It will act upon that belief, passing back to you in the form of *faith*, followed by definite plans for procuring your goal.

The method by which one develops *faith*, where it does not already exist, is extremely difficult to describe. Almost as difficult, in fact, as it would be to describe the colour of red to a blind man. Faith is a state of mind that you may develop at will, after you have mastered the 13 steps to riches in this book.

Making repeated affirmations to your subconscious mind is the only known method of developing the emotion of faith voluntarily. Perhaps the meaning may be made clearer through the following explanation as to the way people sometimes become criminals. Stated in the words of a famous criminologist, 'When people first come into contact with crime, they abhor it. If they remain in contact with crime for a time, they become accustomed to it, and endure it. If they remain in contact with it long enough, they finally embrace it, and become influenced by it.'

This is the equivalent of saying that any impulse of thought which is repeatedly passed on to the subconscious mind is finally accepted and acted upon. The subconscious mind proceeds to translate that impulse into its physical equivalent by the most practical procedure available. In connection with this, consider again the statement, ALL THOUGHTS WHICH HAVE BEEN EMOTIONALISED (given feeling) AND MIXED WITH FAITH begin immediately to translate themselves into their physical equivalent or counterpart.

The emotions, or the 'feeling' portion of thoughts, are the factors that give thoughts vitality, life and action. The emotions of faith, love and sex, when mixed with any thought impulse, give it greater action than any of these emotions can do singly. Not only thought impulses which have been mixed with *faith*, but also those that have been mixed with any of the positive emotions – or any of the negative emotions – may reach and influence the subconscious mind.

From this statement you will understand that the subconscious mind will translate a thought impulse of a negative or destructive nature into its physical equivalent, just as readily as it will act upon thought impulses of a positive or constructive nature. This accounts for the strange phenomenon so many millions of people experience, referred to as 'misfortune', or 'bad luck'.

Millions of people *believe* themselves 'doomed' to poverty and failure, because of some strange force over which they *believe* they have no control. They are the creators of their own 'misfortunes' because of this negative *belief*, which is picked up by the subconscious mind and translated into its physical equivalent.

This is an appropriate place at which to suggest again that you may benefit by passing on to your subconscious mind any *desire* that you wish translated into its physical or monetary equivalent, in a state of expectancy or *belief* that the transmutation will actually take place. Your *belief* or *faith* is the element that determines the action of your subconscious mind. There is nothing to hinder you from 'deceiving' your subconscious mind when giving it instructions through autosuggestion, as I deceived my son's subconscious mind. To make this 'deceit' more realistic, conduct yourself just as you would if you were ALREADY IN POSSESSION OF THE MATERIAL THING WHICH YOU ARE DEMANDING when you call upon your subconscious mind. The subconscious mind will transmute into its physical equivalent, by the most direct and practical media available, any order given to it in a state of *belief* or *faith* that the order will be carried out.

Surely enough has been stated to give a starting point from which one may, through experiment and practice, acquire the ability to mix *faith* with any order given to the subconscious mind. Perfection will come through practice. It cannot come by merely reading instructions.

If it is true that one may become a criminal by association with crime (and this is a known fact), it is equally true that one may develop faith by voluntarily suggesting to the subconscious mind that one has faith. The mind comes, finally, to take on the nature of the influences that dominate it. Understand this truth and you will know why it is essential for you to encourage the positive emotions as dominating forces of your mind, and discourage – and eliminate – negative emotions.

A mind dominated by positive emotions becomes a favourable abode for the state of mind known as faith. A mind so dominated may, at will, give the subconscious mind instructions, which it will accept and act upon immediately.

Faith is a State of Mind which May Be Induced by Autosuggestion

All through the ages, religious leaders have admonished struggling humanity to 'have faith' in this, that and the other dogma or creed, but they have failed to tell people *how* to have faith. They have not stated that faith is a state of mind, and that it may be induced by self-suggestion.

In language any normal human being can understand we will describe all that is known about the principle through which *faith* may be developed, where it does not already exist.

Have Faith in yourself; Faith in the Infinite.

Before we begin, you should be reminded again that:

> *FAITH is the 'eternal elixir' which gives life, power and action to the impulse of thought!*

> The foregoing sentence is worth reading a second time, and a third, and a fourth. It is worth reading aloud!

> FAITH is the starting point of all accumulation of riches!

> FAITH is the basis of all 'miracles' and mysteries that cannot be analysed by the rules of science!

> FAITH is the only known antidote to FAILURE!

> FAITH is the element, the 'chemical' which, when mixed with prayer, gives one direct communication with Infinite Intelligence.

> FAITH is the element that transforms the ordinary vibration of thought, created by the finite mind of man, into the spiritual equivalent.

FAITH is the only agency through which the cosmic force of Infinite Intelligence can be harnessed and used.

EVERY ONE OF THE FOREGOING STATEMENTS IS CAPABLE OF PROOF!

The proof is simple and easily demonstrated. It is wrapped up in the principle of autosuggestion. Let us centre our attention, therefore, upon the subject of self-suggestion, and find out what it is capable of achieving.

It is a well-known fact that one comes, finally, to *believe* whatever one repeats to one's self, whether the statement be true or false. If a person repeats a lie over and over, the lie will eventually be accepted as truth. Moreover, it will be *believed* to be the truth. Each of us is what we are because of the *dominating thoughts* we permit to occupy our minds. Thoughts which are deliberately placed in our own mind, and encouraged with sympathy, and with which are mixed any one or more of the emotions, constitute the motivating forces. These forces direct and control our every movement, act and deed!

THOUGHTS WHICH ARE MIXED WITH ANY OF THE FEELINGS OR EMOTIONS CONSTITUTE A 'MAGNETIC' FORCE WHICH ATTRACTS, FROM THE VIBRATIONS OF THE ETHER, OTHER SIMILAR OR RELATED THOUGHTS.

A thought thus 'magnetised' with emotion may be compared to a seed that, when planted in fertile soil, germinates, grows and multiplies itself over and over again, until that one small seed becomes countless millions of seeds of the *same brand*!

The ether is a great cosmic mass of eternal forces of vibration. It is made up of both destructive vibrations and constructive vibrations. It carries, at all times, vibrations of fear, poverty, disease, failure, misery; and vibrations of prosperity, health, success and happiness. It does this just as surely as it carries the sound of hundreds of orchestrations of music and hundreds of human voices, all of which maintain their individuality and means of identification, through the medium of radio.

From the great storehouse of the ether, the human mind is constantly attracting vibrations that harmonise with that which *dominates* the mind. Any thought, idea, plan or purpose which one holds in one's mind attracts, from the vibrations of the ether, a host of its relatives. It adds these 'relatives' to its own force, and grows until it becomes the dominating *motivating master* of the individual in whose mind it has been housed.

Now, let us go back to the starting point, and find out how the original seed of an idea, plan or purpose may be planted in the mind. The information is easily conveyed: any idea, plan or purpose may be placed in the mind through repetition of thought. This is why you are asked to write out a statement of your major purpose, or Definite Chief Aim, commit it to memory and repeat it – in audible words, day after day – until these vibrations of sound have reached your subconscious mind.

We are what we are because of the vibrations of thought that we pick up and register through the stimuli of our daily environment.

Resolve to throw off the influences of any unfortunate environment and to build your own life to *order*. Taking an inventory of mental assets and liabilities, you will discover that your greatest weakness is lack of self-confidence. This handicap can be surmounted – and timidity translated into courage – through the aid of the principle of autosuggestion. The application of this principle may be made through a simple arrangement of positive thought impulses stated in writing, memorised and repeated, until they become a part of the working equipment of the subconscious faculty of your mind.

Self-confidence Formula

1. I know that I have the ability to achieve the object of my Definite Purpose in life. Therefore I *demand* of myself persistent, continuous action towards its attainment, and I here and now promise to take such action.

2. I realise the dominating thoughts of my mind will eventually reproduce themselves in outward, physical action and gradually transform themselves into physical reality. Therefore I will concentrate my thoughts for 30 minutes daily upon the task of thinking of the person I intend to become, thereby creating in my mind a clear mental picture of that person.

3. I know through the principle of autosuggestion that any desire I persistently hold in my mind will eventually seek expression through some practical means of attaining the object. Therefore I will devote 10 minutes daily to demanding of myself the development of *self-confidence*.

4. I have clearly written down a description of my *Definite Chief Aim* in life. I will never stop trying until I have developed sufficient self-confidence for its attainment.

5. I fully realise that no wealth or position can long endure unless built upon truth and justice. Therefore I will engage in no transaction that does not benefit all whom it affects. I will succeed by attracting to myself the forces I wish to use, and the cooperation of other people. I

will induce others to serve me because of my
willingness to serve others. I will eliminate hatred, envy,
jealousy, selfishness and cynicism by developing love for
all humanity because I know that a negative attitude
towards others can never bring me success. I will cause
others to believe in me, because I will believe in them,
and in myself. I will sign my name to this formula,
commit it to memory and repeat it aloud once a day,
with full *faith* that it will gradually influence my *thoughts*
and *actions* so that I will become a self-reliant and
successful person.

Underpinning this formula is a law of Nature that no one has yet
been able to explain. It has baffled the scientists of all ages.
Psychologists have named this law 'autosuggestion', and let it go at
that. The name by which one calls this law is of little importance.
The important fact about it is it *works* for the glory and success of
humankind *if* it is used constructively. If used destructively, on the
other hand, it will destroy just as readily. In this statement may be
found a significant truth: those who go down in defeat and end
their lives in poverty, misery and distress do so because of negative
application of the principle of autosuggestion. The cause may be
found in the fact that ALL IMPULSES OF THOUGHT HAVE
A TENDENCY TO CLOTHE THEMSELVES IN THEIR
PHYSICAL EQUIVALENT.

The subconscious mind (the chemical laboratory in which
all thought impulses are combined and made ready for translation into physical reality) makes no distinction between
constructive and destructive thought impulses. It works with
the material we feed it through our thought impulses. The
subconscious mind will translate into reality a thought driven

by *fear* just as readily as it will translate into reality a thought driven by *courage* or *faith*.

The pages of medical history are rich with illustrations of cases of 'suggestive suicide'. A person may commit suicide through negative suggestion, just as effectively as by any other means. In a Midwestern city, a bank official named Joseph Grant borrowed a large sum of the bank's money without the consent of the directors. He lost the money through gambling. One afternoon, the Bank Examiner came and began to check the accounts. Grant left the bank and took a room in a local hotel. When they found him, three days later, he was lying in bed, wailing and moaning, repeating over and over these words, 'My God, this will kill me! I cannot stand the disgrace.' In a short time he was dead. The doctors pronounced the case one of 'mental suicide'.

Just as electricity will turn the wheels of industry and provide useful service if used constructively, or snuff out life if wrongly used, so will the law of autosuggestion lead you to peace and prosperity or down into the valley of misery, failure and death. It all depends on your degree of understanding and application of it.

If you fill your mind with *fear*, doubt and disbelief in your ability to connect with and use the forces of Infinite Intelligence, the law of autosuggestion will take this spirit of unbelief and use it as a pattern which your subconscious mind will translate into its physical equivalent.

THIS STATEMENT IS AS TRUE AS THE STATEMENT THAT TWO AND TWO ARE FOUR!

Like the wind that carries one ship east and another west, the law of autosuggestion will lift you up or pull you down, according to the way you set your sails of *thought*.

The law of autosuggestion, through which any person may rise to altitudes of achievement that stagger the imagination, is well described in the following verse:

> If you *think* you are beaten, you are,
> If you *think* you dare not, you don't
> If you like to win, but you *think* you can't,
> It is almost certain you won't.
>
> If you *think* you'll lose, you're lost
> For out of the world we find,
> Success begins with a person's will –
> It's all in the *state of mind*.
>
> If you *think* you are outclassed, you are,
> You've got to *think* high to rise.
> You've got to be *sure of yourself* before
> You can ever win a prize.
>
> Life's battles don't always go
> To the stronger or faster man
> But soon or late the one who wins
> Is the one WHO THINKS HE CAN!

Observe the words which have been emphasised, and you will catch the deep meaning the poet had in mind.

Somewhere in your make-up (perhaps in the cells of your brain) lies sleeping the seed of achievement. If aroused and put into action, this would carry you to heights such as you may never have hoped to attain.

Just as a master musician may cause the most beautiful strains of music to pour forth from the strings of a violin, so may you arouse the genius which lies asleep in your brain, and cause it to drive you upward to whatever goal you may wish to achieve.

Abraham Lincoln was a failure at everything he tried until he was well past the age of 40. He was a Mr Nobody from Nowhere until a great experience came into his life, aroused the sleeping genius within his heart and brain, and gave the world one of its really great men. That 'experience' was mixed with the emotions of sorrow and *love*. It came to him through Anne Rutledge, the only woman he ever truly loved.

It is a known fact that the emotion of *love* is closely akin to the state of mind known as *faith*. Love comes very near to translating one's thought impulses into their spiritual equivalent. During his research, the author discovered, from the analysis of the work and achievements of hundreds of men of outstanding accomplishment, that there was the influence of a woman's love behind nearly *every one of them*.

The emotion of love, in the human heart and brain, creates a favourable field of magnetic attraction, This causes an influx of the higher and finer vibrations that are afloat in the ether.

Let us consider the power of *faith* as it is was demonstrated by a man well known to all of civilisation, Mahatma Gandhi of India. In this man the world experienced one of the most astounding examples of the possibilities of FAITH. Gandhi wielded more potential power than any man living in his time, and this despite the fact that he had none of the orthodox tools of power, such as money, battleships, soldiers and materials of warfare. Gandhi had no money. He had no home. He didn't even own a suit of clothes but *he did have power*. How did he come by that power?

HE CREATED IT OUT OF HIS UNDERSTANDING

OF THE PRINCIPLE OF FAITH. AND THROUGH HIS ABILITY TO TRANSPLANT THAT FAITH INTO THE MINDS OF 200 MILLION PEOPLE.

Gandhi accomplished, through the influence of *faith*, something that the strongest military power on earth could not, and never will, achieve through soldiers and military equipment. He accomplished the astounding feat of *influencing* 200 million minds to *coalesce and move in unison, as a single mind*. What other force on earth, except *faith*, could do as much?

In the mid-20th century, Martin Luther King, through his deep faith in his belief in human rights and dignity for all people, led men and women of all races, religions and beliefs to join in his struggle for civil rights. His dream that people will not be judged by the colour of their skin but the content of their character has not been fully realised, but his work and his death have led to significant improvements in civil rights and an impetus to keep fighting for their achievement.

The watchword of the future will be *human happiness and contentment*. When this state of mind has been attained, the production will take care of itself more effectively than anything ever accomplished where people did not, and could not, mix *faith* and individual interest with their labour.

Because of the need for faith and cooperation in business and industry, it will be both interesting and profitable to analyse a particular event. This provides an excellent understanding of the method by which industrialists and leaders of business accumulate great fortunes, by giving before they try to get.

The event chosen for this illustration dates back to 1900, when the United States Steel Corporation was being formed. As you read the story, keep in mind these fundamental facts and you will understand how *ideas* have been converted into huge fortunes.

First, the huge United States Steel Corporation was born in the mind of Charles M. Schwab, in the form of an *idea* he created through his *imagination*. Second, he mixed *faith* with his idea. Third, he formulated a *plan* for the transformation of his idea into physical and financial reality. Fourth, he put his plan into action with his famous speech at the University Club. Fifth, he applied and followed through on his plan with *persistence*, and backed it with firm *decision* until it had been fully carried out. Sixth, he prepared the way for success by a *burning desire* for success.

If you have often wondered how great fortunes are accumulated, this story of the creation of the United States Steel Corporation will be enlightening. If you have any doubt that people can *think and grow rich*, this story should dispel that doubt, because in it you can plainly see the application of a major portion of the 13 principles described in this book.

John Lowell, in the *New York World-Telegram*, with whose courtesy it is here reprinted, dramatically told this astounding story of the power of an *idea*.

A Pretty After-dinner Speech for a Billion Dollars

'When, on the evening of December 12, 1900, some eighty of the nation's financial nobility gathered in the banquet hall of the University Club on Fifth Avenue to do honor to a young man from out of the West, not half a dozen of the guests realized they were to witness the most significant episode in American industrial history.

'J. Edward Simmons and Charles Stewart Smith, their hearts full of gratitude for the lavish hospitality bestowed on them by

Charles M. Schwab during a recent visit to Pittsburgh, had arranged the dinner to introduce the thirty-eight-year-old steel man to eastern banking society. But they didn't expect him to stampede the convention. They warned him, in fact, that the bosoms within New York's stuffed shirts would not be responsive to oratory, and that, if he didn't want to bore the Stilimans and Harrimans and Vanderbilts, he had better limit himself to fifteen or twenty minutes of polite vaporings and let it go at that.

'Even John Pierpont Morgan, sitting on the right hand of Schwab as became his imperial dignity, intended to grace the banquet table with his presence only briefly. And so far as the press and public were concerned, the whole affair was of so little moment that no mention of it found its way into print the next day.

'So the two hosts and their distinguished guests ate their way through the usual seven or eight courses. There was little conversation and what there was of it was restrained. Few of the bankers and brokers had met Schwab, whose career had flowered along the banks of the Monongahela, and none knew him well. But before the evening was over, they – and with them Money Master Morgan – were to be swept off their feet, and a billion dollar baby, the United States Steel Corporation, was to be conceived.

'It is perhaps unfortunate, for the sake of history, that no record of Charlie Schwab's speech at the dinner ever was made. He repeated some parts of it at a later date during a similar meeting of Chicago bankers. And still later, when the Government brought suit to dissolve the Steel Trust, he gave his own version, from the witness stand, of the remarks that stimulated Morgan into a frenzy of financial activity.

'It is probable, however, that it was a "homely" speech,

somewhat ungrammatical (for the niceties of language never bothered Schwab), full of epigrams and threaded with wit. But aside from that it had a galvanic force and effect upon the five billions of estimated capital that was represented by the diners. After it was over and the gathering was still under its spell, although Schwab had talked for ninety minutes, Morgan led the orator to a recessed window where, dangling their legs from the high, uncomfortable seat, they talked for an hour more.

'The magic of the Schwab personality had been turned on, full force, but what was more important and lasting was the full-fledged, clear-cut program he laid down for the aggrandizement of Steel. Many other men had tried to interest Morgan in slapping together a steel trust after the pattern of the biscuit, wire and hoop, sugar, rubber, whisky, oil or chewing gum combinations. John W. Gates, the gambler, had urged it, but Morgan distrusted him. The Moore boys, Bill and Jim, Chicago stockjobbers who had glued together a match trust and a cracker corporation, had urged it and failed. Elbert H. Gary, the sanctimonious country lawyer, wanted to foster it, but he wasn't big enough to be impressive. Until Schwab's eloquence took J. P. Morgan to the heights from which he could visualize the solid results of the most daring financial undertaking ever conceived, the project was regarded as a delirious dream of easy-money crackpots.

'The financial magnetism that began, a generation ago, to attract thousands of small and sometimes inefficiently managed companies into large and competition-crushing combinations, had become operative in the steel world through the devices of that jovial business pirate, John W. Gates. Gates already had formed the American Steel and Wire Company out of a chain of small concerns, and together with Morgan had created the

Federal Steel Company. The National Tube and American Bridge companies were two more Morgan concerns, and the Moore Brothers had forsaken the match and cookie business to form the "American" group – Tin Plate, Steel Hoop, Sheet Steel – and the National Steel Company.

'But by the side of Andrew Carnegie's gigantic vertical trust, a trust owned and operated by fifty-three partners, those other combinations were picayune. They might combine to their heart's content but the whole lot of them couldn't make a dent in the Carnegie organization, and Morgan knew it.

'The eccentric old Scot knew it, too. From the magnificent heights of Skibo Castle he had viewed, first with amusement and then with resentment, the attempts of Morgan's smaller companies to cut into his business. When the attempts became too bold, Carnegie's temper was translated into anger and retaliation. He decided to duplicate every mill owned by his rivals. Hitherto, he hadn't been interested in wire, pipe, hoops, or sheet. Instead, he was content to sell such companies the raw steel and let them work it into whatever shape they wanted. Now, with Schwab as his chief and able lieutenant, he planned to drive his enemies to the wall.

'So it was that in the speech of Charles M. Schwab, Morgan saw the answer to his problem of combination. A trust without Carnegie – giant of them all – would be no trust at all, a plum pudding, as one writer said, without the plums. Schwab's speech on the night of December 12, 1900, undoubtedly carried the inference, though not the pledge, that the vast Carnegie enterprise could be brought under the Morgan tent. He talked of the world future for steel, of reorganization for efficiency, of specialization, of the scrapping of unsuccessful mills and concentration of effort on the flourishing properties, of economies in the ore traffic, of economies in overhead and administrative departments, of capturing foreign markets.

'More than that, he told the buccaneers among them wherein lay the errors of their customary piracy. Their purposes, he inferred, had been to create monopolies, raise prices, and pay themselves fat dividends out of privilege. Schwab condemned the system in his heartiest manner. The shortsightedness of such a policy, he told his hearers, lay in the fact that it restricted the market in an era when everything cried for expansion. By cheapening the cost of steel, he argued, an ever-expanding market would be created; more uses for steel would be devised, and a goodly portion of the world trade could be captured. Actually, though he did not know it, Schwab was an apostle of modern mass production.

'So the dinner at the University Club came to an end. Morgan went home to think about Schwab's rosy predictions. Schwab went back to Pittsburgh to run the steel business for Andrew Carnegie, while Gary and the rest went back to their stock tickers, to fiddle around in anticipation of the next move.

'It was not long coming. It took Morgan about one week to digest the feast of reason Schwab had placed before him. When he had assured himself that no financial indigestion was to result, he sent for Schwab – and found that young man rather coy. Mr Carnegie, Schwab indicated, might not like it if he found his trusted company president had been flirting with the Emperor of Wall Street, the street upon which Carnegie was resolved never to tread. Then it was suggested by John W. Gates, the go-between, that if Schwab "happened" to be in the Bellevue Hotel in Philadelphia, J.P. Morgan might also "happen" to be there. When Schwab arrived, however, Morgan was inconveniently ill at his New York home, and so, on the elder man's pressing invitation, Schwab went to New York and presented himself at the door of the financier's library.

'Now certain economic historians have professed the belief that from the beginning to the end of the drama, the stage was set by Andrew Carnegie – that the dinner, the famous speech, the Sunday night conference between Schwab and the Money King, were events arranged by the canny Scot. The truth is exactly the opposite. When Schwab was called in to consummate the deal, he didn't even know whether "the little boss", as Andrew was called, would so much as listen to an offer to sell, particularly to a group of men whom Andrew regarded as being endowed with something less than holiness. But Schwab did take into the conference with him, in his own handwriting, six sheets of copperplate figures, representing to his mind the physical worth and the potential earning capacity of every steel company he regarded as an essential star in the new metal firmament.

'Four men pondered over these figures all night. The chief, of course, was Morgan, steadfast in his belief in the Divine Right of Money. With him was his aristocratic partner, Robert Bacon, a scholar and a gentleman. The third was John W. Gates whom Morgan scorned as a gambler and used as a tool. The fourth was Schwab, who knew more about the processes of making and selling steel than any whole group of men then living. Throughout that conference, the Pittsburgher's figures were never questioned. If he said a company was worth so much, then it was worth that much and no more. He was insistent, too, upon including in the combination only those concerns he nominated. He had conceived a corporation in which there would be no duplication, not even to satisfy the greed of friends who wanted to unload their companies upon the broad Morgan shoulders. Thus he left out, by design, a number of the larger concerns upon which the Walruses and Carpenters of Wall Street had cast hungry eyes.

'When dawn came, Morgan rose and straightened his back. Only one question remained.

'"Do you think you can persuade Andrew Carnegie to sell?" he asked.

'"I can try," said Schwab.

'"If you can get him to sell, I will undertake the matter," said Morgan.

'So far so good. But would Carnegie sell? How much would he demand? (Schwab thought about $320,000,000.) What would he take payment in? Common or preferred stocks? Bonds? Cash? Nobody could raise a third of a billion dollars in cash.

'There was a golf game in January on the frost-cracking heath of the St Andrews links in Westchester, with Andrew bundled up in sweaters against the cold, and Charlie talking volubly, as usual, to keep his spirits up. But no word of business was mentioned until the pair sat down in the cozy warmth of the Carnegie cottage hard by. Then, with the same persuasiveness that had hypnotized eighty millionaires at the University Club, Schwab poured out the glittering promises of retirement in comfort, of untold millions to satisfy the old man's social caprices. Carnegie capitulated, wrote a figure on a slip of paper, handed it to Schwab and said, "All right, that's what we'll sell for."

'The figure was approximately $400,000,000, and was reached by taking the $320,000,000 mentioned by Schwab as a basic figure, and adding to it $80,000,000 to represent the increased capital value over the previous two years.

'Later, on the deck of a trans-Atlantic liner, the Scotsman said ruefully to Morgan, "I wish I had asked you for $100,000,000 more."

"'If you had asked for it, you'd have gotten it," Morgan told him cheerfully.

'The thirty-eight-year-old Schwab had his reward. He was made president of the new corporation and remained in control until 1930.'

This dramatic story of big business was included in this book because it is a perfect illustration of the method by which *desire can be transmuted into its physical equivalent*. I imagine some readers will question the statement that a mere, intangible *desire* can be converted into its physical equivalent. Doubtless some will say, 'You cannot convert *nothing* into *something*!' The answer is in the story of United States Steel. That giant organisation was created in the mind of one man. The plan by which the organisation was provided with the steel mills that gave it financial stability was created in the mind of the same man. His *faith*, his *desire*, his *imagination*, his *persistence* were the real ingredients that went into United States Steel. The steel mills and mechanical equipment acquired by the corporation *after it had been brought into legal existence* were incidental, but careful analysis will disclose the fact that the appraised value of the properties acquired by the corporation increased in value by an estimated *six hundred million dollars* by the mere transaction that consolidated them under one management.

In other words, Charles M. Schwab's *idea*, plus the *faith* with which he conveyed it to the minds of J.P. Morgan and the others, was marketed for a profit of approximately $600,000,000. Not an insignificant sum for a single idea!

What happened to some of the people who took their share

of the millions of dollars of profit made by this transaction is a matter with which we are not now concerned. The important feature of the astounding achievement is that it serves as unquestionable evidence of the soundness of the philosophy described in this book. Moreover, the practicality of the philosophy has been established by the fact that the United States Steel Corporation prospered. It became one of the richest and most powerful corporations in America, employing thousands of people, developing new uses for steel and opening new markets; thus proving that the $600,000,000 in profit which the Schwab *idea* produced was earned.

Riches begin in the form of *thought*. The amount is limited only by the person in whose mind the thought is put into motion. *Faith* removes limitation. Remember this when you are ready to bargain with Life for whatever it is that you ask as your price for having passed this way. Remember, also, that the man who created the United States Steel Corporation was practically unknown at the time. He was merely Andrew Carnegie's 'Man Friday' until he gave birth to his famous idea. After that, he quickly rose to a position of power, fame and riches.

Now for another example of how faith *in an idea made millions for one man and through it helped countless others increase their wealth. Sir John Templeton is a man with great faith in his talent to make sound and profitable investments.*

Templeton was better than most people at investing money because people often made investments based on emotion and ignorance and not common sense. He felt that by using his skill in investing, he could not only provide a needed service to the small investor, but make a good deal of money for himself as well.

To accomplish this he started a group of mutual funds to manage other people's money. This was a pioneering project as mutual funds were a relatively new concept at the time. Templeton honed that concept into what it is today.

He reminisced that at the Templeton Growth Fund's first annual meeting the participants consisted of John Templeton, one part-time employee and one shareholder. 'We held the meeting in the dining room of a retired General Foods executive, to save money.'

The Templeton funds now have more than 6,000 employees worldwide and $36 billion in assets. Driving that growth is the Templeton Group's well-earned reputation as the premier fund group for investing. A $10,000 investment in the Templeton Growth Fund 40 years ago is worth $3 million today.

By the time he retired and sold his Templeton Group fund interests in 1992 (estimated at $400 million), John Templeton estimated that he had helped a million people make money, in addition to his own success.

*THERE ARE NO LIMITATIONS
TO THE MIND EXCEPT THOSE
WE ACKNOWLEDGE.*

*BOTH POVERTY AND RICHES
ARE THE OFFSPRING OF
THOUGHT.*

CHAPTER 4

AUTO-SUGGESTION:

the Medium for Influencing the Subconscious Mind

(The Third Step to Riches)

Autosuggestion is a term that applies to all suggestions and all self-administered stimuli that reach one's mind through the five senses. Stated in another way, autosuggestion is self-suggestion. It is the agency of communication between that part of the mind where conscious thought takes place, and that which serves as the seat of action for the subconscious mind. Through the dominating thoughts one permits to remain in the conscious mind (whether these thoughts be negative or positive is immaterial), the principle of autosuggestion voluntarily reaches the subconscious mind and influences it with these thoughts.

NO THOUGHT, whether it is negative or positive, CAN ENTER THE SUBCONSCIOUS MIND WITHOUT THE AID OF THE PRINCIPLE OF AUTOSUGGESTION, with the exception of thoughts picked up from the ether. Stated differently, all sense impressions which are perceived through the five senses are stopped by the *conscious* thinking mind, and may be either passed on to the subconscious mind or rejected at will. The conscious faculty serves, therefore, as an outer guard to the approach of the subconscious.

Nature has so built us that we have *absolute control* over the material which reaches our subconscious mind through our five senses, although this is not meant to be construed as a statement that we always *exercise* this control. In the great majority of instances, we do *not* exercise it, which explains why so many people go through life in poverty.

Recall what has been said about the subconscious mind resembling a fertile garden spot in which weeds will grow in abundance if the seeds of more desirable crops are not sown there. Autosuggestion is the agency of control through which an individual may voluntarily feed the subconscious mind thoughts of a creative nature or, by neglect, permit thoughts of a destructive nature to find their way into this rich garden of the mind.

You were instructed, in the last of the six steps described in Chapter 2, to read aloud twice daily the written statement of your desire for money, and to see and feel yourself already in possession of the money, By following these instructions, you communicate the object of your *desire* directly to your *subconscious* mind in a spirit of absolute *faith*. Through repetition of this procedure, you voluntarily create thought habits favourable to your efforts to transmute desire into its monetary equivalent.

Go back to these six steps described in Chapter 2, and read them again, very carefully, before you proceed further. Then (when you come to it), read very carefully the four instructions for the organisation of your 'Master Mind' group, described in

Chapter 7. By comparing these two sets of instructions with that which has been stated on autosuggestion, you will see that the instructions involve the application of the principle of auto-suggestion.

Remember, therefore, when reading aloud the statement of your desire (through which you are endeavouring to develop a 'money consciousness'), that the mere reading of the words is of no consequence unless you mix emotion, or feeling, with your words. If you repeat a million times the famous Emil Coué formula, 'Day by day, in every way, I am getting better and better', without mixing emotion and *faith* with your words, you will experience no desirable results. Your subconscious mind recognises and acts *only* upon thoughts that have been well mixed with emotion or feeling.

This is a fact of such importance as to warrant repetition in practically every chapter. The lack of understanding of this is the main reason the majority of people who try to apply the principle of autosuggestion get no desirable results.

Plain, unemotional words do not influence the subconscious mind. You will get no appreciable results until you learn to reach your subconscious mind with thoughts or spoken words that have been well emotionalised with *belief*. Do not become discouraged if you cannot control and direct your emotions the first time you try to do so. Remember, there is no such possibility as *something for nothing*. Ability to reach and influence your subconscious mind has its price, and you *must pay that price*. You cannot cheat, even if you desire to do so. The price of ability to influence your subconscious mind is everlasting *persistence* in applying the principles described here. You cannot develop the desired ability for a lower price. You, and *you alone*, must decide whether or not the reward for which you are striving (the 'money consciousness') is worth the price you must pay for it in effort.

Wisdom and cleverness alone will not attract and retain money except in a few very rare instances where the law of averages favours the attraction of money through these sources. The method of attracting money described here does not depend upon the law of averages. Moreover, the method plays no favourites. It will work for one person as effectively as it will for another. Where failure is experienced, it is the individual, not the method, which has failed. If you try and fail, make another effort, and still another, until you succeed.

Your ability to use the principle of autosuggestion will depend, very largely, upon your capacity to *concentrate* upon a given *desire* until that desire becomes a *burning obsession*.

When you begin to carry out the instructions in connection with the six steps described in the second chapter, it will be necessary for you to make use of the principle of *concentration*.

Let us here offer suggestions for the effective use of concentration. When you begin to carry out the first of the six steps, which instructs you to 'fix in your own mind the *exact* amount of money you desire', hold your thoughts on that amount of money by *concentration*, or fixation of attention, with your eyes closed, until you can *actually see* the physical appearance of the money. Do this at least once each day. As you go through these exercises, follow the instructions given in the chapter on *faith*, and see yourself actually *in possession of the money*.

Here is a most significant fact – the subconscious mind takes any orders given it in a spirit of absolute *faith* and acts upon those orders, although the orders often have to be presented over and over again, through repetition, before they are interpreted by the subconscious mind. Consider the possibility of playing a perfectly legitimate 'trick' on your subconscious mind by making it believe – because you believe it – that you must have the amount of money you are visualising, that this money is already awaiting your claim, that the subconscious mind *must* hand over to you practical plans for acquiring the money which is yours. Hand over this thought to your *imagination*, and see what your imagination can, or will, do to create practical plans for the accumulation of money through transmutation of your desire.

Do not wait for a definite plan through which you intend to exchange services or merchandise in return for the money you are visualising. Begin at once to see yourself in possession of the money, *demanding* and *expecting* meanwhile that your subconscious mind will hand over the plan, or plans, you need. Be on the alert for these plans, and when they appear, put them into action immediately. They will probably 'flash' into your mind through the sixth sense, in the form of an 'inspiration'. This inspiration may be considered a direct message from Infinite Intelligence. Treat it with respect, and act upon it as soon as you receive it. Failure to do this will be *fatal* to your success.

In the fourth of the six steps, you were instructed to 'Create a definite plan for carrying out your desire, and begin at once to put this plan into action.' You should follow this instruction in the manner described in the preceding paragraph. Do not trust to your 'reason' when creating your plan. Your reason is faulty. Moreover, your reasoning faculty may be lazy, and, if you depend entirely upon it to serve you, it may disappoint you.

When visualising the money you intend to accumulate (with closed eyes), see yourself rendering the service, or delivering the merchandise you intend to give in return for this money. This is important!

Summary of Instructions

The fact you are reading this book is an indication that you earnestly seek knowledge. It is also an indication that you are a student of this subject. If you are only a student, there is a chance you may learn much, but you will learn only by assuming an attitude of humility. If you choose to follow some of the instructions but neglect or refuse to follow others, you will fail! To get satisfactory results, you must follow *all* instructions in a spirit of *faith*.

The instructions given in connection with the six steps in Chapter 2 will now be summarised and blended with the principles covered by this chapter:

1. Go into some quiet spot (preferably in bed at night) where you will not be disturbed or interrupted. Close your eyes and repeat aloud (so you may hear your own words) the written statement of the amount of money you intend to accumulate, the time limit for its accumulation, and a description of the service or merchandise you intend to give in return for the money. As you carry out these instructions, *see yourself already in possession of the money*. For example: suppose you intend to accumulate $100,000 by the first of January, five years hence, and that you intend to give personal services in return for the money in the capacity of a sales representative. Your written statement of your purpose should be similar to the following:

   'By the first day of January 20 . . . I will have in my possession $100,000, which will come to me in various amounts from time to time during the interim.

'In return for this money I will give the most efficient service of which I am capable, rendering the fullest possible quantity and the best possible quality of service as a sales representative of (describe the service or merchandise you intend to sell).

'I believe I will have this money in my possession. My faith is so strong that I can now see this money before my eyes. I can touch it with my hands. It is now awaiting transfer to me in the proportion that I deliver the service I intend to render in return for it. I am awaiting a plan by which to accumulate this money, and I will follow that plan when it is received.'

2. Repeat this programme night and morning until you can see (in your imagination) the money you intend to accumulate.

3. Place a written copy of your statement where you can see it night and morning. Read it just before retiring and upon rising until it has been memorised.

As you carry out these instructions, remember that you are applying the principle of autosuggestion for the purpose of giving orders to your subconscious mind. Remember, also, that your subconscious mind will act *only* upon instructions that are emotionalised and handed over to it with 'feeling'. *Faith* is the strongest and most productive of the emotions. Follow the instructions given in Chapter 3.

These instructions may, at first, seem abstract. Do not let this disturb you. Follow them anyway. The time will soon come, if you do as you have been instructed in spirit as well as in action, when a whole new universe of power will unfold to you. Scepticism, in connection with *all* new ideas, is characteristic of all human beings. But if you follow the instructions outlined, your scepticism will soon be replaced by belief, and this in turn will soon become crystallised into *absolute faith*. Then you will have arrived at the point where you may truly say, 'I am the Master of my Fate, I am the Captain of my Soul!'

Many philosophers have made the statement that people have control over their own earthly destinies, but most of them have failed to say why this is. The reason why one may control one's own earthly status, and especially one's financial status, is thoroughly explained in this chapter. People may gain control of themselves and their environment because they have the *power to influence their own subconscious minds*, and through it gain the cooperation of Infinite Intelligence.

You are now reading the chapter that represents the keystone to the arch of this philosophy. The instructions contained in this chapter must be understood and *applied with persistence* if you are to succeed in transmuting desire into money.

The actual performance of transmuting *desire* into money involves the use of autosuggestion as an agency by which one may reach, and influence, the subconscious mind. The other principles are simply tools with which to apply autosuggestion. Keep this thought in mind, and you will, at all times, be conscious of the important part the principle of autosuggestion is to play in your efforts to accumulate money through the methods described in this book.

Carry out these instructions as though you were a small child. Inject into your efforts something of the *faith* of a child. The author has been most careful to see that no impractical instructions have been included because of his sincere desire to be helpful.

After you have read the entire book, come back to this chapter, and follow in spirit, and in action, this instruction:

READ THE ENTIRE CHAPTER ALOUD ONCE EVERY NIGHT, UNTIL YOU BECOME THOROUGHLY CONVINCED THAT THE PRINCIPLE OF AUTO-SUGGESTION IS SOUND, THAT IT WILL ACCOMPLISH FOR YOU ALL THAT HAS BEEN CLAIMED FOR IT. AS YOU READ, UNDERSCORE WITH A PENCIL EVERY SENTENCE THAT IMPRESSES YOU FAVOURABLY.

Follow this instruction to the letter and it will open the way for a complete understanding and mastery of the principles of success.

CHAPTER 5

SPECIALISED KNOWLEDGE:

Personal Experiences or Observations

(The Fourth Step to Riches)

There are two kinds of knowledge. One is general, the other is specialised. General knowledge, no matter how great in quantity or variety it may be, is of but little use in the accumulation of money. The faculties of the great universities possess, in the aggregate, practically every form of general knowledge known to civilisation. They specialise in teaching knowledge, but they do not specialise in the organisation, or the use, of knowledge.

Knowledge will not attract money unless it is organised and intelligently directed through practical *plans of action* to the *definite end* of accumulation of money. Lack of understanding of this fact has been the source of confusion to millions of people who falsely believe that 'knowledge is power'. It is nothing of the sort! Knowledge is only potential power. It becomes power only when, and if, it is organised into definite plans of action and directed to a definite end.

This 'missing link' in all systems of education known to civilisation today may be found in the failure of educational institutions to teach their students HOW TO ORGANISE AND USE KNOWLEDGE AFTER THEY ACQUIRE IT.

Many people make the mistake of assuming that, because Henry Ford had but little 'schooling', he is not a man of 'education'. Those who make this mistake do not know Henry Ford, nor do they understand the real meaning of the word 'educate'. That word is derived from the Latin 'educo', meaning to educe, to draw out, to *develop from within*.

An educated person is not necessarily one who has an abundance of general or specialised knowledge. Educated people have developed the faculties of their minds so that they may acquire anything they want, or its equivalent, without violating the rights of others. Henry Ford comes well within the meaning of this definition.

During World War I, a Chicago newspaper published certain editorials in which, among other statements, Henry Ford was called 'an ignorant pacifist'. Mr Ford objected to the statements, and brought a suit against the paper for libelling him. When the suit was tried in the courts, the attorneys for the paper pleaded justification, and placed Mr Ford himself on the witness stand for the purpose of proving to the jury that he was ignorant. The attorneys asked Mr Ford a great variety of questions, all of them intended to prove, by his own evidence, that while he might possess considerable specialised knowledge pertaining to the manufacture of cars, he was, in the main, ignorant.

Mr Ford was plied with such questions as the following:

'Who was Benedict Arnold?' and 'How many soldiers did the

British send over to America to put down the Rebellion of 1776?' In answer to the last question, Mr Ford replied, 'I do not know the exact number of soldiers the British sent over, but I have heard that it was a considerably larger number than ever went back.'

Finally, Mr Ford became tired of this line of questioning. In reply to a particularly offensive question, he leaned over, pointed his finger at the lawyer who had asked the question, and said, 'If I should really *want* to answer the foolish question you have just asked, or any of the other questions you have been asking me, let me remind you that I have a row of electric push-buttons on my desk, and by pushing the right button, I can summon to my aid people who can answer *any* question I desire to ask concerning the business to which I am devoting most of my efforts. Now, will you kindly tell me *why* I should clutter up my mind with general knowledge, for the purpose of being able to answer questions, when I have people around me who can supply any knowledge I require?'

There certainly was good logic to that reply.

That answer floored the lawyer. Every person in the courtroom realised it was the answer not of an ignorant man, but of a man of *education*. Any person is educated who knows where to get knowledge when needed, and how to organise that knowledge into definite plans of action. Through the assistance of his 'Master Mind' group, Henry Ford had at his command all the specialised knowledge he needed to enable him to become one of the wealthiest men in America. It was not essential that he have this knowledge in his own mind. Surely no person who has sufficient inclination and intelligence to read a book of this nature can possibly miss the significance of this illustration.

Before you can be sure of your ability to transmute *desire* into

81

its monetary equivalent, you will require *specialised knowledge* of the service, merchandise or profession you intend to offer in return for fortune. Perhaps you may need much more specialised knowledge than you have the ability or the inclination to acquire, and if this should be true, you may bridge your weakness through the aid of your 'Master Mind' group.

Andrew Carnegie stated that he, personally, knew nothing about the technical end of the steel business; moreover, he did not particularly care to know anything about it. The specialised knowledge he required for the manufacture and marketing of steel he found available through the individual units of his MASTER MIND GROUP.

The accumulation of great fortunes calls for *power*, and power is acquired through highly organised and intelligently directed specialised knowledge, but that knowledge does not necessarily have to be in the possession of the person who accumulates the fortune.

The preceding paragraph should give hope and encouragement to individuals with ambition to accumulate a fortune who have not acquired the necessary 'education' to supply such specialised knowledge as may be needed. People sometimes go through life suffering from 'inferiority complexes' because they do not have formal education. The person who can organise and direct a 'Master Mind' group of people who possess knowledge useful in the accumulation of money is just as much an educated person as anyone in the group. Remember this if you suffer from a feeling of inferiority because your schooling has been limited.

Thomas A. Edison had only three months of 'schooling' during his entire life. He did not lack education, neither did he die poor. Henry Ford had limited 'schooling' but he managed to do pretty well by himself, financially. The fact that Ford and Edison did not have much formal schooling does not give today's young people an excuse to drop out of school. Today a minimum standard of formal education is necessary to get a good start in the world of business.

Of course, there are exceptions. Dave Thomas, who founded the Wendy Restaurant chain, was a dropout. But after he achieved success, he encouraged youngsters to continue their schooling. He backed this up by choosing to be an example to dropouts by working to get his own high school diploma 45 years after he left school.

He took, and passed, his General Educational Development (GED) exam – the equivalent of a high school diploma. He was awarded the diploma during a special ceremony at a school in the community in which he resides in Florida. Thomas addressed more than 500 students from the school, as well as GED candidates from across the state. 'Being a high school dropout has always bothered me, but I guess I always thought it was too late to get my diploma,' said an enthusiastic Thomas. 'Now I know it's never too late and maybe this will inspire others to do the same.'

The inspiration to get his diploma came to Thomas during a cross-country book tour promoting his autobiography, Dave's Way. In many cities, Thomas met with high school journalists, answering their questions, offering advice and encouraging students to stay in school and succeed. 'These high school journalists were very sharp,' said Thomas. 'They kept asking me why I say education is so important, yet I never finished school – why didn't I practise what I preached? I didn't have a good answer, so I decided to get my high school diploma.'

His goal now is to publicise to school dropouts – whether they've recently dropped out or whether it's been years since they've been in school – that it's never too late to graduate.

'I tell people to get all the education they possibly can. The fact that I got my diploma 45 years after dropping out shows that it's never too late,' said Thomas. 'Even with everything that's happened in my life, getting this diploma is one of my most important accomplishments.'

It Pays to Know how to Purchase Knowledge

First of all, decide on the sort of specialised knowledge you require, and the purpose for which it is needed. To a large extent your major purpose in life, the goal towards which you are working, will help determine what knowledge you need. With this question settled, your next move requires that you have accurate information concerning dependable sources of knowledge. The more important of these are:

(a) One's own experience and education

(b) Experience and education available through cooperation of others

(c) Colleges and universities

(d) Public libraries (through books and periodicals in which may be found all the knowledge organised by civilisation)

(e) Special training courses (through evening classes and distance-learning courses in particular)

As knowledge is acquired it must be organised and put into use, for a definite purpose, through practical plans. Knowledge has no value except that which can be gained from its application towards some worthy end. This is one reason why university degrees are not guarantees of successful careers. If you contemplate taking additional schooling, first determine the purpose for which you want the knowledge you are seeking, then learn where this particular sort of knowledge can be obtained from reliable sources.

Successful people, in all callings, never stop acquiring specialised knowledge related to their major purpose, business or profession.

Those who are not successful usually make the mistake of believing that the knowledge-acquiring period ends when they finish school. The truth is that schooling does little more than point one in the direction of how to acquire practical knowledge.

Year after year, university careers advisers report that recruiters who come to their campuses are chiefly interested in hiring students who have studied in a specialised field such as business management, computer science, mathematics, chemistry, and other areas that prepare them to move rapidly into productive jobs, rather than the liberal arts students, who have broader but unspecialised schooling.

However, there are many students with great potential who did not choose a specialisation because they were not sure at age 18 to 20 in what areas they wanted to make their careers. Many of these men and women have a diversified education as undergraduates, but choose a career-oriented postgraduate qualification. Young readers of this book should not rush into choosing a speciality until they learn enough about what the field entails, its opportunities and its disadvantages.

Most universities and colleges provide information and guidance to students to help them make this key decision. Whether or not such guidance is available, students should explore a variety of fields, read as much as possible about that field and talk with people who currently are engaged in that work.

Not all careers require university degrees. Other types of training are available. Most universities have continuing education programmes for people who want specialised knowledge. Some offer certificate programmes in which people desirous of either learning a new field or honing their skills in that field can take a series of carefully designed courses to obtain the necessary knowledge. These courses are given in the evening or at weekends and are usually attended by adults rather than college-age students.

Home study programmes – often referred to as 'distance learning' –

are available by correspondence or through the Internet. One advantage of home study is the flexibility of the programme that permits one to study during spare time. Another stupendous advantage (if the provider is carefully chosen) is the fact that most courses offered provide opportunity for students to obtain clarification or additional information by mail or e-mail, which can be of priceless value to those needing specialised knowledge. No matter where you live, you can share the benefits.

The *self-discipline* one receives from a definite programme of specialised study makes up to some extent for the wasted opportunity when knowledge was available without cost. The home study method of training is especially suited to the needs of employed people who find, after leaving school, that they must acquire additional specialised knowledge, but cannot spare the time to go back to school. The continuously changing economic conditions in our society have made it necessary for thousands of people to find additional, or new, sources of income. For the majority, the solution to their problem may be found only by acquiring specialised knowledge. Many will be forced to change their occupations entirely. When a merchant finds that a certain line of merchandise is not selling, he usually supplants it with another that is in demand. The person whose business is that of marketing their services must also be an efficient merchant. If their services do not bring adequate returns in one occupation, they must change to another, where broader opportunities are available.

The person who stops studying merely because they have finished school is forever hopelessly doomed to mediocrity, no matter what their calling. The way of success is the way of continuous pursuit of knowledge. Let us consider a specific instance.

During an economic downturn, a salesman in a grocery store was made redundant. Rather than seek a job in an economy where jobs were scarce, he chose to create a business of his own. Having had some book-keeping experience, he took a special course in accounting, familiarising himself with the latest book-keeping techniques and office equipment.

Starting with the grocer for whom he had formerly worked, he made contracts with more than 100 small merchants to keep their books, at a very nominal monthly fee. His idea was so practical that he soon found it necessary to set up a portable office in a light delivery truck, which he equipped with modern office equipment. He now has a fleet of these book-keeping offices 'on wheels' and employs a large staff of assistants, thus providing small merchants with accounting service equal to the best money can buy, at very nominal cost.

Specialised knowledge, plus imagination, were the ingredients that went into this unique and successful business. Last year the owner of that business paid income tax almost ten times as much as he was paid by the merchant for whom he once worked. The loss of his job forced upon him a temporary adversity that proved to be a blessing in disguise.

The beginning of this successful business was an *idea*. Inasmuch as I had the privilege of supplying the unemployed salesman with that idea, I now assume the further privilege of suggesting another idea that has within it the possibility of even greater income, plus the possibility of rendering useful service to thousands of people who badly need that service.

The idea was suggested to the salesman who gave up selling and went into the business of keeping books on a wholesale basis. When the plan was suggested as a solution to his unemployment problem, he quickly exclaimed, 'I like the idea, but I would not know how to turn it into cash.' In other words, he complained he would not know how to market his book-keeping knowledge after he acquired it.

So, that brought up another problem to be solved. With the aid of a young woman clever at hand-lettering, and who could put the story together, a very attractive book was prepared, describing the advantages of the new system of book-keeping. The pages were neatly typed and pasted in an ordinary scrapbook, which was used as a sales tool. The story of this new business was so effectively told that its owner soon had more accounts than he could handle.

Thousands of people need the services of a merchandising specialist capable of preparing an attractive brief for use in marketing their services. The aggregate annual income from such a service might easily exceed that received by the largest employment agency, and the benefits of the service might be made far greater to the purchaser than any to be obtained from an employment agency.

The *idea* here described was born of necessity, to bridge an emergency that had to be covered, but it did not stop by merely serving one person. The woman who created the idea has a keen *imagination*. She saw in her newly born brainchild the making of a new profession, one destined to provide a valuable service to thousands of people who need practical guidance in marketing their services.

Spurred to action by the instantaneous success of her first 'prepared plan to market services', this energetic woman turned next to the solution of a similar problem for her son, who had just finished college, but had been totally unable to find a market for his services. The plan she originated for his use was the finest specimen of merchandising of services I have ever seen.

When the plan book had been completed, it contained nearly 50 pages of beautifully typed, properly organised information, telling the story of her son's natural ability, schooling, personal experiences, and a great variety of other information too extensive for description. The plan book also contained a complete description of the position her son desired, together with a marvellous word picture of the exact plan he would use in filling the position.

The preparation of the plan book required several weeks' labour, during which time its creator sent her son to the public library almost daily to procure data needed in selling his services to best advantage. She also sent him to all the competitors of his prospective employer, and gathered from them vital information concerning their business methods which was of great value in the formation of the plan he intended to use in filling the position he sought. When the plan had been finished, it contained more than half a dozen very fine suggestions for the use and benefit of the prospective employer, which were put to use by the company after he was hired.

One may be inclined to ask, 'Why go to all this trouble to secure a job?' The answer is straight to the point. It is also dramatic because it deals with a subject which assumes the proportion of a tragedy with millions of men and women whose sole source of income is their services.

The answer is, DOING A THING WELL IS NEVER TROUBLE! THE PLAN PREPARED BY THIS WOMAN FOR THE BENEFIT OF HER SON HELPED HIM GET THE JOB FOR WHICH HE APPLIED, AT THE FIRST INTERVIEW, AT A SALARY FIXED BY HIMSELF.

Moreover – and this, too, is important – THE POSITION

DID NOT REQUIRE THE YOUNG MAN TO START AT THE BOTTOM. HE BEGAN AS A JUNIOR EXECUTIVE, AT AN EXECUTIVE'S SALARY.

'Why go to all this trouble?' do you ask? Well, for one thing, the *planned presentation* of this young man's application for a position clipped off no less than 10 years of time he would have required to get to where he began, had he 'started at the bottom and worked his way up'.

This idea of starting at the bottom and working one's way up may appear sound, but the major objection to it is this — too many of those who begin at the bottom never manage to lift their heads high enough to be seen by *opportunity*, so they remain at the bottom. It should be remembered, also, that the outlook from the bottom is not so very bright or encouraging. It has a tendency to kill off ambition. We call it 'getting into a rut', which means we accept our fate because we form the *habit* of daily routine, a habit that finally becomes so strong we cease to try to throw it off. And that is another reason why it pays to start one or two steps above the bottom. By so doing one forms the *habit* of looking around, of observing how others get ahead, of seeing *opportunity*, and of embracing it without hesitation.

Dan Halpin is a splendid example of what I mean. During his college days, he was student-manager of the famous 1930 National Championship Notre Dame football team, when it was under the direction of the great football coach, Knute Rockne. Perhaps he was inspired by Rockne to aim high and *not mistake temporary defeat for failure*, just as Andrew Carnegie, the great industrial leader, inspired his young business lieutenants to set high goals for themselves. At any rate, young Halpin finished college at a mighty unfavourable time, when the Depression had made jobs scarce, so, after a fling at investment banking and motion pictures, he took the first opening with a potential future he could find – selling electrical hearing aids on a commission basis. Anyone could start in that sort of job, and Halpin knew it, but it was enough to open the door of opportunity to him.

For almost two years, he continued in a job not to his liking, and he would never have risen above that job if he had not done something about his dissatisfaction. He aimed, first, at the job of Assistant Sales Manager of his company, and got the job. That one step upwards placed him high enough above the crowd to enable him to see still greater opportunity. In addition, it placed him where *opportunity could see him*.

He made such a fine record selling hearing aids that A.M. Andrews, Chairman of the Board of the Dictograph Products Company, a business competitor, took notice. He wanted to know something about that man Dan Halpin who was taking big sales away from the long-established Dictograph Company. He sent for Halpin. When the interview was over, Halpin was the new Sales Manager, in charge of Dictograph's Acousticon Division.

Then, to test young Halpin's mettle, Mr Andrews went away to Florida for three months, leaving him to sink or swim in his new job. He did not sink! Knute Rockne's spirit of 'All the world loves a winner and has no time for a loser' inspired him to put so much into his job that he was elected Vice-President of the company, and General Manager of the Acousticon and Silent Radio Division, a job which most men would be proud to earn through 10 years of loyal effort. Halpin turned the trick in little more than six months.

It is difficult to say whether Mr Andrews or Mr Halpin is

more deserving of eulogy, as both showed evidence of having an abundance of that very rare quality known as *imagination*. Mr Andrews deserves credit for seeing, in young Halpin, a 'go-getter' of the highest order. Halpin deserves credit for refusing to compromise with life by accepting and keeping a job he did not want. That is one of the major points I am trying to emphasise through this entire philosophy – that we rise to high positions or remain at the bottom *because of conditions we can control if we desire to control them.*

I am also trying to emphasise another point, namely that both success and failure are largely the results of *habit*! I have not the slightest doubt that Dan Halpin's close association with the greatest football coach America ever knew planted in his mind the same brand of *desire* to excel which made the Notre Dame football team world famous. Truly, there is something to the idea that hero-worship is helpful, provided one worships a *winner*. Halpin tells me that Rockne was one of the world's greatest leaders of men in all history.

My belief in the theory that business associations are vital factors, both in failure and in success, was demonstrated when my son Blair was negotiating with Dan Halpin for a position. Mr Halpin offered him a starting salary of about one half what he could have got from a rival company. I brought parental pressure to bear, and induced him to accept the place with Mr Halpin because I believe that close association with one who refuses to compromise with circumstances he does not like is an asset that can never be measured in terms of money.

Honing one's skills to become top in one's field is not limited to people in business. Michael Jordan planned every step to becoming one of the greatest athletes of his generation.

He has always had the determination to win and the willpower to keep in shape and play his very best. He is committed to maintaining high standards and improving his own records.

Jordan learned this lesson early. In high school, he was dropped from the team, but his determination to be reinstated led to him starting a heavy practice regime daily – which he still follows. He takes each doubt as a challenge, and each year he's had a new incentive.

When he returned to basketball after a few years away from the game, his critics said he was past his prime, that he was slower and couldn't win another championship. He took this as a challenge. It just honed his determination to show them they were wrong.

He worked harder than ever. He designed a year-round training programme with his personal trainer and his own gym and weight room He recognised that as one grows older, the body starts giving signals you must listen to, and that it is essential to do things correctly to stay in the best shape possible to consistently play at championship level.

The results were astounding. Jordan led his team to the championship in 1996 and 1997, and in both years was named the Most Valuable Player.

Michael Jordan's determination is a lesson to all of us that if we are determined to achieve our goals, neither our age nor the scepticism of others can deter us. But determination is only the first step. It must be followed by hard work, a regime of physical and mental exercise and whatever it takes to bring us to peak performance.

The bottom is a monotonous, dreary, unprofitable place for any person. That is why I have taken the time to describe how proper planning may circumvent lowly beginnings. Also, that is why so much space has been devoted to a description of this new profession, created by a woman who was inspired to do a fine job of *planning* because she wanted her son to have a favourable 'break'.

When the economy slows down and jobs become scarce, a

means of creating newer and better ways of marketing our services is needed. It is hard to determine why someone had not previously discovered this stupendous need, in view of the fact that more money changes hands in return for services than for any other purpose. The sum paid out monthly to people who work for wages and salaries is so huge that it runs into hundreds of millions, and the annual distribution amounts to billions.

Perhaps some will find, in the *idea* here briefly described, the nucleus of the riches they *desire*! Ideas with much less merit have been the seedlings from which great fortunes have grown. Woolworth's Five and Ten Cent Store idea, for example, had far less merit, but it piled up a fortune for its creator.

Those seeing *opportunity* lurking in this suggestion will find valuable aid in the chapter on Organised Planning. Incidentally, an efficient marketer of services would find a growing demand for *his* services wherever there are men and women who seek better markets for *their* services. By applying the Master Mind principle (see page 193), a few people with suitable talent could form an alliance, and have a paying business very quickly. One would need to be a fair writer with a flair for advertising and selling, one handy at graphic design, and one should be a first-class business getter who would let the world know about the service. If one person possessed all these abilities, he or she might carry on the business alone until it became too big for one person to handle.

The woman who prepared the sales plan for her son received requests from all parts of the country for her cooperation in preparing similar plans for others who desired to market their services for more money. She eventually supervised a staff of expert typists, artists, and writers who had the ability to dramatise the case history so effectively that one's services could be marketed for much more money than the prevailing wages for similar services. She was so confident of her ability that she accepted, as the major portion of her fee, a percentage of the increased pay she helped her clients earn.

It must not be supposed that her plan merely consisted of clever salesmanship by which she helped men and women to demand and receive more money for the same services they formerly sold for less pay. She looked after the interests of the purchaser as well as the seller of services, and so prepared her plans that the employer would receive full value for the additional money paid. The method by which she accomplished this astonishing result is a professional secret that she disclosed to no one except her own clients.

If you have the *imagination* and seek a more profitable outlet for your services, this suggestion may be the stimulus for which you have been searching. The *idea* is capable of yielding an income far greater than that of the 'average' doctor, lawyer or engineer whose education required several years in college. The idea is saleable to those seeking new positions in practically all positions calling for managerial or executive ability, and those desiring rearrangement of incomes in their present positions.

There is no fixed price for sound ideas! Underpinning all ideas is specialised knowledge. For those who do not find riches in abundance, specialised knowledge is more abundant and more easily acquired than ideas. Because of this very truth, there is a universal demand and an ever-increasing opportunity for the person capable of helping men and women sell their services advantageously. Capability means imagination, the one quality needed to combine specialised knowledge with ideas in the form of *organised plans* designed to yield riches.

If you have imagination, this chapter may present you with an idea sufficient to serve as the beginning of the riches you desire. Remember, the idea is the main thing. Specialised knowledge may be found just around the corner – any corner!

CHAPTER 6

IMAGINATION:
the Workshop of the Mind

(The Fifth Step to Riches)

The imagination is literally the workshop wherein are fashioned all plans created by people. The impulse, the *desire*, is given shape, form and *action* through the aid of the imaginative faculty of the mind.

It has been said that we can create anything we can imagine. Of all the ages of civilisation, this is the most favourable for the development of the imagination because it is an age of rapid change. Everywhere we come into contact with stimuli that develop the imagination. Through the aid of the imaginative faculty, humankind has discovered, and harnessed, more of Nature's forces during the past 50 years than during the entire history of the human race previous to that time. We have conquered the air so completely that the birds are a poor match for us in flying. We have harnessed the ether, and made it serve as a means of instantaneous communication with any part of the world. We have analysed and weighed the sun at a distance of millions of miles, and have determined, through the aid of *imagination*, the elements of which it consists. We have discovered that our own brain is both a broadcasting and a receiving station for the vibration of thought, and we are beginning now to learn how to make practical use of this discovery. We have increased the speed of locomotion until we may now travel at a speed of more than 600 miles an hour.

Our only limitation, within reason, *Lies in the development and use of our imagination*. We have not yet reached the apex of development in the use of our imaginative faculty. We have merely discovered that we have an imagination, and have commenced to use it in a very elementary way.

Two Forms of Imagination

The imaginative faculty functions in two forms. One is known as 'synthetic imagination', and the other as 'creative imagination'.

SYNTHETIC IMAGINATION: Through this faculty one may arrange old concepts, ideas or plans into new combinations. This faculty creates nothing. It merely works with the material of experience, education and observation with which it is fed. It is the faculty used most by the inventor, with the exception of the 'genius' who draws upon the creative imagination when they cannot solve a problem through synthetic imagination.

CREATIVE IMAGINATION: Through the faculty of creative imagination, the finite mind of humankind has direct communication with Infinite Intelligence. It is the faculty through which 'hunches' and 'inspirations' are received. It is by this faculty that all basic or new ideas are developed. It is through this faculty that thought vibrations from the minds of others are received. And it is through this faculty that one individual may 'tune in to', or communicate with the subconscious minds of others.

The creative imagination works automatically, in the manner described in subsequent pages. This faculty functions *only* when the conscious mind is vibrating at an exceedingly rapid rate, as for example when the conscious mind is stimulated through the emotion of a strong desire.

The creative faculty becomes more alert, more receptive to vibrations from the sources mentioned, in proportion to its development through *use*. Indeed, both the synthetic and creative faculties of imagination become more alert with use, just as any muscle or organ of the body develops through use. Your imaginative faculty may have become weak through inaction. It can be revived and made alert through *use*. This faculty does not die, though it may become quiescent through lack of use. This statement is significant! Ponder on it before continuing.

Keep in mind as you follow these principles that the entire story of how one may convert *desire* into money cannot be told in one statement. The story will be complete only when one has *mastered, assimilated* and *begun to make use* of all the principles.

The great leaders of business, industry and finance and the great artists, musicians, poets and writers became great because they developed the faculty of creative imagination.

Desire is only a thought, an impulse. It is nebulous and ephemeral. It is abstract and of no value until it has been transformed into its physical counterpart. While the synthetic imagination is the one used most frequently in the process of transforming the impulse of *desire* into money, you must keep in mind that you may face circumstances which demand use of the creative imagination as well.

Centre your attention, for the time being, on the development of the synthetic imagination. Transformation of the intangible impulse of *desire* into the tangible reality of *money* calls for the use of a plan, or plans. These plans must be formed with the aid of the imagination, and mainly with the synthetic faculty.

Read the entire book through, then come back to this chapter and begin at once to put your imagination to work on building a plan, or plans, for the transformation of your *desire* into money. Detailed instructions for building plans have been given in almost every chapter. Carry out the instructions best suited to your needs. Put your plan in writing, if you have not already done so. The moment you complete this, you will have *definitely* given concrete form to the intangible *desire*. Read the preceding sentence once more. Read it aloud, very slowly. As you do so, remember that the moment you put in writing the statement of your desire and a plan for its realisation, you have actually *taken the first* of a series of steps that will enable you to convert the thought into its physical counterpart.

The earth on which you live, you yourself and every other material thing are the result of evolutionary change, through which microscopic bits of matter have been organised and arranged in an orderly fashion. Moreover – and this statement is of stupendous importance – this earth, every one of the billions of individual cells of your body and every atom of matter *began as an intangible form of energy.*

Desire is a thought impulse! Thought impulses are forms of energy. When you begin with the thought impulse *desire* to accumulate money, you are drafting into your service the same 'stuff' that nature used in creating this earth and every material form in the universe, including the body and brain in which the thought impulses function.

As far as science has been able to determine, the entire universe consists of but two elements – matter and energy. Through the combination of energy and matter has been created everything perceptible, from the largest star that floats in the heavens down to and including humankind.

You are now engaged in the task of trying to profit by Nature's method. You are (sincerely and earnestly, we hope) trying to adapt yourself to Nature's laws by endeavouring to convert *desire* into its physical and monetary equivalent. YOU CAN DO IT! IT HAS BEEN DONE BEFORE!

You can build a fortune through the aid of immutable laws. But first you must become familiar with these laws, and learn to *use* them. Through repetition, and by approaching the description of these principles from every conceivable angle, the author hopes to reveal to you the secret through which great fortunes have been accumulated. Strange and paradoxical as it may seem, the 'secret' is *not a secret*. Nature, herself, advertises it on the earth on which we live, the stars, the planets suspended within our view, in the elements above and around us, in every blade of grass and every form of life within our vision.

Nature advertises this 'secret' in the terms of biology, in the conversion of a tiny cell, so small that it may be lost on the point of a pin, into the *human being* now reading this line. The conversion of desire into its physical equivalent is certainly no more miraculous!

Do not become discouraged if you do not fully comprehend all that has been stated. Unless you have long been a student of the mind, it is not to be expected that you will assimilate all that is in the chapter upon a first reading.

But you will, in time, make good progress.

The principles that follow will open the way for an understanding of imagination. Assimilate that which you understand, as you read this philosophy for the first time, then, when you reread and study it, you will discover that something has happened to clarify it, and give you a broader understanding of the whole. Above all, *do not stop* nor hesitate in your study of these principles until you have read the book at least *three* times, for then you will not want to stop.

How to Make Practical Use of Imagination

Ideas are the beginning points of all fortunes. Ideas are products of the imagination. Let us examine a few well-known ideas that have yielded huge fortunes, with the hope that these illustrations will convey definite information concerning the method by which imagination may be used in accumulating riches.

The Enchanted Kettle

Many years ago, an old country doctor drove to town, hitched his horse, quietly slipped into a drug store by the back door and began 'dickering' with the young drug clerk. His mission was destined to yield great wealth to many people. It was destined to bring to the South the most far-flung benefit since the Civil War.

For more than an hour, behind the prescription counter, the old doctor and the clerk talked in low tones. Then the doctor left. He went out to the buggy and brought back a large, old-fashioned kettle and a big wooden paddle (used for stirring the contents of the kettle), and deposited them in the back of the store.

The clerk inspected the kettle, reached into his inside pocket, took out a roll of bills and handed it over to the doctor. The roll contained exactly $500 – the clerk's entire savings!

The doctor handed over a small slip of paper on which was written a secret formula. The words on that small slip of paper were worth a king's ransom! *But not to the doctor!* Those magic words were needed to start the kettle boiling, but neither the doctor nor the young clerk knew what fabulous fortunes were destined to flow from that kettle.

The old doctor was glad to sell the outfit for $500. The money would pay off his debts and give him freedom of mind. The clerk was taking a big chance by staking his entire life's savings on a mere scrap of paper and an old kettle! He never dreamed his investment would start a kettle overflowing with gold that would surpass the miraculous performance of Aladdin's lamp.

What the clerk really purchased was an *idea*!

The old kettle and the wooden paddle, and the secret message on a slip of paper were incidental. The strange performance of that kettle began to take place after the new owner mixed with the secret instructions an ingredient of which the doctor knew nothing.

Read this story carefully, and give your imagination a test! See if you can discover what it was that the young man added to the secret message which caused the kettle to overflow with gold. Remember, as you read, that this is not a story from Arabian Nights. Here you have a story of facts, stranger than fiction, facts which began in the form of an *idea*.

Let us take a look at the vast fortunes of gold this idea has produced. It has paid, and still pays, huge fortunes to men and women all over the world who distribute the contents of the kettle to millions of people.

The old kettle is now one of the world's largest consumers of sugar, thus providing jobs of a permanent nature to thousands of men and women engaged in growing sugar cane, and in refining and marketing sugar.

The old kettle consumes, annually, millions of glass bottles, providing jobs to huge numbers of glass workers. The old kettle gives employment to an army of clerks, copy-writers and advertising experts throughout the nation. It has brought fame and fortune to scores of artists who have created magnificent pictures describing the product. The old kettle has converted a small southern city into the business capital of the South, which now benefits – directly or indirectly – every business and practically every resident of the city. The influence of this idea now benefits every civilised country in the world, pouring out a continuous stream of gold to all who touch it.

Gold from the kettle built and maintains one of the most prominent colleges of the South, where thousands of young people receive the training essential for success.

The old kettle has done other marvellous things.

All through the Depression of the 1930s, when factories, banks and business houses were folding up and quitting by the thousands, the owner of this enchanted kettle went marching on, *giving continuous employment* to an army of men and women all over the world, and paying out extra portions of gold to those who, long ago, *had faith in the idea*.

If the product of that old brass kettle could talk it would tell thrilling tales of romance in every language: romances of love, romances of business, romances of professional men and women who are daily stimulated by it.

The author is sure of at least one such romance, for he was a part of it, and it all began not far from the very spot on which the drug clerk purchased the old kettle. It was here that the author met his wife, and it was she who first told him of the enchanted kettle. It was the product of that kettle they were drinking when he asked her to accept him 'for better or worse'.

Now that you know the content of the enchanted kettle is a world-famous drink, it is fitting that the author confess that the home city of the drink supplied him with a wife, also that the drink itself provides him with stimulation of thought without intoxication, and thereby serves to give the refreshment of mind an author must have to do his best work.

Whoever you are, wherever you may live, whatever occupation you may be engaged in, just remember in the future, every time you see the words 'Coca-Cola', that its vast empire of wealth and influence grew out of a single *idea*, and that the mysterious ingredient the drug clerk – Asa Candler – mixed with the secret formula was . . . *imagination*!

Stop and think about that for a moment.

Remember, also, that the 13 steps to riches described in this book were the media through which the influence of Coca-Cola has been extended to every city, town, village and crossroads of the world. *Any idea* you may create, as sound and *meritorious* as Coca-Cola, has the possibility of duplicating the stupendous record of this worldwide thirst-killer.

Truly, thoughts are things, and their scope of operation is the world itself.

What I Would Do If I Had a Million Dollars

This story proves the truth of that old saying, 'where there's a will, there's a way'. It was told to me by that beloved educator and clergyman, Frank W. Gunsaulus, who began his preaching career in the stockyards region of South Chicago.

While Dr Gunsaulus was going through college, he observed many defects in our educational system, defects which he believed he could correct if he were the head of a college. His deepest desire was to become the directing head of an educational institution in which young men and women would be taught to 'learn by doing'.

He made up his mind to organise a new college in which he could carry out his ideas without being handicapped by orthodox methods of education. He needed a million dollars to put the project across! Where was he to lay his hands on so large a sum of money? That was the question that absorbed most of this ambitious young preacher's thought.

But he couldn't seem to make any progress.

Every night he took that thought to bed with him. He got up with it in the morning. He took it with him everywhere he went. He turned it over and over in his mind until it became a consuming obsession with him. A million dollars is a lot of money. He recognised that fact, but he also recognised the truth that the only limitation is that which one sets up in one's own mind.

Being a philosopher as well as a preacher, Dr Gunsaulus recognised, as do all who succeed in life, that *definiteness of purpose* is the point from which one must begin. He recognised, too, that definiteness of purpose takes on animation, life and power when backed by a *burning desire* to translate that purpose into its material equivalent.

He knew all these great truths, yet he did not know where or how to lay his hands on a million dollars. The natural procedure would have been to give up and quit, saying, 'Ah well, my idea is a good one, but I cannot do anything with it because I never can procure the necessary million dollars.' That is exactly what the majority of people would have said, but it is not what Dr Gunsaulus said. What he said, and what he did, are so important that I now introduce him, and let him speak for himself.

'One Saturday afternoon I sat in my room thinking of ways and means of raising the money to carry out my plans. For nearly two years, I had been thinking, but I had done nothing but think!'

The time had come for *action*!

'I made up my mind, then and there, that I would get the necessary million dollars within a week. How? I was not concerned about that. The main thing of importance was the decision to get the money within a specified time. The moment I reached that decision, a strange feeling of assurance came over me, such as I had never before experienced. Something inside me seemed to say, "Why didn't you reach that decision a long time ago? The money was waiting for you all the time!"

'Things began to happen in a hurry. I called the newspapers and announced I would preach a sermon the following morning, entitled, "What I would do if I had a million dollars".

'I went to work on the sermon immediately. I must tell you, frankly, the task was not difficult because I had been preparing that sermon for almost two years. The spirit of it was a part of me!

'Long before midnight I had finished writing the sermon. I went to bed and slept with a feeling of confidence, for *I could see myself already in possession of the million dollars.*

'Next morning I arose early, went into the bathroom, read the sermon, then knelt and prayed that my sermon might come to the attention of someone who would supply the needed money.

'While I was praying I again had that feeling of assurance that the money would be forthcoming. In my excitement, I walked out without my sermon, and did not discover the oversight until I was in my pulpit and about ready to begin delivering it.

'It was too late to go back for my notes, and what a blessing that was, Instead, my own subconscious mind yielded the material I needed. When I arose to begin my sermon, I closed my eyes and spoke with all my heart and soul of my dreams. I not only talked to my audience, but I fancy I talked also to God. I told what I would do with a million dollars if that amount were placed in my hands. I described the plan I had in mind for organising a great educational institution where young people would learn to do practical things, and at the same time develop their minds.

'When I had finished and sat down, a man slowly arose from his seat, about three rows from the rear, and made his way towards the pulpit. I wondered what he was going to do. He came into the pulpit, extended his hand, and said, "Reverend, I liked your sermon. I believe you can do everything you said you would, if you had a million dollars. To prove that I believe in you and your sermon, if you will come to my office tomorrow morning, I will give you the million dollars. My name is Phillip D. Armour."'

Young Gunsaulus went to Mr Armour's office and the million dollars was presented to him. With the money, he founded the Armour Institute of Technology. That is more money than the majority of preachers ever see in an entire lifetime, yet the thought impulse behind the money was created in the young preacher's mind in a fraction of a minute. The necessary million dollars came as a result of an idea. Behind the idea was a *desire* that young Gunsaulus had been nursing in his mind for almost two years.

Observe this important fact: HE GOT THE MONEY WITHIN 36 HOURS OF REACHING A DEFINITE DECISION IN HIS OWN MIND TO GET IT, AND DECIDING UPON A DEFINITE PLAN FOR GETTING IT!

There was nothing new or unique about young Gunsaulus' vague thinking about a million dollars, and weakly hoping for it. Others before him, and many since his time, have had similar thoughts. But there was something unique and different about the decision he reached on that memorable Saturday, when he put vagueness into the background, and definitely said, 'I *will* get that money within a week!'

God seems to throw Himself on the side of people who know exactly what they want, if they are determined to get *just that*!

Moreover, the principle through which Dr Gunsaulus got his million dollars is still alive! It is available to you! This universal law is as workable today as it was when the young preacher made use of it so successfully. This book describes, step by step, the 13 elements of this great law, and suggests how they may be put to use.

Observe that Asa Candler and Dr Frank Gunsaulus had one characteristic in common. Both knew the astounding truth that IDEAS CAN BE TRANSMUTED INTO CASH THROUGH THE POWER OF DEFINITE PURPOSE, PLUS DEFINITE PLANS.

If you are one of those who believe that hard work and honesty alone will bring riches, perish the thought! It is not true! Riches, when they come in huge quantities, are never the result of *hard* work! Riches come, if they come at all, in response to definite demands, based upon the application of definite principles, and not by chance or luck.

Generally speaking, an idea is an impulse of thought that impels action by an appeal to the imagination. All master sales reps know that ideas can be sold where merchandise cannot. Ordinary sales reps do not know this – that is why they are 'ordinary'.

A publisher of books made a discovery that should be worth much to publishers generally. He learned that many people buy titles, and not contents of books. By merely changing the name of one book that was not moving, his sales on that book jumped upwards more than a million copies. The inside of the book was not changed in any way. He merely ripped off the cover bearing the title that did not sell, and put on a new cover with a title that had 'box-office' value.

That, as simple as it may seem, was an *idea*! It was *imagination*. There is no standard price on ideas. Creators of ideas make their own price, and, if they are smart, they get it.

The moving picture industry created a whole flock of millionaires. Most of them were men who couldn't create ideas – *but* they had the imagination to recognise ideas when they saw them.

Andrew Carnegie knew very little about making steel – I have Carnegie's own word for this – but he made practical use of two of the principles described in this book, and made the steel business yield him a fortune.

The story of practically every great fortune starts with the day when a creator of ideas and a seller of ideas got together and worked in harmony. Carnegie surrounded himself with experts who could do all that he could not do, people who created ideas and men who put ideas into operation and made themselves and the others fabulously rich.

Millions of people go through life hoping for favourable 'breaks'. Perhaps a favourable break can get one an opportunity, but the safest plan is not to depend upon luck. It was a favourable 'break' that gave me the biggest opportunity of my life – but 25 years of determined effort had to be devoted to that opportunity before it became an asset.

The 'break' consisted of my good fortune in meeting and gaining the cooperation of Andrew Carnegie. On that occasion Carnegie planted in my mind the idea of organising the principles of achievement into a philosophy of success. Thousands of people have profited by the discoveries made in the 25 years of research, and several fortunes have been accumulated through the application of the philosophy. The beginning was simple. It was an *idea* that anyone might have developed.

The favourable break came through Carnegie, but what about the *determination, definiteness of purpose,* the *desire to attain the goal* and the *persistent effort of 25 years?* It was no ordinary desire that survived disappointment, discouragement, temporary defeat, criticism and the constant accusation of 'waste of time'. It was a *burning desire,* an *obsession!*

When Mr Carnegie first planted the idea in my mind, it was coaxed, nursed and enticed to remain alive. Gradually, the idea became a giant under its own power, and it coaxed, nursed and drove me. Ideas are like that. First you give life, action and guidance to ideas, and then they take on a power of their own and sweep aside all opposition.

Like Andrew Carnegie, Herb Kelleher, one of the founders of Southwest Airlines, is a good example of a 'seller of ideas'. He was a lawyer in San Antonio, Texas, when Rollin King, the creator of an idea, asked for his help in founding a new airline.

Rollin King was an investment adviser. As a side business, he ran an unprofitable air charter service between small Texas cities. At that time, most Americans who travelled by air were business executives or wealthy pleasure seekers. King was frustrated when he wanted to fly from one city in Texas to another. He could never get a seat on the airlines that currently flew those routes – and besides, prices were too high.

He recognised the need to create an airline that would fly just between the three biggest cities in the state. King knew his little airline wasn't up to the task so he decided to start one. He put together a feasibility study and business plan. He raised $100,000 and then went to Herb Kelleher, his lawyer, to arrange for the necessary paperwork to create Air Southwest Co. (later Southwest Airlines Co.).

Although Kelleher was at first sceptical, he worked with King to gain additional capital and some political support. On 20 February 1968, the Texas Aeronautics Commission approved Southwest's petition to fly between the three cities. However, on 21 February, competing airlines – Braniff, Trans Texas and Continental – blocked the approval with a temporary restraining order.

Kelleher, his enthusiasm for the airline ignited by the efforts to quash it, put his litigation skills to work. The competition argued that Texas didn't need a new carrier. It took a three-and-a-half-year legal battle, including three trips to three courts, for Southwest to prove otherwise and gain the necessary permission to start operating.

Although they made a good start, it wasn't enough. The company lost $3.7 million that year, and the losses continued for another year and a half. Southwest was trying to keep costs down and attract customers without compromising its original goals.

By this time Kelleher had become so enthralled with the concept that he gave up his law practice to run Southwest. His aim was to make Southwest the airline of choice in the market it served.

One of his innovations was peak and off-peak airline pricing. Another was the 10-minute turnaround. After landing, each plane would pull into the gate, get checked by maintenance, unload passengers, reload, and leave the gate within 10 minutes instead of the 45 minutes other airlines took. The 10-minute turnaround allowed the three-plane airline to maintain a busy schedule and improve its on-time performance.

Because of their very limited budget, they couldn't advertise in the usual media, so they chose to promote the airline by word of mouth. To do this the company decided to cultivate a sensational, off-the-wall image.

Customer service became their top priority. Flight attendants were trained to give 'tender loving care' to the passengers. The company's slogan was 'Now there's somebody else up there who loves you'.

In addition, Kelleher eliminated the annoying, time-consuming methods the major airlines used in issuing boarding passes by creating open-seating on all flights. No seat reservations were needed and passengers were given numbered boarding cards which were issued and collected at the gate.

With passenger satisfaction as their main objective, Kelleher and his team built up a loyal following and a reputation for passenger consideration.

Southwest began to climb its way up.

By 1978, it was one of the country's most profitable airlines. In the early 2000s when many airlines suffered major setbacks, some going into bankruptcy and even out of business, Southwest not only survived, but led the industry in profitability.

Herb Kelleher gives this advice to success-minded people:

- *Stick to your ideas. Despite the efforts of its giant competitors to keep Southwest from entering the business, a positive attitude kept them going during three years of court fights and no operating income.*
- *Think of what the customers want and then give it to them.*
- *Overcome obstacles put in your path by taking positive steps to break them down – even while the battle is being fought, find ways to get around them.*
- *Keep open to new opportunities, and when they arise, take positive steps to meet them.*

SUCCESS REQUIRES NO
EXPLANATION.

FAILURE PERMITS NO ALIBIS.

CHAPTER 7

ORGANISED PLANNING:
the Crystallisation of Desire into Action

(The Sixth Step to Riches)

You have learned that everything that is created or acquired begins in the form of *desire*, that desire is taken on the first lap of its journey, from the abstract to the concrete, into the workshop of the *imagination* where *plans* for its transition are created and organised.

In Chapter 2, you were instructed to take six definite, practical steps as your first move in translating desire into money. One of these steps is the formation of a *definite*, practical plan, or plans, through which this transformation may be made.

You will now be instructed on how to build practical plans:

1. Ally yourself with a group of as many people as you may need for the creation and carrying out of your plan, or plans, for the accumulation of money, making use of the 'Master Mind' principle described in Chapter 9.

(Compliance with this instruction is absolutely essential. Do not neglect it.)

2. Before forming your 'Master Mind' alliance, decide what advantages and benefits you may offer the individual members of your group in return for their cooperation. No one will work indefinitely without some form of compensation. No intelligent person will either request or expect another to work without adequate compensation, although this may not always be in the form of money

3. Arrange to meet with the members of your 'Master Mind' group at least twice a week, and more often if possible, until you have collectively perfected the necessary plan, or plans, for the accumulation of money.

4. Maintain *perfect harmony* between yourself and every member of your 'Master Mind' group. If you fail to carry out this instruction to the letter, you may expect to meet with failure. The 'Master Mind' principle cannot operate where perfect harmony does not prevail. Keep in mind these facts:

   (a) You are engaged in an undertaking of major importance to you. To be sure of success, you must have plans that are faultless.

   (b) You must have the advantage of the experience, education, natural ability and imagination of other minds. This is in harmony with the methods followed by every person who has accumulated a great fortune.

No individual has sufficient experience, education, natural ability and knowledge to ensure the accumulation of a great fortune without the cooperation of other people. Every plan you adopt in your endeavour to accumulate wealth should be the collective creation of yourself and every other member of your Master Mind group. You may originate your own plans, either in whole or in part, but *see that those plans are checked and approved by the members of your 'Master Mind' alliance.*

If the first plan you adopt does not work successfully, replace it with a new plan. If this new plan fails to work, replace it, in turn, with still another, and so on until you find a plan which *does work.* Right here is the point at which the majority of people meet with failure because of their lack of *persistence* in creating new plans to take the place of those which fail.

The most intelligent person living cannot succeed in accumulating money – nor in any other undertaking – without plans that are practical and workable. Just keep this fact in mind, and remember when your plans fail that temporary defeat is not permanent failure. It may only mean that your plans have not been sound. Build other plans. Start all over again.

Thomas A. Edison 'failed' 10,000 times before he perfected the incandescent electric light bulb. That is, he met with temporary defeat 10,000 times before his efforts were crowned with success.

Temporary defeat should mean only one thing – the certain knowledge that there is something wrong with your plan. Millions of people go through life in misery and poverty because they lack a sound plan through which to accumulate a fortune.

Henry Ford accumulated a fortune, not because of his superior mind, but because he adopted and followed a *plan* which proved to be sound. A thousand people could be pointed out with a better education than Ford's, yet they live in poverty because they do not possess the *right* plan for the accumulation of money.

James J. Hill met with temporary defeat when he first endeavoured to raise the necessary capital to build a railroad from the East to the West, but he turned defeat into victory through new plans.

Henry Ford met with temporary defeat, not only at the beginning of his career, but after he had gone far towards the top. He created new plans and went marching on to financial victory.

We see people who have accumulated great fortunes, but we often recognise only their triumph, overlooking the temporary defeats they had to surmount before 'arriving'.

NO FOLLOWER OF THIS PHILOSOPHY CAN REASONABLY EXPECT TO ACCUMULATE A FORTUNE WITHOUT EXPERIENCING 'TEMPORARY DEFEAT'. When defeat comes, accept it as a signal that your plans are not sound, rebuild those plans and set sail once more towards your coveted goal. If you give up before your goal has been reached, you are a 'quitter'.

A QUITTER NEVER WINS – AND A WINNER NEVER QUITS.

Lift this sentence out, write it on a piece of paper in letters an inch high, and place it where you will see it every night before you go to sleep, and every morning before you go to work.

When you begin to select members for your 'Master Mind' group, endeavour to select those who do not take defeat seriously.

Some people foolishly believe that only *money* can make money. This is not true! *Desire*, transmuted into its monetary equivalent through the principles laid down here, is the agency through which money is 'made'. Money, of itself, is nothing but inert matter. It cannot move, think, or talk, but it can 'hear' when one who *desires* it calls it to come!

Planning the Sale of Services

The remainder of this chapter has been given over to a description of ways and means of marketing services. The information here conveyed will be of practical help to any person having any form of service to market, but it will be of priceless benefit to those who aspire to leadership in their chosen occupations.

Intelligent planning is essential for success in any undertaking designed to accumulate riches. Here will be found detailed instructions to those who must begin the accumulation of riches by selling their services.

It should be encouraging to know that practically all the great fortunes began in the form of compensation for services, or from the sale of *ideas*. What else, except ideas and services, would one not possessed of property have to give in return for riches?

Broadly speaking, there are two types of people in the world, *leaders* and *followers*. Decide at the outset whether you intend to become a leader in your chosen calling or remain a follower. The difference in compensation is vast. The follower cannot reasonably expect the compensation to which a leader is entitled, although many followers make the mistake of expecting such pay.

It is no disgrace to be a follower. On the other hand, it is no credit to remain a follower. Most great leaders began in the capacity of followers. They became great leaders because they were *intelligent followers*. With few exceptions, people who cannot follow a leader intelligently cannot become efficient leaders. People who can follow a leader most efficiently are usually those who develop into leadership most rapidly. An intelligent follower has many advantages, among them the *opportunity to acquire knowledge from the leader.*

The Major Attributes of Leadership

The following are important factors of leadership:

1. UNWAVERING COURAGE based upon knowledge of self and of one's occupation. No follower wishes to be dominated by a leader who lacks self-confidence and courage. No intelligent follower will be dominated by such a leader for very long.

2. SELF-CONTROL. People who cannot control themselves can never control others. Self-control sets a mighty example for one's followers, which the more intelligent will emulate.

3. A KEEN SENSE OF JUSTICE. Without a sense of fairness and justice, no leader can command and retain the respect of his or her followers.

4. DEFINITENESS OF DECISION. People who waver in decisions show that they are not sure of themselves. They cannot lead others successfully.

5. DEFINITENESS OF PLANS. The successful leader must plan the work, and work the plan. A leader who moves by guesswork without practical, definite plans is comparable to a ship without a rudder. Sooner or later it will land on the rocks.

6. THE HABIT OF DOING MORE THAN PAID FOR. One of the penalties of leadership is the necessity of willingness, upon the part of the leaders, to do more than they require of their followers.

7. **A PLEASING PERSONALITY.** No slovenly, careless person can become a successful leader. Leadership calls for respect. Followers will not respect leaders who do not score highly on all factors of a pleasing personality.

8. **SYMPATHY AND UNDERSTANDING.** Successful leaders must be in sympathy with their followers. Moreover, they must understand them and their problems.

9. **MASTERY OF DETAIL.** Successful leadership calls for mastery of details of the leader's position.

10. **WILLINGNESS TO ASSUME FULL RESPONSIBILITY.** Successful leaders must be willing to assume responsibility for the mistakes and shortcomings of their followers. If they try to shift this responsibility, they will not remain leaders. If followers make mistakes and become incompetent, it is the leader who has failed.

11. **COOPERATION.** Successful leaders must understand and apply the principle of cooperative effort and be able to induce followers to do the same. Leadership calls for *power*, and power calls for *cooperation*.

There are two forms of leadership. The first, and by far the most effective, is *leadership by consent* of, and with the sympathy of, the followers. The second is *leadership by force*, without the consent and sympathy of the followers.

History is filled with evidence that leadership by force cannot endure. The downfall and disappearance of 'dictators' and kings is significant. It means that people will not follow forced leadership indefinitely. The world has entered a new era of relationship between leaders and followers, which very clearly calls for new leaders and a new brand of leadership in business and industry. Those who belong to the old school of leadership by force must acquire an understanding of the new brand of leadership (cooperation) or be relegated to the rank and file of the followers. There is no other way out for them.

The relationship of employer and employee, or of leader and follower, in the future will be one of mutual cooperation, based upon an equitable division of the profits of business. In the future, the relationship of employer and employee will be more like a partnership than it has been in the past. Hitler and Stalin are examples of leaders who ruled by force. Their leadership passed. People may follow the forced leadership temporarily, but they will not do so willingly. *Leadership by consent* of the followers is the only brand that can endure!

The new brand of leadership will embrace the 11 attributes described earlier in this chapter, as well as some other factors. People who make these attributes the basis of their leadership will find abundant opportunity to lead in any walk of life.

The 10 Major Causes of Failure in Leadership

We come now to the major faults of leaders who fail, because it is just as essential to know *what not to do* as it is to know what to do.

1. INABILITY TO ORGANISE DETAILS. Efficient leadership calls for ability to organise and to master details. No genuine leader is ever 'too busy' to do anything which may be required as a leader. When a leader or follower is 'too busy' to change plans or give attention to any emergency, it is an indication of

inefficiency. The successful leader must be the master of all details connected with the position. That means, of course, that the habit of delegating details to capable lieutenants must be acquired.

2. UNWILLINGNESS TO RENDER HUMBLE SERVICE. Truly great leaders are willing, when occasion demands, to perform any sort of labour that they would ask another to perform. 'The greatest among ye shall be the servant of all' is a truth that all able leaders observe and respect.

3. EXPECTATION OF PAY FOR WHAT THEY 'KNOW' INSTEAD OF WHAT THEY DO WITH WHAT THEY KNOW. The world does not pay for what people 'know'. It pays them for what they *do*, or induce others to do.

4. FEAR OF COMPETITION FROM FOLLOWERS. The leader who fears that one of his followers may take his position is practically sure to realise that fear sooner or later. Able leaders train understudies to whom they may delegate at will. Only in this way may leaders multiply themselves and prepare to be at many places, and give attention to many things, at one time. It is an eternal truth that people receive more pay for their *ability to get others to perform* than they could possibly earn by their own efforts. Efficient leaders may, through knowledge of their jobs and the magnetism of their personalities, greatly increase the efficiency of others, and induce them to render more service and better service than they could by themselves.

5. LACK OF IMAGINATION. Without imagination, leaders are incapable of meeting emergencies, and of

creating plans by which to guide followers efficiently.

6. SELFISHNESS. Leaders who claim all the honour for the work of their followers are sure to be met by resentment. Really great leaders *claim none of the honours*. They are content to see the honours go to their followers because they know that most people will work harder for commendation and recognition than they will for money alone.

7. INTEMPERANCE. Followers do not respect an intemperate leader. Moreover, intemperance in any of its various forms destroys the endurance and the vitality of all who indulge in it.

8. DISLOYALTY. Perhaps this should have come at the head of the list. Leaders who are not loyal to their trust and to their associates – those above and below them – cannot long maintain their leadership. Disloyalty marks people as being less than the dust of the earth, and brings down on their head the contempt they deserve. Lack of loyalty is one of the major causes of failure in every walk of life.

9. EMPHASIS OF THE 'AUTHORITY' OF LEADERSHIP. Efficient leaders lead by encouraging, not by trying to instil fear in the hearts of their followers. Leaders who try to impress followers with their 'authority' come within the category of leadership through *force*. Real leaders have no need to advertise that fact except by their conduct, sympathy, understanding, fairness and a demonstration of knowledge of the job..

10. EMPHASIS OF TITLE. Competent leaders require no 'title' to gain the respect of their followers. Leaders who make too much of their title generally have little else to

emphasise. The doors to the office of real leaders are open to all who wish to enter, and their working quarters are free from formality or ostentation.

These are among the more common causes of failure in leadership. Any one of these faults is sufficient to induce failure. Study the list carefully if you aspire to leadership, and make sure you are free of these faults.

Some Fertile Fields in which 'New Leadership' Will Be Required

Before leaving this chapter, your attention is called to a few of the fertile fields in which there has been a decline of leadership, and in which the new type of leader may find an abundance of *opportunity*.

1. In the field of politics there is a most insistent demand for new leaders; a demand that indicates nothing less than an emergency. Too many politicians have, seemingly, become high-grade, legalised racketeers. They have increased taxes and debauched the machinery of industry and business until the people can no longer stand the burden.

2. The financial industry is undergoing a reform. The leaders in this field have almost entirely lost the confidence of the public. Already financial executives have sensed the need for reform, and have set the wheels in motion.

3. Industry calls for new leaders. The old type of leaders thought and moved in terms of dividends instead of

thinking and moving in terms of human equations! The future leaders in industry, to endure, must regard themselves as quasi–public officials whose duty it is to manage their trust in such a way that it will bring hardship on no individual or group. Exploitation of workers is a thing of the past. Let those who aspire to leadership in the field of business, industry and labour remember this.

4. Religious leaders of the future will be forced to give more attention to the temporal needs of their followers in the solution of their economic and personal problems of the present, and less attention to the dead past and the yet unborn future.

5. In the professions of law, medicine and education, a new brand of leadership, and to some extent new leaders, will become a necessity. This is especially true in the field of education. Leaders in that field must, in the future, find ways and means of teaching people *how to apply* the knowledge they receive in school. They must deal more with *practice* and less with *theory*.

6. New leaders will be required in the field of journalism. The media of the future, to be conducted successfully, must be divorced from 'special privilege' and relieved from the subsidy of advertising.

These are but a few of the fields in which opportunities for new leaders and a new brand of leadership are now available. The world is undergoing a rapid change. This means that the media, through which the changes in human habits are promoted, must be adapted to the changes. The media here described are the ones that, more than any others, determine the trend of civilisation.

When and How to Apply for a Position

The information described here is the net result of many years of experience during which thousands of men and women were helped to market their services effectively. It can, therefore, be relied upon as sound and practical.

Media through which Services May be Marketed

Experience has proved that the following media offer the most direct and effective methods of bringing the buyer and seller of services together:

1. EMPLOYMENT AGENCIES. Care must be taken to select only reputable agencies, the management of which can show adequate records of achievement of satisfactory results.

2. ADVERTISING in newspapers, trade journals, magazines and on the Internet. Classified advertising may usually be relied upon to produce satisfactory results in the case of those who apply for clerical or ordinary salaried positions. Display advertising is more desirable in the case of those who seek executive connections, the copy to appear in the section of the paper most likely to come to the attention of the class of employer being sought. When preparing the advertisement it is advantageous to get advice from an expert who understands how to inject sufficient selling qualities to produce replies.

3. PERSONAL LETTERS OF APPLICATION, directed to particular firms or individuals most likely to need the services being offered. Letters should be neatly typed, ALWAYS, and signed by hand. With the letter should be

sent a complete CV or outline of the applicant's qualifications. Both the letter of application and the CV should be prepared with advice from an expert (below).

4. APPLICATION THROUGH PERSONAL ACQUAINTANCES. When possible, the applicant should endeavour to approach prospective employers through some mutual acquaintance. This method of approach is particularly advantageous in the case of those who seek executive connections and do not wish to appear to be 'peddling' themselves.

5. APPLICATION IN PERSON. In some instances it may be more effective if applicants offer their services personally to prospective employers. In such cases a complete written statement of qualifications for the position should be presented so that prospective employers may discuss the applicant's record with associates.

Information to be Supplied in a Written CV

This CV should be prepared as carefully as a lawyer would prepare the brief of a case to be tried in court. Unless the applicant is experienced in the preparation of CVs, an expert should be consulted. Successful merchants employ men and women who understand the art and psychology of advertising to present the merits of their merchandise. One who has services for sale should do the same. The following information should appear in the CV.

1. Education. State briefly, but definitely, what schooling you have had, and in what subjects you specialised, giving the reasons for that specialisation.

2. Experience. If you have had experience in connection with positions similar to the one you seek, describe it fully, stating names and addresses of former employers. Be sure to bring out clearly any special experience you may have had which would equip you to fill the position you seek.

3. References. Practically every business firm desires to know all about the previous records of prospective employees who seek positions of responsibility. Be prepared to present to the employer, if asked, the names of people who can provide information about your experience and capabilities, such as:

(a) Former employers

(b) Teachers under whom you studied

(c) Prominent people whose judgment may be relied upon

4. Apply for a specific position. Avoid application for a position without describing *exactly* what position you seek. Never apply for 'just a position'. That indicates you lack specialised qualifications.

5. State your qualifications for the particular position for which you are applying. Give full details as to the reason you believe you are qualified for the particular position you seek. This is THE MOST IMPORTANT DETAIL OF YOUR APPLICATION. It will determine, more than anything else, what consideration you receive.

6. Offer to go to work on probation. In the majority of instances, if you are determined to have the position for which you apply, it will be most effective if you offer to work for a week, or a month or for a sufficient length of time to enable your prospective employer to judge your

value WITHOUT PAY. This may appear to be a radical suggestion, but experience has proved that it seldom fails to win at least a trial. If you are *sure of your qualifications*, a trial is all you need. Incidentally, such an offer indicates that you have confidence in your ability to fill the position you seek. It is most convincing. If your offer is accepted and you make good, more than likely you will be paid for your 'probation' period. Make clear the fact that your offer is based upon:

(a) Your confidence in your ability to fill the position

(b) Your confidence in your prospective employer's decision to employ you after trial

(c) Your *determination* to have the position you seek

7. Knowledge of your prospective employer's business. Before applying for a position, do sufficient research in connection with the business to familiarise yourself thoroughly with that business, and indicate in your brief the knowledge you have acquired in this field. This will be impressive, as it will indicate that you have imagination and a real interest in the position you seek.

Remember that it is not the lawyer who knows the most law, but the one who best prepares the case, who wins. If your 'case' is properly prepared and presented, your victory will have been more than half won at the outset.

8. Do not be afraid of making your CV too long. Employers are just as interested in purchasing the services of well-qualified applicants as you are in securing employment. In fact, the success of most successful employers is due, in the main, to their ability to select well-qualified lieutenants. They want all the information available.

Remember another thing; neatness in the preparation of your CV will indicate that you are a painstaking person. I have helped to prepare CVs for clients that were so striking and out of the ordinary that they resulted in the employment of the applicant without a personal interview.

Once the CV is completed, have it printed on the finest paper you can obtain, Carefully check the spelling and grammar. Follow these instructions to the letter, improving upon them wherever your imagination suggests.

Successful salespeople groom themselves with care. They understand that first impressions are lasting. Your CV is your sales representative. Give it a good suit of clothes so it will stand out in bold contrast to anything your prospective employer ever saw in the way of an application for a position. If the position you seek is worth having, it is worth going after with care. Moreover, if you sell yourself to an employer in a manner that impresses them with your individuality, you will probably receive more money for your services from the very start than you would if you applied for employment in the usual conventional way.

If you seek employment through an advertising agency or an employment agency, get the agent to use copies of your CV in marketing your services. This will help to gain preference for you, both with the agent and the prospective employers.

How to Get the Exact Position You Desire

Everyone enjoys doing the kind of work for which they are best suited. An artist loves to work with paints, mechanics with their hands, a writer loves to write. Those with less definite talents have their preferences for certain fields of business and industry. There is a full range of occupations to choose from in manufacturing, marketing and the professions.

1. Decide *exactly* what kind of job you want. If the job doesn't already exist, perhaps you can create it.
2. Choose the company, or individual, for whom you wish to work.
3. Study your prospective employer as to policies, personnel and chances of advancement.
4. By analysis of yourself, your talents and capabilities, work out *what you can offer*, and plan ways and means of giving advantages, services, developments and ideas that you believe you can successfully deliver.
5. Forget about 'a job'. Forget whether or not there is an opening. Forget the usual routine of 'have you got a job for me?' Concentrate on what you can give.
6. Once you have your plan in mind, arrange with an experienced writer to help you put it on paper in neat form, and in full detail.
7. Present it to the proper person with authority to make the decision. Every company is looking for people who can give something of value, whether it is ideas, services or 'connections'. Every company has room for the person who has a definite plan of action to the advantage of that company.

This line of procedure may take a few days or weeks of extra time, but the difference in income, in advancement and in gaining recognition will save years of hard work at low pay. It has many advantages, the main one being that it will often save from one to five years of time in reaching a chosen goal.

Every person who starts or 'gets in' half way up the ladder does so by deliberate and careful planning (excepting, of course, the Boss's son).

The New Way of Marketing Services
'Jobs' Are Now 'Partnerships'

Men and women who want to market their services to best advantage in the future must recognise the stupendous change that has taken place in the relationship between employer and employee.

The time will come when the 'Golden Rule' and not the 'Rule of Gold' will be the dominating factor in the marketing of merchandise as well as services. The future relationship between employers and their employees will be more in the nature of a partnership consisting of:

(a) The employer
(b) The employee
(c) The public they serve

This new way of marketing services is called new for many reasons. First, both the employer and the employee of the future will be considered as fellow-employees whose business it will be to *serve the public efficiently*. In times past, employers and employees have bartered among themselves, driving the best bargains they could with one another, not considering that in the final analysis they were, in reality, *bargaining at the expense of the third party, the public they served*.

In the future both employers and employees will recognise that they are *no longer privileged to drive bargains at the expense of those whom they serve.* The real employer of the future will be the public. This should be kept uppermost in mind by every person seeking to market their services effectively.

'Courtesy' and 'service' are the watchwords of merchandising today. They apply to the person who is marketing their services even more directly than to the employer they serve, because, in the final analysis, both employer and employee are *employed by the public they serve.* If they fail to serve well, they pay by the loss of their privilege of serving.

What is Your 'QQS' Rating?

The causes of success in marketing services *effectively* and permanently have been clearly described. Unless those causes are studied, analysed, understood and *applied*, no one can market their services effectively and permanently. It is up to *you* to sell your own services. The *quality* and the *quantity* of service rendered, and the *spirit* in which it is rendered, determine to a large extent the price and the duration of employment. To market services effectively (which means a permanent market, at a satisfactory price, under pleasant conditions), one must adopt and follow the QQS formula, which means that QUALITY, plus QUANTITY, plus the proper SPIRIT of cooperation equals perfect marketing of service. Remember the 'QQS' formula, but do more – *apply it as a habit!*

Let us analyse the formula to make sure we understand exactly what it means:

1. QUALITY of service means the performance of every detail, in connection with your position, in the most efficient manner possible, with the object of greater efficiency always in mind.

2. QUANTITY of service means the HABIT of giving all the service of which you are capable, at all times, with the purpose of increasing the amount of service as you develop greater skill through practice and experience. Emphasis is again placed on the word HABIT.

3. SPIRIT of service means the HABIT of agreeable, harmonious conduct that will induce cooperation from associates and fellow employees.

   Adequacy of QUALITY and QUANTITY of service is not sufficient to maintain a permanent market for your services. The conduct, or the SPIRIT, in which you deliver service is a strong determining factor in connection with both the price you receive and the duration of employment.

Andrew Carnegie stressed this point more than others in his description of the factors that lead to success in the marketing of services. He emphasised again and again the necessity for *harmonious conduct*. He stressed that he would not retain any person, no matter how great a *quantity* or how efficient the *quality* of their work, unless that person worked in a spirit of *harmony*. Mr Carnegie insisted upon everybody being *agreeable*. To prove that he placed a high value upon this quality, he permitted many people who conformed to his standards to become very wealthy. Those who did not conform had to make room for others.

The importance of a pleasing personality has been stressed because it enables one to provide service in the proper *spirit*. If one has a personality which *pleases* and serves in a spirit of *harmony*, these assets often make up for deficiencies in both the *quality* and the *quantity* of service one gives. Nothing, however, can be *successfully substituted for pleasing conduct*.

The Capital Value of Your Services

The person whose income is derived entirely from the sale of their services is no less than a merchant who sells commodities. It might well be added that such a person is subject to *exactly the same rules* of conduct as the merchant who sells merchandise.

This has been emphasised because the majority of people who live by the sale of their services make the mistake of considering themselves free from the rules of conduct and the responsibilities attached to those engaged in marketing commodities.

The actual capital value of your brains may be determined by the amount of income you can produce (by marketing your services). A fair estimate of the capital value of your services may be made by multiplying your annual income by 16 and two-thirds, as it is reasonable to estimate that your annual income represents six per cent of your capital value. Money rents for six per cent per annum. Money is worth no more than brains. It is often worth much less.

Competent 'brains', if effectively marketed, represent a much more desirable form of capital than that required to conduct a business dealing in commodities. This is because 'brains' are a form of capital that cannot be permanently depreciated through depressions, nor can this form of capital be stolen or spent. Moreover, the money essential for the conduct of business is as worthless as a sand dune until it has been mixed with efficient 'brains'.

The 30 Major Causes of Failure
How Many of These are Holding You Back?

Life's greatest tragedy consists of men and women who earnestly try, and fail! The tragedy lies in the overwhelmingly large majority of people who fail, as compared to the few who succeed.

I have had the privilege of analysing several thousand men and women, 98 per cent of whom were classed as 'failures'. There is something radically wrong with a civilisation and a system of education which permit so many people to go through life as failures. But I did not write this book for the purpose of moralising on the rights and wrongs of the world; that would require a book 100 times the size of this one.

My analysis work proved that there are 30 major reasons for failure. As you go over the list, check yourself by it, point by point, to discover how many of these causes of failure stand between you and success.

1. UNFAVOURABLE HEREDITARY BACKGROUND. Little, if anything, can be done for people who are born with a deficiency in brainpower. This philosophy offers but one method of bridging this weakness – through the aid of the Master Mind (see page 193). Observe with profit, however, that this is the *only* one of the 30 causes of failure that may not be easily corrected by any individual.

2. LACK OF A WELL-DEFINED PURPOSE IN LIFE. There is no hope of success for the person who does not have a central purpose, or definite goal, at which to aim. Ninety-eight out of every hundred of those whom I have analysed had no such aim. Perhaps this was the *major cause of their failure.*

3. LACK OF AMBITION TO AIM ABOVE MEDIOCRITY. We offer no hope for the person who is so indifferent as not to want to get ahead in life, and who is not willing to pay the price.

4. INSUFFICIENT EDUCATION. This is a handicap that may be overcome with comparative ease. Experience has proven that the best-educated people are often those who are known as 'self-made' or self-educated. It takes more than a university degree to make one a person of education. Any person who is educated has learned to get whatever they want in life without violating the rights of others. Education consists not so much of knowledge, but of knowledge effectively and persistently *applied*. People are paid not merely for what they know, but more particularly for *what they do with what they know*.

5. LACK OF SELF-DISCIPLINE. Discipline comes through self-control. This means that you must control all negative qualities. Before you can control conditions, you must first control yourself. Self-mastery is the hardest job you will ever tackle. If you do not conquer self, you will be conquered by self. You may see at one and the same time both your best friend and your greatest enemy, by stepping in front of a mirror.

6. ILL HEALTH. No person may enjoy outstanding success without good health. Many of the causes of ill health are subject to mastery and control. These, in the main are:
   • Overeating of foods not conducive to health
   • Wrong habits of thought; giving expression to negatives
   • Wrong use of, and overindulgence in sex
   • Lack of proper physical exercise
   • An inadequate supply of fresh air, due to improper breathing

7. UNFAVOURABLE ENVIRONMENTAL INFLUENCES DURING CHILDHOOD. 'As the twig is bent, so shall the tree grow.' Most people who have criminal tendencies acquire them as the result of bad environment and improper associates during childhood.

8. PROCRASTINATION. This is one of the most common causes of failure. 'Old Man Procrastination' stands within the shadow of all people, awaiting the opportunity to spoil their chances of success. Most of us go through life as failures because we are waiting for the 'time to be right' to start doing something worthwhile. Do not wait. The time will never be 'just right'. Start where you stand, work with whatever tools you may have at your command, and better tools will be found as you go along.

9. LACK OF PERSISTENCE. Most of us are good 'starters' but poor 'finishers' of everything we begin. Moreover, people are prone to give up at the first signs of defeat. There is no substitute for *persistence*. The persistent person discovers that 'Old Man Failure' finally becomes tired and goes away. Failure cannot cope with persistence.

10. NEGATIVE PERSONALITY. There is no hope of success for the person who repels people through a negative personality. Success comes through the application of *power*, and power is attained through the cooperative efforts of other people. A negative personality will not induce cooperation.

11. LACK OF CONTROLLED SEXUAL URGE. Sex energy is the most powerful of all the stimuli that move

people into *action*. Because it is the most powerful of the emotions, it must be controlled through transmutation, and converted into other channels.

12. UNCONTROLLED DESIRE FOR 'SOMETHING FOR NOTHING'. The gambling instinct drives millions of people to failure. *Evidence of this may be found in a study of the dot.com fiasco of the early 2000s, during which millions of people tried to make money by investing in fly-by-night companies.*

13. LACK OF A WELL-DEFINED POWER OF DECISION. People who succeed reach decisions promptly, and change them – if at all – very slowly. People who fail reach decisions – if at all – very slowly, and change them frequently and quickly. Indecision and procrastination are twins. Where one is found, the other may usually be found also. Kill off this pair before they completely tie you to the treadmill of *failure*.

14. ONE OR MORE OF THE SIX BASIC FEARS. These fears have been analysed for you in Chapter 15. They must be mastered before you can market your services effectively.

15. WRONG SELECTION OF A MATE IN MARRIAGE. This is a most common cause of failure. The relationship of marriage brings people intimately into contact. Unless this relationship is harmonious, failure is likely to follow. Moreover, it will be a form of failure marked by misery and unhappiness, destroying all signs of *ambition*.

16. OVER-CAUTION. The person who takes no chances generally has to take whatever is left when others have

finished choosing. Over-caution is as bad as under-caution. Both are extremes to be guarded against. Life itself is filled with the element of chance.

17. WRONG SELECTION OF ASSOCIATES IN BUSINESS. This is one of the most common causes of failure in business. In marketing your services, you should take great care to select an employer who will be an inspiration, and who is intelligent and successful. We emulate those with whom we associate most closely. Pick an employer who is worth emulating.

18. SUPERSTITION AND PREJUDICE. Superstition is a form of fear. It is also a sign of ignorance. People who succeed keep open minds and are afraid of nothing.

19. WRONG SELECTION OF A VOCATION. No one can succeed in a line of endeavour they do not like. The most essential step in marketing your services is selecting an occupation into which you can throw yourself wholeheartedly.

20. LACK OF CONCENTRATION OF EFFORT. The 'jack-of-all-trades' is seldom good at any. Concentrate all your efforts on one *definite chief aim*.

21. THE HABIT OF INDISCRIMINATE SPENDING. Spendthrifts cannot succeed, mainly because they stand eternally in *fear of poverty*. Form the habit of systematic saving by putting aside a definite percentage of your income. Money in the bank gives you a very safe foundation of *courage* when bargaining for the sale of your services. Without money, you must take what you are offered, and be glad to get it.

22. LACK OF ENTHUSIASM. Without enthusiasm one cannot be convincing. Moreover, enthusiasm is

contagious, and the person who has it, under control, is generally welcome in any group of people.

23. INTOLERANCE. The person with a 'closed' mind on any subject seldom gets ahead. Intolerance means that one has stopped acquiring knowledge. The most damaging forms of intolerance are those connected with religious, racial and political differences of opinion.

24. INTEMPERANCE. The most damaging forms of intemperance are connected with eating, strong drink and sexual activities. Overindulgence in any of these is fatal to success.

25. INABILITY TO COOPERATE WITH OTHERS. More people lose their positions and their big opportunities in life because of this fault than for all other reasons combined. It is a fault which no well-informed business executive or leader will tolerate.

26. POSSESSION OF POWER NOT ACQUIRED THROUGH SELF-EFFORT. (Sons and daughters of wealthy families, and others who inherit money that they did not earn.) Power in the hands of one who did not acquire it gradually is often fatal to success. *Quick riches* are more dangerous than poverty.

27. INTENTIONAL DISHONESTY. There is no substitute for honesty. One may be temporarily dishonest by force of circumstances over which one has no control, without permanent damage. But there is *no hope* for people who are dishonest by choice. Sooner or later, their deeds will catch up with them, and they will pay by loss of reputation, and perhaps even loss of liberty.

28. **EGOTISM AND VANITY.** These qualities serve as red lights that warn others to keep away. *They are fatal to success.*
29. **GUESSING INSTEAD OF THINKING.** Most people are too indifferent or lazy to acquire *facts* with which to *think accurately*. They prefer to act on 'opinions' created by guesswork or snap-judgments.
30. **LACK OF CAPITAL.** This is a common cause of failure among those who start out in business for the first time without sufficient reserve of capital to absorb the shock of their mistakes, and to carry them over until they have established a *reputation*.
31. Under this, name any particular cause of failure from which you have suffered that has not been included in the foregoing list.

In these 30 major causes of failure is found a description of the tragedy of life, which is relevant for practically every person who tries and fails. It will be helpful if you can induce someone who knows you well to go over this list with you, and help to analyse you by the 30 causes of failure. It may be more beneficial than if you try this alone. Most people cannot see themselves as others see them. You may be one who cannot.

The oldest of admonitions is 'Know thyself!' If you market merchandise successfully, you must know the merchandise. The same is true in marketing your services. You should know all of your weaknesses so that you may either bridge them or eliminate them entirely. You should know your strengths so that you may call attention to them when selling your services. You can know yourself only through accurate analysis.

The folly of ignorance in connection with self was displayed by a young man who applied to the manager of a well-known business for a position. He made a very good impression until the manager asked him what salary he expected. He replied that he had no fixed sum in mind (lack of a definite aim). The manager then said, 'We will pay you all you are worth, after we try you out for a week.'

'I will not accept it,' the applicant replied, 'because *I am getting more than that where I am now employed.*'

Before you even start to negotiate for a readjustment of your salary in your present position, or to seek employment elsewhere, *be sure that you are worth more than you now receive.*

It is one thing to *want* money – everyone wants more – but it is something entirely different to be *worth more*! Many people mistake their *wants* for their *just dues.* Your financial requirements or wants have nothing whatever to do with your *worth.* Your value is established entirely by your ability to provide useful service or your capacity to induce others to provide such service.

Take an Inventory of Yourself
28 Questions You Should Answer

Annual self-analysis is as essential in the effective marketing of services as is annual inventory in merchandising. Moreover, the yearly analysis should disclose a *decrease in faults* and an *increase in virtues.* One goes ahead, stands still, or goes backward in life. One's object should be, of course, to go ahead. Annual self-analysis will disclose whether advancement has been made, and if so, how much. It will also disclose any backward steps one may have made. The effective marketing of services requires one to move forwards, even if the progress is slow.

Your annual self-analysis should be made at the end of each year so you can include in your New Year's resolutions any improvements that the analysis indicates should be made. Take this inventory by asking yourself the following questions, and by checking your answers with the aid of someone who will not permit you to deceive yourself as to their accuracy.

Self-analysis Questionnaire for Personal Inventory

1. Have I attained the goal that I established as my objective for this year? (You should work with a definite yearly objective to be attained as a part of your major life objective.)

2. Have I delivered service of the best possible *quality* of which I was capable, or could I have improved any part of this service?

3. Have I delivered service in the greatest possible *quantity* of which I was capable?

4. Has the spirit of my conduct been harmonious and cooperative at all times?

5. Have I permitted the habit of *procrastination* to decrease my efficiency, and if so, to what extent?

6. Have I improved my *personality*, and if so, in what ways?

7. Have I been *persistent* in following my plans through to completion?

8. Have I reached *decisions promptly and definitely* on all occasions?

9. Have I permitted any one or more of the six basic fears (see Chapter 15) to decrease my efficiency?

10. Have I been either 'over-cautious' or 'under-cautious'?

11. Has my relationship with my colleagues in work been pleasant or unpleasant? If it has been unpleasant, has the fault been partly or wholly mine?

12. Have I dissipated any of my energy through lack of *concentration* of effort?

13. Have I been open-minded and tolerant in connection with all subjects?
14. In what way have I improved my ability to provide service?
15. Have I been intemperate in any of my habits?
16. Have I expressed, either openly or secretly, any form of *egotism*?
17. Has my conduct towards my colleagues been such that it has induced them to *respect* me?
18. Have my opinions and *decisions* been based upon guesswork, or accuracy of analysis and *thought*?
19. Have I followed the habit of budgeting my time, my expenses and my income, and have I been conservative in these budgets?
20. How much time have I devoted to *unprofitable* effort which I might have used to better advantage?
21. How may I *re-budget* my time and change my habits so I will be more efficient during the coming year?
22. Have I been guilty of any conduct that was not approved by my conscience?
23. In what ways have I provided *more service and better service* than I was paid for?
24. Have I been unfair to anyone, and if so, in what way?
25. If I had been the purchaser of my own services for the year, would I have been satisfied with my purchase?
26. Has the purchaser of my services been satisfied with the service I have provided, and if not, why not?
27. Am I in the right vocation, and if not, why not?
28. What is my present rating on the fundamental principles of success? (Make this rating fairly and frankly, and have it checked by someone who is courageous enough to do it accurately.)

Having read and assimilated the information conveyed in this chapter, you are now ready to create a practical plan for marketing your services. Those who have lost their fortunes, and those who are just beginning to earn money, have nothing but their services to offer in return for riches. It is therefore essential that they have available the practical information needed to market their services to best advantage.

The information contained in this chapter will be of great value to all who aspire to attain leadership in any calling. It will be particularly helpful to those aiming to market their services as business or industrial executives.

Complete assimilation and understanding of the information here conveyed will be helpful in marketing one's own services, and it will also help one to become more analytical and capable of judging people. The information will be priceless to personnel directors, employment managers and other executives charged with the selection of employees and the maintenance of efficient organisations. If you doubt this statement, test its soundness by answering in writing the 28 self-analysis questions. Indeed, that might be both interesting and profitable even if you do not doubt the soundness of the statement.

Where and How to Find Opportunities to Accumulate Riches

Now that we have analysed the principles by which riches may be accumulated, we naturally ask, 'Where may one find favourable opportunities to apply these principles?' Very well, let us take an inventory and see what the Western economy may offer the person seeking riches, great or small.

To begin with, let us remember, all of us, that we live in a society where every law-abiding citizen enjoys freedom of thought and freedom of deed. Most of us have never taken stock of the advantages of this freedom. We have never compared our unlimited freedom with the curtailed freedom in some other societies.

Here we have freedom of thought, freedom in the choice and enjoyment of education, freedom in religion, freedom in politics, freedom in the choice of a business, profession or occupation, freedom to accumulate and own without molestation *all the property we can accumulate*, freedom to choose our place of residence, freedom in marriage, freedom through equal opportunity to all races, freedom of travel, freedom in our choice of foods, and freedom to *aim for any station in life for which we have prepared ourselves*. We have other forms of freedom, but this list will give a bird's eye view of the most important, which constitute *opportunity* of the highest order.

Next, let us recount some of the blessings that our widespread freedom has placed within our hands. Take the average family in Western society for example (meaning the family of average income) and sum up the benefits available to every member of the family.

- FOOD. Because of our universal freedom, the average family has available, at its very door, a choice selection of food, and at prices within its financial range.
- SHELTER. This family lives in a comfortable home, heated by gas, lighted with electricity, with gas for cooking, all for a reasonable rate. The toast they had for

breakfast was toasted on an electric toaster; the carpets
are cleaned with a vacuum cleaner run by electricity.
Hot and cold water is available, at all times, in the
kitchen and the bathroom. The food is kept cool in a
refrigerator run by electricity. The wife styles her hair,
washes her clothes and irons them with easily operated
electrical equipment, on power obtained by sticking a
plug in the wall. The husband shaves with an electric
shaver. They receive entertainment from all over the
world, 24 hours a day if they want it, by merely
switching on their television.

- CLOTHING. Men and women in Western society can
  meet their clothing requirements and dress very
  comfortably at prices within the range of an average
  family's salary.

Only the three basic necessities of food, clothing and shelter have
been mentioned. The average citizen has other privileges and
advantages available in return for modest effort, not exceeding
eight hours per day of labour. Among these is the privilege of
owning a car, with which one can come and go at will, at very
small cost.

The 'Miracle' that Has Provided
These Blessings

Having no axe to grind, no grudge to express and no ulterior
motives, I have the privilege of analysing frankly that mysterious,
abstract, greatly misunderstood SOMETHING which provides
us with the aforementioned blessings, opportunities to accumulate wealth and freedom of every nature.

I have the right to analyse the source and nature of this *unseen power* because I know, and have known for more than a quarter of a century, many of the people who organised that power, and many who are now responsible for its maintenance.

The name of this mysterious benefactor of humankind is CAPITAL!

Capital consists not of money alone, but more particularly of highly organised, intelligent groups of people who plan ways and means of using money efficiently for the good of the public, and profitably for themselves.

These groups consist of scientists, educators, chemists, inventors, business analysts, public relations experts, transportation experts, accountants, lawyers, doctors, and both men and women who have highly specialised knowledge in all fields of industry and business. They pioneer, experiment and blaze trails in new fields of endeavour. They support colleges, hospitals and schools, build good roads, publish newspapers, pay most of the cost of government, and take care of the multitudinous detail essential to human progress. Stated briefly, the capitalists are the brains of civilisation because they supply the entire fabric of which all education, enlightenment and human progress consist.

Money without brains is always dangerous. Properly used, it is the most important essential of civilisation. A simple breakfast for a city family consisting of grapefruit juice, cereal, eggs, bread and butter and tea with sugar could not be provided at a reasonable price if organised capital had not supplied the machinery, the ships, the railways, and the huge armies of trained people to operate them.

Some slight idea of the importance of *organised capital* may be had by trying to imagine yourself burdened with the responsibility of collecting and delivering a simple breakfast to the above-mentiioned city family, without the aid of capital.

To supply the tea, you would have to make a trip to China or India. Unless you are an excellent swimmer, you would become rather tired before making the round trip. Then another problem would confront you. What would you use for money, even if you had the physical endurance to swim the ocean?

To supply the sugar, you would have to take another long swim to a Caribbean island, or a long walk to a sugar beet farm. But even then you might come back without the sugar, because organised effort and money are necessary to produce sugar, to say nothing of what is required to refine, transport and deliver it to the breakfast table.

The eggs you could deliver easily enough but you would have a very long journey before you could serve the two glasses of grapefruit juice.

You would have another long walk to a wheat-growing area when you went after the four slices of wheat bread.

The cereal would have to be omitted from the menu because it would not be available except through the labour of a trained organisation of people and suitable machinery, *all of which call for capital*.

While resting, you could take off for another little swim down to South America, where you would pick up a couple of bananas, and on your return you could take a short walk to the nearest dairy farm and pick up some butter and cream. Then your city family would be ready to sit down and enjoy breakfast.

Seems absurd, doesn't it? Well, the procedure described would be the only possible way these simple items of food could be delivered to the heart of the city if we had no capitalistic system.

The sum of money required for the building and maintenance

of the railways and ships used in the delivery of that simple breakfast is so huge that it staggers one's imagination. It runs into hundreds of millions of dollars, not to mention the armies of trained employees required to man the ships and trains. But transportation is only a part of the requirements of modern civilisation. Before there can be anything to haul, something must be grown from the ground, or manufactured and prepared for market. This calls for more millions of dollars for equipment, machinery, boxing, marketing, and for the wages of millions of men and women.

Ships and railways do not spring up from the earth and function automatically. They come in response to the call of civilisation, through the labour and ingenuity and organising ability of people who have *imagination, faith, enthusiasm, decision* and *persistence*! These people are known as capitalists. They are motivated by the desire to build, construct, achieve, provide useful service, earn profits and accumulate riches. And, because they *provide service without which there would be no civilisation*, they put themselves in the way of great riches.

Just to keep the record simple and understandable, I will add that these capitalists are the selfsame people of whom most of us have heard soapbox orators speak. They are the same people to whom radicals, racketeers, dishonest politicians and union leaders refer as 'the predatory interests'.

I am not attempting to present a brief for or against any group of people or any system of economics. I am not attempting to condemn collective bargaining when I refer to 'union leaders', nor do I aim to give a clean bill of health to all individuals known as capitalists.

The purpose of this book – a purpose to which I have faithfully devoted over a quarter of a century – is to present to all who want the knowledge the most dependable philosophy through which individuals may accumulate riches in whatever amounts they desire.

I have here analysed the economic advantages of the capitalistic system for the two-fold purpose of showing:

1. that all who seek riches must recognise and adapt themselves to the system that controls all approaches to fortunes, large or small, and
2. that they must present the side of the picture opposite to that being shown by politicians and demagogues who refer to organised capital as if it were something poisonous.

This is a capitalistic society. It was developed through the use of capital, and we who claim the right to partake of the blessings of freedom and opportunity, we who seek to accumulate riches here, may as well know that neither riches nor opportunity would be available to us if *organised capital* had not provided these benefits.

If you are one of those who believe that riches can be accumulated by the mere act of people who organise themselves into groups and demand *more pay* for *less service*, if you are one of those who *demand* Government relief without early morning disturbance when the money is delivered to you, if you are one of those who believe in trading their votes to politicians in return for the passing of laws which permit the raiding of the public treasury, you may rest securely on your belief, with certain knowledge that no one will disturb you because *this is a free country where everyone may think as they please*, where nearly everybody can live with but little effort, where many may live well without doing any work whatsoever.

However, you should know the full truth concerning this

freedom of which so many people boast and so few understand. As great as it is, as far as it reaches, as many privileges as it provides, *it does not and cannot bring riches without effort.*

There is but one dependable method of accumulating and legally holding riches, and that is by providing useful service. No system has ever been created by which people can legally acquire riches through mere force of numbers, or without giving in return an equivalent value of one form or another.

There is a principle known as the law of *economics*! This is more than a theory. It is a law no person can beat.

Mark well the name of the principle and remember it, because it is far more powerful than all the politicians and political machines. It is above and beyond the control of all the labour unions. It cannot be swayed, influenced or bribed by racketeers or self-appointed leaders in any calling. Moreover, *it has an all-seeing eye and a perfect system of bookkeeping* in which it keeps an accurate account of the transactions of every human being engaged in the business of trying to get without giving. Sooner or later its auditors come around, look over the records of individuals both great and small, and demand an accounting.

'Big business', 'capital predatory interests' or whatever name you choose to give the system which has given us *freedom* represents a group of people who understand, respect and adapt themselves to this powerful *law of economics*. Their financial continuation depends upon their respecting the law.

Remember, also, that this is but the beginning of the available sources for the accumulation of wealth. Only a few of the luxuries and non-essentials have been mentioned. But remember that the business of producing, transporting and marketing these few items of merchandise gives regular employment to *many millions of men and women* who receive for their services *many millions of dollars monthly* and spend it freely on both the luxuries and the necessities.

Especially remember that behind all this exchange of merchandise and personal services may be found an abundance of *opportunity* to accumulate riches. Here our *freedom* comes to our aid. There is nothing to stop you or anyone from engaging in any portion of the effort necessary to carry on these businesses. If one has superior talent, training, or experience, one may accumulate riches in large amounts. Those not so fortunate may accumulate smaller amounts. Anyone may earn a living in return for a very nominal amount of labour.

So – there you are!

Opportunity has spread its wares before you. Step up to the front, select what you want, create your plan, put the plan into action and follow through with *persistence*. 'Capitalistic' society will do the rest. You can depend upon this much – CAPITALISTIC SOCIETY GUARANTEES EVERY PERSON THE OPPORTUNITY TO PROVIDE USEFUL SERVICE AND TO COLLECT RICHES IN PROPORTION TO THE VALUE OF THE SERVICE.

The 'system' denies no one this right, but it does not and cannot promise *something for nothing*. The *law of economics* itself irrevocably controls the system that neither recognises nor tolerates for long *getting without giving*.

The law of economics was passed by Nature! There is no court to which violators of this law may appeal. The law hands out both penalties for its violation and appropriate rewards for its observance, without interference or the possibility of inter-ference by any human being. The law cannot be repealed. It is as fixed as the stars in the heavens, and subject to, and a part of, the same system that controls the stars.

May one refuse to adapt oneself to the law of economics?

Certainly! This is a free society, where all are born with equal rights, including the privilege of ignoring the law of economics. What happens then?

Well, nothing happens until large numbers of people join forces for the avowed purpose of ignoring the law, and taking what they want by force. *Then comes the dictator, with well-organised firing squads and machine guns!*

We have not yet reached that stage, but we have learned all we want to know about how the system works. Perhaps we shall be fortunate enough not to demand personal knowledge of so gruesome a reality. Doubtless we shall prefer to continue with our *freedom of speech, freedom of deed* and *freedom to provide useful service in return for riches.*

These observations are not founded upon short-time experience. They are the result of 25 years of careful analysis of the methods of both the most successful and the most unsuccessful men America has known.

CHAPTER 8

DECISION:
the Mastery of Procrastination

(The Seventh Step to Riches)

ACCURATE analysis of over 25,000 men and women who had experienced failure disclosed the fact that *lack of decision* was near the head of the list of the 30 major causes of *failure*. This is no mere statement of a theory – it is a fact.

Procrastination, the opposite of *decision*, is a common enemy that practically everybody must conquer.

You will have an opportunity to test your capacity to reach quick and definite *decisions* when you finish reading this book, and are ready to begin putting into *action* the principles it describes.

Analysis of several hundred people who accumulated fortunes well beyond the million-dollar mark disclosed the fact that every one of them had the habit of *reaching decisions promptly* and of changing these decisions *slowly*, if and when they were changed. People who fail to accumulate money, without exception, have the habit of reaching decisions, *if at all*, very slowly, and of changing these decisions quickly and often.

One of Henry Ford's most outstanding qualities was his habit of reaching decisions quickly and definitely, and changing them slowly. This quality was so pronounced in Mr Ford that it gave him the reputation of being obstinate. It was this quality which prompted Mr Ford to continue to manufacture his famous Model 'T' (the world's ugliest car), when all of his advisers, and many of the purchasers of the car, were urging him to change it.

Perhaps Mr Ford delayed too long in making the change, but the other side of the story is that Mr Ford's firmness of decision yielded a huge fortune before the change in model became necessary. There is but little doubt that Mr Ford's habit of definiteness of decision assumed the proportion of obstinacy, but this quality is preferable to slowness in reaching decisions and quickness in changing them.

The majority of people who fail to accumulate money sufficient for their needs are, generally, easily influenced by the 'opinions' of others. They permit the newspapers and the 'gossiping' neighbours to do their 'thinking' for them. 'Opinions' are the cheapest commodities on earth. Everyone has a flock of opinions ready to be wished upon anyone who will accept them. If you are influenced by 'opinions' when you reach *decisions*, you will not succeed in any undertaking, much less in that of transmuting *your own desire* into money.

If you are influenced by the opinions of others, you will have no *desire* of your own.

Keep your own counsel, when you begin to put into practice the principles described here, by reaching your own decisions and following them. Take no one into your confidence *except* the members of your 'Master Mind' group, and be very sure in your selection of this group that you choose *only* those who will be in *complete sympathy and harmony with your purpose*.

Close friends and relatives, while not meaning to do so, often handicap one through 'opinions' and sometimes through ridicule, which is meant to be humorous. Thousands of men and women carry inferiority complexes with them all through life because some well-meaning but ignorant person destroyed their confidence through 'opinions' or ridicule.

You have a brain and mind of your own. Use it and reach your own decisions. If you need facts or information from other people to enable you to reach decisions, as you probably will in many instances, acquire these facts or secure the information you need quietly, without disclosing your purpose.

It is characteristic of people who have but a smattering or a veneer of knowledge to try to give the impression that they have much knowledge. Such people generally do *too much* talking and *too little* listening. Keep your eyes and ears wide open and your mouth *closed* if you wish to acquire the habit of prompt decision. Those who talk too much do little else. If you talk more than you listen, you not only deprive yourself of many opportunities to accumulate useful knowledge, but you also disclose your *plans* and *purposes* to people who will take great delight in defeating you, because they envy you.

Remember, also, that every time you open your mouth in the presence of a person who has an abundance of knowledge, you display to that person your exact stock of knowledge or your *lack* of it! Genuine wisdom is usually conspicuous through modesty and silence.

Keep in mind the fact that every person with whom you associate is, like yourself, seeking the opportunity to accumulate money. If you talk about your plans too freely, you may be surprised when you learn that some other person has beaten you to your goal by *putting into action ahead of you* the plans of which you talked unwisely.

Let one of your first decisions be to *keep a closed mouth and open ears and eyes*.

As a reminder to yourself to follow this advice, it will be helpful if you copy the following epigram in large letters and place it where you will see it daily:

TELL THE WORLD WHAT YOU INTEND TO DO, BUT FIRST SHOW IT

This is the equivalent of saying that 'deeds, and not words, are what count most'.

Freedom or Death on a Decision

The value of decisions depends upon the courage required to make them. The great decisions which served as the foundation of civilisation were reached by assuming great risks, which often meant the possibility of death.

Lincoln's decision to issue his famous Proclamation of Emancipation, which gave freedom to the enslaved people of America, was taken with full understanding that his act would turn thousands of friends and political supporters against him. He knew, too, that the carrying out of that proclamation would mean death to thousands of men on the battlefield. In the end, it cost Lincoln his life. That required courage.

Socrates' decision to drink the cup of poison, rather than

compromise in his personal belief, was a decision of courage. It turned time ahead a thousand years, and gave to people then unborn the right to freedom of thought and of speech.

The decision of General Robert E. Lee, when he came to the parting of the way with the Union and took up the cause of the South, was one of courage, for he well knew it might cost him his own life, and that it would surely cost the lives of others.

But the greatest decision of all time, as far as any American citizen is concerned, was reached in Philadelphia on 4 July 1776, when 56 men signed their names to a document they well knew would bring freedom to all Americans, or leave every one of the 56 hanging from a gallows!

You have heard of this famous document, but you may not have drawn from it the great lesson in personal achievement it so plainly taught.

We all remember the date of this momentous decision, but few of us realise what courage that decision required. We remember history as it was taught; we remember dates, and the names of the men who fought; we remember Valley Forge and Yorktown; we remember George Washington and Lord Cornwallis. But we know little of the real forces behind these names, dates and places. We know still less of that intangible *power*, which guaranteed freedom for Americans long before Washington's armies reached Yorktown.

We read the history of the Revolution and falsely imagine that George Washington was the father of America, that it was he who won Americans their freedom. The truth is that Washington was only an accessory after the fact, because victory for his armies had been ensured long before Lord Cornwallis surrendered. This is not intended to rob Washington of any of the glory he so richly merited. Its purpose, rather, is to give greater attention to the astounding *power* that was the real cause of his victory.

It is nothing short of tragedy that the writers of history have entirely missed even the slightest reference to the irresistible *power* that gave birth and freedom to the nation destined to set up new standards of independence for all the peoples of the earth. I say it is a tragedy because it is the self-same *power* that must be used by every individual who surmounts the difficulties of Life, and forces Life to pay the price asked.

Let us briefly review the events that gave birth to this *power*. The story begins with an incident in Boston on 5 March 1770. British soldiers were patrolling the streets, openly threatening the citizens by their presence. The colonists resented armed men marching in their midst. They began to express their resentment openly, hurling stones as well as epithets at the marching soldiers, until the commanding officer gave orders, 'Fix bayonets . . . Charge!'

The battle was on. It resulted in the death and injury of many. The incident aroused such resentment that the Provincial Assembly (made up of prominent colonists) called a meeting for the purpose of taking definite action. Two of the members of that Assembly were John Hancock and Samuel Adams. They spoke up courageously and declared that a move must be made to eject all British soldiers from Boston.

Remember this – a *decision*, in the minds of two men, might properly be called the beginning of the freedom that Americans now enjoy. Remember, too, that the *decision* of these two men called for *faith* and *courage*, because it was dangerous.

Before the Assembly adjourned, Samuel Adams was appointed to call on the Governor of the province, Hutchinson, and demand the withdrawal of British troops. The request was granted and the troops were removed from Boston, but the incident was not closed. It had caused a situation destined to change the entire trend of civilisation. Strange, is it not, how the great changes, such as the American Revolution and many wars, often have their beginnings in circumstances which seem unimportant? It is interesting, also, to observe that these important changes usually begin in the form of a *definite decision* in the minds of a relatively small number of people. Few of us know the history of America well enough to realise that John Hancock, Samuel Adams and Richard Henry Lee (of the Province of Virginia) were the real fathers of the country.

Richard Henry Lee became an important factor in this story due to the fact that he and Samuel Adams communicated frequently (by correspondence), sharing freely their fears and their hopes concerning the welfare of the people of their provinces. From this practice, Adams conceived the idea that a mutual exchange of letters between the 13 colonies might help to bring about the coordination of effort so badly needed in connection with the solution of their problems. In March 1772, two years after the clash with the soldiers in Boston, Adams presented this idea to the Assembly in the form of a motion that a Correspondence Committee be established among the colonies, with definitely appointed correspondents in each colony, 'for the purpose of friendly cooperation for the betterment of the Colonies of British America'.

Mark well this incident! It was the beginning of the organisation of the far-flung *power* destined to give freedom to Americans. The Master Mind had already been organised. It consisted of Adams, Lee and Hancock. The Committee of Correspondence was organised. Observe that this move provided the way for increasing the power of the Master Mind by adding to it men from all the colonies. Take notice that this procedure constituted the first *organised planning* of the disgruntled colonists.

In union there is strength! The citizens of the colonies had been waging disorganised warfare against the British soldiers through incidents similar to the Boston riot, but nothing of benefit had been accomplished. Their individual grievances had not been consolidated under one Master Mind. No group of individuals had put their hearts, minds, souls and bodies together in one definite *decision* to settle their difficulty with the British once and for all, until Adams, Hancock and Lee got together.

Meanwhile, the British were not idle. They, too, were doing some *planning* and Master-Minding on their own account, with the advantage of having money and organised soldiery behind them.

The Crown appointed Gage to supplant Hutchinson as the Governor of Massachusetts. One of the new Governor's first acts was to send a messenger to call on Samuel Adams, for the purpose of endeavouring to stop his opposition – by *fear*.

We can best understand the spirit of what happened by quoting the conversation between Colonel Fenton (the messenger sent by Gage) and Adams.

Colonel Fenton: 'I have been authorised by Governor Gage to assure you, Mr Adams, that the Governor has been empowered to confer upon you such benefits as would be satisfactory [endeavour to win Adams by promise of bribes] upon the condition that you engage to cease in your opposition to the measures of the government. It is the Governor's advice to you, Sir, not to incur the further displeasure of His Majesty. Your conduct has been such as makes you liable to penalties of an Act of Henry VIII, by which persons can be sent to England for trial for treason, or misprision of treason, at the discretion of a governor of a province. But, *by changing your political course*, you will not only receive great personal advantages, but you will make your peace with the King.'

Samuel Adams had the choice of two *decisions*. He could cease his opposition and receive personal bribes, or he could *continue, and run the risk of being hanged*!

Clearly, the time had come when Adams was forced to reach instantly a *decision* that could have cost his life. The majority of people would have found it difficult to reach such a decision. The majority would have sent back an evasive reply, but not Adams! He insisted Colonel Fenton give his word of honour to deliver to the Governor the answer exactly as Adams gave it to him.

Adams' answer was, 'Then you may tell Governor Gage that I trust I have long since made my peace with the King of Kings. No personal consideration shall induce me to abandon the righteous cause of my country. And, *tell Governor Gage it is the advice of Samuel Adams to him*, no longer to insult the feelings of an exasperated people.'

Comment as to the character of this man seems unnecessary. It must be obvious to all who read this astounding message that its sender possessed loyalty of the highest order. This is important. (Racketeers and dishonest politicians have prostituted the honour for which such men as Adams died.)

When Governor Gage received Adams' caustic reply, he flew into a rage and issued a proclamation which read, 'I do, hereby, in His Majesty's name, offer and promise his most gracious pardon to all persons who shall forthwith lay down their arms and return to the duties of peaceable subjects, excepting only from the benefit of such pardon, *Samuel Adams and John Hancock*, whose offences are of too flagitious a nature to admit of any other consideration but that of condign punishment.'

As one might say in modern slang, Adams and Hancock were 'on the spot'! The threat of the irate Governor forced the two men to reach another *decision*, equally as dangerous. They hurriedly called a secret meeting of their staunchest followers. (Here the Master Mind began to take on momentum.) After the meeting had been called to order, Adams locked the door, placed the key in his pocket and informed all present that it was imperative that a Congress of the Colonists be organised, and that *no man should leave the room until the decision for such a Congress had been reached.*

Great excitement followed. Some weighed the possible consequences of such radicalism (fear). Some expressed grave doubt as to the wisdom of so definite a decision in defiance of the Crown. Locked in that room were *two men* immune to fear, blind to the possibility of failure. Hancock and Adams. Through the influence of their minds, the others were induced to agree that, through the Correspondence Committee, arrangements should be made for a meeting of the First Continental Congress, to be held in Philadelphia on 5 September 1774.

Remember this date. It is more important than 4 July 1776. If there had been no *decision* to hold a Continental Congress, there could have been no signing of the Declaration of Independence.

Before the first meeting of the new Congress, another leader, in a different section of the country, was deep in the throes of publishing a *Summary View of the Rights of British America*. He was Thomas Jefferson of the Province of Virginia, whose relationship to Lord Dunmore (representative of the Crown in Virginia) was as strained as that of Hancock and Adams with their governor.

Shortly after his famous *Summary of Rights* was published, Jefferson was informed that he was subject to prosecution for high treason against His Majesty's Government. Inspired by the threat, one of Jefferson's colleagues, Patrick Henry, boldly spoke his mind, concluding his remarks with a sentence that shall remain forever a classic, 'If this be treason, then make the most of it.'

It was such men as these who, without power, without authority, without military strength, without money, sat in solemn consideration of the destiny of the colonies, beginning at the opening of the First Continental Congress, and continuing at intervals for two years until, on 7 June 1776, Richard Henry Lee arose, addressed the Chair, and to the startled Assembly made this motion:

'Gentlemen, I make the motion that these United Colonies are, and of right ought to be free and independent states, that they be absolved from all allegiance to the British Crown, and that all political connection between them and the state of Great Britain is, and ought to be totally dissolved.'

Lee's astounding motion was discussed fervently and at such length that he began to lose patience. Finally, after days of argument, he again took the floor and declared, in a clear, firm voice, 'Mr President, we have discussed this issue for days. It is the only course for us to follow. Why then, Sir, do we longer delay? Why still deliberate? Let this happy day give birth to an American Republic. Let her arise, not to devastate and to conquer, but to re-establish the reign of peace and of law. The eyes of Europe are fixed upon us. She demands of us a living example of freedom that may exhibit a contrast, in the felicity of the citizen, to the ever increasing tyranny.'

Before his motion was finally voted upon, Lee was called back to Virginia because of serious family illness, but before leaving he placed his cause in the hands of his friend, Thomas Jefferson, who promised to fight until favourable action was taken. Shortly thereafter the President of the Congress (Hancock) appointed Jefferson as chairman of a committee to draw up a Declaration of Independence.

Long and hard the Committee laboured on a document which would mean, when accepted by the Congress, that EVERY MAN WHO SIGNED IT WOULD BE SIGNING HIS OWN DEATH WARRANT, should the Colonies lose in the fight with Great Britain, which was sure to follow.

The document was drawn, and on 28 June the original draft was read before the Congress. For several days it was discussed, altered and made ready. On 4 July 1776, Thomas Jefferson stood before the Assembly and fearlessly read the most momentous *decision* ever placed upon paper.

'When in the course of human events it is necessary for one people to dissolve the political bands which have connected them with another, and to assume, among the powers of the earth, the separate and equal station to which the laws of Nature, and of Nature's God entitle them, a decent respect to the opinions of mankind requires that they should declare the causes which impel them to the separation . . .'

When Jefferson finished, the document was voted upon, accepted and signed by the 56 men, every one staking his own life upon his *decision* to write his name. By that *decision* came into existence a nation destined to bring to humankind forever the privilege of making *decisions*.

By decisions made in a similar spirit of faith, and only by such decisions, can people solve their personal problems and win for themselves high estates of material and spiritual wealth. Let us not forget this!

Analyse the events that led to the Declaration of Independence, and be convinced that the American nation was born of a *decision* created by a Master Mind consisting of 56 men. Note well the fact that it was their *decision* that ensured the success of Washington's armies, because the spirit of that decision was in the heart of every soldier who fought with him, and served as a spiritual power that recognises no such thing as *failure*.

Note, also (with great personal benefit), that the *power* that gave America its freedom is the self-same power that must be used by every individual who becomes self-determining. This *power* is made up of the principles described in this book. In the story of the Declaration of Independence it will not be difficult to detect at least six of these principles: DESIRE, DECISION, FAITH, PERSISTENCE, THE MASTER MIND and ORGANISED PLANNING.

Throughout this philosophy will be found the suggestion that thought, backed by strong *desire*, has a tendency to transmute itself into its physical equivalent. Before passing on, I wish to leave with you the suggestion that one may find in this story, and in the story of the organisation of the United States Steel Corporation, a perfect description of the method by which thought makes this astounding transformation.

In your search for the secret of the method, do not look for a miracle because you will not find it. You will find only the eternal laws of Nature. These laws are available to every person who has the *faith* and the *courage* to use them. They may be used to bring freedom to a nation or to accumulate riches. There is no charge save the time necessary to understand and appropriate them.

Those who reach *decisions* promptly and definitely know what they want, and generally get it. The leaders in every walk of life *decide* quickly and firmly. That is the major reason why they are leaders. The world has the habit of making room for people whose words and actions show they know where they are going.

Indecision is a habit that usually begins in youth. The habit takes on permanency as the youth goes through school and even through university or college without *definiteness of purpose*. The major weakness of all educational systems is that they neither teach nor encourage the habit of *definite decision*.

It would be beneficial if no university or college would permit the enrolment of any student unless and until the student declared their major purpose in graduating. It would be of still greater benefit if every student starting school were compelled to accept training in the *habit of decision*, and forced to pass a satisfactory examination on this subject before being permitted to advance.

The habit of *indecision* acquired because of the deficiencies of our school systems goes with the students into the occupations they choose, if in fact they choose their occupations. Generally, young people just out of school seek any job that can be found. They take the first place they find because they have fallen into the habit of *indecision*. Ninety-eight out of every hundred people working for wages today are in the positions they hold because they lacked the *definiteness of decision* to *plan a definite position*, and the knowledge of how to choose an employer.

Definiteness of decision always requires courage, sometimes very great courage. The 56 men who signed the Declaration of Independence staked their lives on the decision to affix their signatures to that document. People who reach a definite decision to procure a particular job and make life pay the price they ask do not stake their life on that decision; they stake their *economic freedom.* Financial independence, riches, desirable business and professional positions are not within reach of the person who neglects or refuses to *expect, plan* and *demand* these things. The person who desires riches in the same spirit that Samuel Adams desired freedom for the Colonies is sure to accumulate wealth.

A modern example of a person who displayed courage in making decisions is Fred Smith, the founder of Federal Express (FEDEX).

When Smith was a student in an economics class at Yale University, his professor stated that airfreight was the wave of the future and would be the primary source of revenue for the airlines.

Smith wrote a paper disagreeing. His argument was that the passenger route patterns that were the primary airline routes were wrong for freight. He noted that because costs would not come down with volume, the only way airfreight could be profitable was through a whole new system that would reach out to smaller cities as well as big ones and be designed for packages, not people. The professor considered this entirely unfeasible and gave Smith's paper a low grade.

Smith's concept was to start an all-freight airline that would fly primarily at night when the airports weren't congested. It would carry small, high-priority packages when speed of delivery was more important than cost. It would bring all the packages to a central point (he chose his home town – Memphis) where, through a specially designed computer program, the packages would be sorted, dispersed and loaded on planes that were flown to the ultimate destinations. By consolidating all shipments to smaller cities, it would enable the company to fly full planeloads to cities all over the country and eventually the world.

Smith believed that venture capitalists would be interested and excited about this innovative idea. But to his shock, little interest was developed in the financial community.

This did not stop Smith. Because of his enthusiasm for the project and the courage of his convictions, he raised $91 million to finance his untested idea.

At this point the competing carriers realised that Smith's concept was a potential threat to their industry. The major airlines tried to forestall this new competition by lobbying the Civil Aeronautics Board to refuse Smith the necessary permission. Smith's team found a loophole in the law. Planes with a payload under 7,500 pounds did not need CAB permission to operate.

Smith went ahead and assembled a fleet of small jets. He began construction of his main facility at Memphis and started servicing 75 airports. FEDEX would pick up packages at airports all over the country and fly them to Memphis, where they were sorted out and processed for immediate reshipment to other cities. Once unloaded, FEDEX trucks delivered them to their destinations. Smith set a goal to get all packages to their destinations within 24 hours of pick-up – and this goal was almost always met.

Despite the hard work and efforts of the company, the first few years were financial disasters. Losses amounted to millions of dollars. The investors were seriously concerned. Federal was falling far short of Smith's projections.

Despite the losses – which the investors blamed on Smith – and even talk of removing him and taking over the company, Smith did not lose faith. His courage never faltered. He hired experts (his 'Master Mind') and worked day and night with them to solve operational problems. This resulted in Federal's revenues reaching $75 million in the next fiscal year, with a profit of $3.6 million.

Although competition from faxes virtually eliminated the use of FEDEX for letters and documents, and despite competition from other airfreight companies and the postal service, which offered overnight service at a much lower price, Smith's continued innovation and dedication to *continuous improvement have kept Federal as the number one carrier in its field.*

In Chapter 7 on organised planning, you will find complete instructions for marketing every type of service. You will also find detailed information on how to choose the employer you prefer, and the particular job you desire. These instructions will be of no value to you UNLESS YOU DEFINITELY DECIDE to organise them into a plan of action.

CHAPTER 9

PERSISTENCE:
the Sustained Effort
Necessary to Induce Faith

(The Eighth Step to Riches)

PERSISTENCE is an essential factor in the procedure of transmuting *desire* into its monetary equivalent. The basis of persistence is the *power of will*.

Willpower and desire, when properly combined, make an irresistible pair. People who accumulate great fortunes are generally known as cold-blooded and sometimes ruthless. Often they are misunderstood. What they have is willpower, which they mix with persistence and use as the basis of their desires to ensure the attainment of their objectives.

Henry Ford has been generally misunderstood to be ruthless and cold-blooded. This misconception grew out of Ford's habit of following through all of his plans with *persistence*.

The majority of people are ready to throw their aims and purposes overboard, and give up at the first sign of opposition or misfortune. A few carry on *despite* all opposition until they attain their goal. These few are the Fords, Carnegies, Rockefellers and Edisons.

There may be no heroic connotation to the word 'persistence', but the quality is to character what carbon is to steel.

The building of a fortune generally involves the application of the entire 13 factors of this philosophy. These principles must be understood – all who accumulate money must apply them with *persistence*.

If you are reading this book with the intention of applying the knowledge it conveys, the first test of your *persistence* will come when you begin to follow the six steps described in the second chapter. Unless you are one of the two out of every hundred who already have a *definite goal* at which you are aiming and a *definite plan* for its attainment, you may read the instructions and then carry on with your daily routine, never complying with those instructions.

The author is checking you up at this point because lack of persistence is one of the major causes of failure. Moreover, experience with thousands of people has proved that lack of persistence is a weakness common to the majority of people. It is a weakness that may be overcome by effort. The ease with which lack of persistence may be conquered will depend entirely upon the *intensity of one's desire*.

The starting point of all achievement is *desire*. Keep this constantly in mind. Weak desires bring weak results, just as a small amount of fire makes a small amount of heat. If you find yourself lacking in persistence, this weakness may be remedied by building a stronger fire under your desires.

Continue to read through to the end, then go back to Chapter 2 and start immediately to carry out the instructions given in the six steps. The eagerness with which you follow these instructions will indicate clearly how much, or how little, you really *desire* to accumulate money. If you find that you are indifferent, you may be sure that you have not yet acquired the 'money consciousness' which you must possess before you can be sure of accumulating a fortune.

Fortunes gravitate to people whose minds have been prepared to 'attract' them, just as surely as water gravitates to the ocean. In this book may be found all the stimuli necessary to 'attune' any normal mind to the vibrations that will attract the object of one's desires.

If you find you are weak in *persistence*, centre your attention upon the instructions contained in Chapter 10 on power. Surround yourself with a 'Master Mind' group, and develop persistence through the cooperative efforts of the members of this group. You will find additional instructions for the development of persistence in Chapter 4 on autosuggestion, and Chapter 12 on the subconscious mind. Follow the instructions outlined in these chapters until your habit nature hands over to your subconscious mind a clear picture of the object of your *desire*. From that point on, you will not be handicapped by lack of persistence.

Your subconscious mind works continuously, while you are awake and while you are asleep. Spasmodic or occasional effort to apply the rules will be of no value to you. To get *results*, you must apply all of the rules until their application becomes a fixed habit with you. In no other way can you develop the necessary 'money consciousness'.

Poverty is attracted to the one whose mind is favourable to it, as money is attracted to one whose mind has been deliberately prepared to attract it, and through the same laws. POVERTY CONSCIOUSNESS WILL VOLUNTARILY SEIZE THE MIND THAT IS NOT OCCUPIED WITH MONEY CONSCIOUSNESS. A poverty consciousness develops without conscious application of habits favourable to it. The money consciousness must be created to order, unless one is born with such a consciousness.

Catch the full significance of the statements in the preceding paragraph and you will understand the importance of *persistence* in the accumulation of a fortune. Without *persistence*, you will be defeated, even before you start. With *persistence*, you will win.

If you have ever experienced a nightmare, you will realise the value of persistence. You are lying in bed, half awake, with a feeling that you are about to suffocate. You are unable to turn over or to move a muscle. You realise that you *must begin* to regain control over your muscles. Through persistent effort of willpower, you finally manage to move the fingers of one hand. By continuing to move your fingers, you extend your control to the muscles of one arm, until you can lift it. Then you gain control of the other arm in the same manner. You finally gain control over the muscles of one leg, and then extend it to the other leg. THEN – WITH ONE SUPREME EFFORT OF WILL – you regain complete control over your muscular system, and 'snap' out of your nightmare. The trick has been turned step by step.

You may find it necessary to 'snap' out of your mental inertia through a similar procedure, moving slowly at first, then increasing your speed until you gain complete control over your will. Be *persistent* no matter how slowly you may, at first, have to move. WITH PERSISTENCE WILL COME SUCCESS.

If you select your 'Master Mind' group with care, you will have in it at least one person who will aid you in the development of persistence. Some people who have accumulated great fortunes did so because of *necessity*. They developed the habit of persistence because they were so closely driven by circumstances they had to become persistent.

THERE IS NO SUBSTITUTE FOR PERSISTENCE! It cannot be supplanted by any other quality! Remember this in the beginning and it will hearten you when the going may seem difficult and slow.

Those who have cultivated the *habit* of persistence seem to enjoy insurance against failure. No matter how many times they are defeated, they finally arrive up near the top of the ladder. Sometimes it appears there is a hidden guide whose duty is to test people through all sorts of discouraging experiences. Those who pick themselves up after defeat and keep on trying arrive; and the world cries, 'Bravo! I knew you could do it!' The hidden guide lets no one enjoy great achievement without passing the *persistence test*. Those who can't take it simply do not make the grade.

Those who can 'take it' are bountifully rewarded for their *persistence*. They receive, as their compensation, whatever goal they are pursuing. That is not all! They receive something infinitely more important than material compensation – the knowledge that EVERY FAILURE BRINGS WITH IT THE SEED OF AN EQUIVALENT ADVANTAGE.

A few people know from experience the soundness of persistence. They are the ones who have not accepted defeat as being anything more than temporary. They are the ones whose *desires* are so *persistently applied* that defeat is finally changed into victory. We who stand on the sidelines of life see the overwhelmingly large number who go down in defeat, never to rise again. We see the few who take the punishment of defeat as an urge to greater effort. These, fortunately, never learn to accept life's reverse gear. But what we *do not see*, what most of us never suspect of existing, is the silent but irresistible *power* which comes to the rescue of those who fight on in the face of discouragement. If we speak of this power at all we call it *persistence*, and let it go at that. One thing we all know, if one does not possess persistence, one does not achieve noteworthy success in any calling.

A good example of the power of persistence is show business. From all over the world people have come to Hollywood seeking fame, fortune, power, love, or whatever it is that human beings call success. Once in a great while someone steps out from the long procession of seekers, and the world hears that another person has mastered Hollywood. But Hollywood is not easily nor quickly conquered. It acknowledges talent, recognises genius and pays off in money only after one has refused to *quit*. The secret is always inseparably attached to one word, *persistence*!

Bruce Lee, the actor who made us conscious of the Asian martial arts, might have been forgotten long ago were it not for his persistence in reaching for movie stardom.

Lee arrived in America from China with nothing but a dream and the capacity for hard work. During his youth he studied and mastered kung fu and later became a teacher of this art. However, his real goal was to be an actor. He obtained minor roles in some films and TV programmes, but he felt his great break came when he learned that the producers of a new television series called Kung Fu *were looking for an actor who knew the martial arts for the starring role. His screen test was successful and he looked forward to being given the role, but to his great disappointment, another actor, David Carradine, was chosen.*

Disillusioned, he was ready to give up acting and go back to teaching. When members of the Asian community heard of this, he was deluged with letters asking him not to give up. Soon the word spread to movie fans of all races and Lee made up his mind to keep seeking new roles.

He never gave up. He took roles in several films and his reputation as an actor and proponent of the martial arts made him a household name throughout the world. He took the study of the martial arts from being limited to Asian countries to becoming universally respected.

Although he died of a cerebral haemorrhage at the age of 32, his fame has lived after him. Bruce Lee is not only still remembered and admired by fans – many of whom were not even born when he made his movies – but TV series and early films have been made into videos and are still highly popular all over the world.

Persistence is a state of mind, so it can be cultivated. Like all states of mind, persistence is based upon definite causes, including:

1. DEFINITENESS OF PURPOSE. Knowing what you want is the first and, perhaps, the most important step towards the development of persistence. A strong motive forces you to surmount many difficulties.

2. DESIRE. It is comparatively easy to acquire and maintain persistence in pursuing the object of intense desire.

3. SELF-RELIANCE. Belief in your ability to carry out a plan encourages you to follow the plan through with persistence. (Self-reliance can be developed through the principle described in Chapter 4 on autosuggestion).

4. DEFINITENESS OF PLANS. Organised plans, even though they may be weak and entirely impractical, encourage persistence.

5. ACCURATE KNOWLEDGE. Knowing that your plans are sound, based upon experience or observation, encourages persistence; 'guessing' instead of 'knowing' destroys persistence.

6. COOPERATION. Sympathy, understanding and harmonious cooperation with others tend to develop persistence.

7. **WILLPOWER.** The habit of concentrating your thoughts upon the building of plans for the attainment of a definite purpose leads to persistence.

8. **HABIT.** Persistence is the direct result of habit. The mind absorbs and becomes a part of the daily experiences upon which it feeds. Fear, the worst of all enemies, can be effectively cured by forced repetition of acts of courage. Everyone who has seen active service in war knows this.

Before leaving the subject of *persistence*, take an inventory of yourself. Determine in what particular, if any, you are lacking in this essential quality. Measure yourself courageously, point by point, and see how many of the eight factors of persistence you lack. The analysis may lead to discoveries that will give you a new grip on yourself.

Symptoms of Lack of Persistence

Here you will find the real enemies that stand between you and noteworthy achievement. Here you will find not only the 'symptoms' indicating weakness of *persistence*, but also the deeply seated subconscious causes of this weakness. Study the list carefully and face yourself squarely IF YOU REALLY WISH TO KNOW WHO YOU ARE AND WHAT YOU ARE CAPABLE OF DOING. These are the weaknesses that must be mastered by all who accumulate riches.

1. Failure to recognise and clearly define exactly what you want.

2. Procrastination, with or without cause (usually backed up with a formidable array of alibis and excuses).

3. Lack of interest in acquiring specialised knowledge.

4. Indecision, the habit of 'passing the buck' on all occasions, instead of facing issues squarely (also backed by alibis).

5. The habit of relying upon alibis instead of creating definite plans for the solution of problems.

6. Self-satisfaction. There is but little remedy for this affliction, and no hope for those who suffer from it.

7. Indifference, usually reflected in your readiness to compromise on all occasions, rather than meet opposition and fight it.

8. The habit of blaming others for your mistakes, and accepting unfavourable circumstances as being unavoidable.

9. *Weakness of desire* due to neglect in the choice of *motives* that impel action.

10. Willingness, even eagerness, to quit at the first sign of defeat (based upon one or more of the six basic fears).

11. Lack of *organised plans*, placed in writing where they may be analysed.

12. The habit of neglecting to move on ideas, or to grasp opportunity when it presents itself.

13. *Wishing* instead of *willing*.

14. The habit of compromising with *poverty* instead of aiming at riches – a general absence of ambition to *be*, to *do* and to *own*.

15. Searching for all the short-cuts to riches, trying to *get* without *giving* a fair equivalent, usually reflected in the habit of gambling or endeavouring to drive 'sharp' bargains.

16. *Fear of criticism*, failure to create plans and to put them into

action because of what other people will think, do or say.
This enemy belongs at the head of the list, because it
generally exists in the subconscious mind without being
recognised (see the six basic fears in Chapter 15).

Let us examine some of the symptoms of the fear of criticism.
The majority of people permit relatives, friends and the public
at large to so influence them that they cannot live their own
lives, because they fear criticism.

Huge numbers of people make mistakes in marriage, stand by
the bargain and go through life miserable and unhappy because
they fear criticism that may follow if they correct the mistake.
(Anyone who has submitted to this form of fear knows the
irreparable damage it does by destroying ambition, self-reliance
and the desire to achieve.)

Millions of people neglect to acquire belated educations, after
having left school, because they fear criticism.

Countless numbers of men and women, both young and old,
permit relatives to wreck their lives in the name of *duty* because
they fear criticism. (Duty does not require any person to submit
to the destruction of their personal ambitions and the right to
live their life in their own way.)

People refuse to take chances in business because they fear the
criticism that may follow if they fail. The fear of criticism in such
cases is stronger than the *desire* for success.

Too many people refuse to set high goals for themselves, or
even neglect selecting a career, because they fear the criticism of
relatives and 'friends' who may say, 'Don't aim so high, people
will think you are crazy.'

When Andrew Carnegie suggested that I devote 20 years to
the organisation of a philosophy of individual achievement, my

first impulse of thought was fear of what people might say. The suggestion set up a goal for me, far out of proportion to any I had ever conceived. As quick as a flash, my mind began to create alibis and excuses, all of them traceable to the inherent *fear of criticism*. Something inside me said, 'You can't do it – the job is too big and requires too much time – what will your relatives think of you? How will you earn a living? No one has ever organised a philosophy of success so what right have you to believe you can do it? Who are you, anyway, to aim so high? Remember your humble birth. What do you know about philosophy? People will think you are crazy (and they did). Why hasn't some other person done this before now?'

These, and many other questions, flashed into my mind and demanded attention. It seemed as if the whole world had suddenly turned its attention to me with the purpose of ridiculing me into giving up all desire to carry out Mr Carnegie's suggestion.

I had a fine opportunity, then and there, to kill off ambition before it gained control of me. Later in life, after having analysed thousands of people, I discovered that MOST IDEAS ARE STILLBORN AND NEED THE BREATH OF LIFE INJECTED INTO THEM THROUGH DEFINITE PLANS OF IMMEDIATE ACTION. The time to nurse an idea is at the time of its birth. Every minute it lives gives it a better chance of surviving. The *fear of criticism* is at the bottom of the destruction of most ideas that never reach the *planning* and *action* stage.

Another good example of a person who refused to accept the criticism of others and persisted in pursuing his dream is Fred Smith, whose success in creating and developing Federal Express was described in the previous chapter.

Many people believe that material success is the result of favourable 'breaks'. There is an element of ground for the belief, but those depending entirely upon luck are nearly always disappointed because they overlook another important factor that must be present before one can be sure of success. It is the knowledge with which favourable 'breaks' can be made to order.

Let's look at Tom Monaghan, who created and grew Domino Pizzas from a one-store pizza parlour to a chain of several thousand home-delivery outlets over a period of about 30 years. In 1989, he decided to sell his hugely successful company to concentrate instead on doing philanthropic work.

However, his plan did not work out. After two-and-a-half years, the company that purchased the chain almost drove it into bankruptcy so Monaghan came back.

It took much hard work and persistence to first rebuild and then expand the organisation. Monaghan had developed the necessary determination early in his life. He had overcome a childhood of deprivation, poverty and abuse to become a great entrepreneur. Now once again he mobilised all his efforts not only to return Domino to its original prominence but to expand it to 6,000 stores – of which 1,100 are in countries other than the United States.

Once the chain was back on its feet, Monaghan faced a new and serious challenge. Domino built its major promotion on its guarantee of fast delivery. It guaranteed the customer would get their pizza within 30 minutes.

This led to a series of law suits from people who claimed injury from accidents caused by Domino delivery drivers who were speeding to make the 30-minute deadline. The family of a woman allegedly killed by a Domino driver was awarded $3 million. The final blow came when another woman was awarded $78 million. After that Domino dropped the 30-minute guarantee.

Despite this financial catastrophe, Monaghan refused to give up. He ploughed more money, time and energy into the company and brought it back once again. By his persistence and positive attitude he forged ahead and inspired his team with the winning spirit that has made Domino number one in its industry.

Examine the next hundred people you meet. Ask them what they want most in life, and 98 of them will not be able to tell you. If you press them for an answer, some will say *security*, many will say *money*, a few will say *happiness*, others will say *fame and power* and still others will say *social recognition, ease in living, ability to sing, dance or write*, but none of them will be able to define these terms, or give the slightest indication of a *plan* by which they hope to attain these vaguely expressed wishes. Riches do not respond to wishes. They respond only to definite plans, backed by definite desires, through constant *persistence*.

How to Develop Persistence

There are four simple steps that lead to the habit of persistence. They call for no great amount of intelligence, no particular level of education and but little time or effort. The necessary steps are:

1. A DEFINITE PURPOSE BACKED BY A BURNING DESIRE FOR ITS FULFILMENT.
2. A DEFINITE PLAN, EXPRESSED IN CONTINUOUS ACTION.
3. A MIND CLOSED TIGHTLY AGAINST ALL NEGATIVE AND DISCOURAGING INFLUENCES, including negative suggestions of relatives, friends and acquaintances.
4. A FRIENDLY ALLIANCE WITH ONE OR MORE PERSONS WHO WILL ENCOURAGE YOU TO

FOLLOW THROUGH WITH BOTH PLAN AND PURPOSE.

These four steps are essential for success in all walks of life. The entire purpose of the 13 principles of this philosophy is to enable you to take these four steps as a matter of *habit*.

They are the steps by which you may control your economic destiny.

They are the steps that lead to freedom and independence of thought.

They are the steps that lead to riches, in small or great quantities.

They are the steps that lead the way to power, fame and worldly recognition.

They are the steps that guarantee favourable 'breaks'.

They are the steps that convert dreams into physical realities.

They are the steps that lead, also, to the mastery of *fear*, *discouragement* and *indifference*.

There is a magnificent reward for all who learn to take these four steps. It is the privilege of writing your own ticket and of making life yield whatever price is asked.

What mystical power gives to people of *persistence* the capacity to master difficulties? Does the quality of persistence set up in your mind some form of spiritual, mental or chemical activity that gives you access to supernatural forces? Does Infinite

Intelligence throw itself on the side of the person who still fights on after the battle has been lost, with the whole world on the opposing side?

These and many other similar questions have arisen in my mind as I have observed men like Henry Ford, who started from scratch and built an industrial empire of huge proportions, with little else in the way of a beginning but *persistence*. Or Thomas A. Edison who, with less than three months of schooling, became the world's leading inventor and converted *persistence* into the talking machine, the moving picture machine and the incandescent light, to say nothing of half a hundred other useful inventions.

I had the happy privilege of analysing both Mr Edison and Mr Ford, year by year, over a long period, and the opportunity to study them at close range. I therefore speak from actual knowledge when I say that I found no quality save *persistence* in either of them that even remotely suggested the major source of their stupendous achievements.

As one makes an impartial study of successful people, one is drawn to the inevitable conclusion that *persistence*, concentration of effort and *definiteness of purpose* are the major sources of their achievements.

A good example of determination and persistence is Howard Schultz, the 'Starbucks man'. It takes a person with vision, fortitude and unswerving confidence to make a new concept succeed.

Schultz was hired to manage retail sales and marketing for a small coffee distributor who had a few retail outlets in Seattle. He was 29 and just married. He and his wife left their home in New York City to accept this new job.

About a year later, Schultz visited Italy on a buying trip. As he wandered around Milan, he noticed how important coffee was to the

Italian culture. Typically, the workday starts with a cup of rich coffee at a coffee bar. After work, friends and colleagues once again meet at the coffee bar for a leisurely stop before heading home. It is a centre of Italian social life. Schultz visualised this transferred to America. It had never been done but he felt it could work because of the high quality of Starbucks coffee.

It became Schultz's obsession. He was determined to build a national chain of cafés based on the Italian coffee bar, but the Starbucks owners were reluctant. They were in the wholesale coffee bean business; the restaurants they owned were only a small part of their operation.

To implement his goal, Schultz left Starbucks and planned a new company. In 1986, Schultz opened his first coffee bar in Seattle. It was an immediate success. Schultz soon opened another in Seattle and a third in Vancouver. The following year he bought the Starbucks company and adopted its name for his enterprise.

Schultz believes that the quality of Starbucks will one day alter how everyday Americans conduct their lives. If Schultz has his way, a cup of Starbucks will become a basic part of American culture. His concept has paid off. Starbucks' sales have increased nine-fold for every year since 1988.

Schultz envisioned hundreds of Starbucks coffee shops across America where business people would stop on their way to work and come to after work to relax. Shoppers would stop for a pick-me-up. Young people would meet their dates over coffee rather than cocktails. Families would come for refreshment before or after the cinema.

Starbucks incurred losses for three straight years – more than $1 million in 1989 alone – but Schultz never gave up. He had a firm conviction that this was the way to build a company and that the losses would soon turn into profits.

Once his Seattle stores were profitable, Starbucks spread slowly into other cities – Vancouver, Portland, Los Angeles, Denver and Chicago –

and later to the eastern cities and overseas. Starbucks has become a household name all over the world and an exemplar of American marketing ingenuity. And it has made Howard Schultz one of the world's richest people.

CHAPTER 10

POWER OF THE MASTER MIND:
the Driving Force

(The Ninth Step to Riches)

Power is essential for success in the accumulation of money.

Plans are inert and useless without sufficient *power* to translate them into *action*. This chapter will describe the method by which an individual may attain and apply power.

Power may be defined as 'organised and intelligently directed *knowledge*'. Power, as the term is here used, refers to *organised* effort, sufficient to enable an individual to transmute *desire* into its monetary equivalent. Organised effort is produced through the coordination of effort of two or more people, who work towards a *definite* end in a spirit of harmony.

POWER IS REQUIRED FOR THE ACCUMULATION OF MONEY! POWER IS NECESSARY FOR THE RETENTION OF MONEY AFTER IT HAS BEEN ACCUMULATED!

Let us ascertain how power may be acquired. If power is 'organised knowledge', let us examine the sources of knowledge:

1. INFINITE INTELLIGENCE. This source of knowledge may be contacted through the procedure described in Chapter 6, with the aid of Creative Imagination.

2. ACCUMULATED EXPERIENCE. The accumulated experience of humankind (or that portion of it which has been organised and recorded) may be found in any well-equipped public library. An important part of this accumulated experience is taught in schools and colleges, where it has been classified and organised.

3. EXPERIMENT AND RESEARCH. In the field of science, and in practically every other walk of life, people are gathering, classifying and organising new facts daily. This is the source to which one must turn when knowledge is not available through 'accumulated experience'. Here, too, the Creative Imagination must often be used.

Knowledge may be acquired from any of the foregoing sources. It may be converted into *power* by organising it into definite *plans* and by expressing those plans in terms of *action*.

Examination of the three major sources of knowledge will readily disclose the difficulty people would have – if they depended upon their efforts alone – in assembling knowledge and expressing it through definite plans in terms of action. If their plans are comprehensive, and if they contemplate large proportions, they must, generally, induce others to cooperate with them, before they can inject into their plans the necessary element of power.

Gaining Power through the 'Master Mind'

The 'Master Mind' may be defined as: 'coordination of knowledge and effort, in a spirit of harmony, between two or more people, for the attainment of a definite purpose'.

No individual may have great power without availing him or herself of the Master Mind. In Chapter 7, instructions were given for the creation of *plans* for the purpose of translating *desire* into its monetary equivalent. If you carry out these instructions with *persistence* and intelligence, and use discrimination in the selection of your 'Master Mind' group, your objective will have been halfway reached before you even begin to recognise it.

So you may better understand the 'intangible' potentialities of power available to you through a properly chosen Master Mind group, we will here explain the two characteristics of the Master Mind principle, one of which is economic in nature, and the other psychic. The economic feature is obvious. Economic advantages may be created by people who surround themselves with the advice, counsel and personal cooperation of a group of people who are willing to lend them wholehearted aid in a spirit of *perfect harmony*. This form of cooperative alliance has been the basis of nearly every great fortune. Your understanding of this great truth may definitely determine your financial status.

The psychic phase of the Master Mind principle is much more abstract, much more difficult to comprehend, because it refers to the spiritual forces with which the human race, as a whole, is not well acquainted. You may catch a significant suggestion from this statement: 'No two minds ever come together without thereby creating a third, invisible, intangible force which may be likened to a third mind.'

Keep in mind the fact that there are only two known elements in the whole universe – energy and matter. Matter may be broken down into units of molecules, atoms and electrons. There are units of matter that may be isolated, separated and analysed.

Likewise, there are units of energy.

The human mind is a form of energy, a part of it being spiritual in nature. When the minds of two people are coordinated in a *spirit of harmony*, the spiritual units of energy of each mind form an affinity, which constitutes the 'psychic' phase of the Master Mind.

The Master Mind principle, or rather the economic feature of it, was first called to my attention by Andrew Carnegie. Discovery of this principle was responsible for the choice of my life's work.

Mr Carnegie's Master Mind group consisted of a staff of approximately 50 men, with whom he surrounded himself for the *definite purpose* of manufacturing and marketing steel. He attributed his entire fortune to the *power* he accumulated through this Master Mind.

Analyse the record of any person who has accumulated a great fortune, and many of those who have accumulated modest fortunes, and you will find that they have either consciously or unconsciously employed the Master Mind principle.

GREAT POWER CAN BE ACCUMULATED THROUGH NO OTHER PRINCIPLE!

Energy is Nature's set of building blocks, out of which she constructs every material thing in the universe, including humankind, and every form of animal and vegetable life. Through a process that only Nature completely understands, she translates energy into matter.

Nature's building blocks are available to us in the energy involved in *thinking*! The brain may be compared to an electric battery. It absorbs energy from the ether, which permeates every atom of matter and fills the entire universe.

A group of electric batteries will provide more energy than a single battery. An individual battery will provide energy in proportion to the number and capacity of the cells it contains. The brain functions in a similar fashion. This accounts for the fact that some brains are more efficient than others, and leads to this significant statement – a group of brains coordinated (or connected) in a spirit of harmony will provide more thought-energy than a single brain, just as a group of electric batteries will provide more energy than a single battery.

Through this metaphor it becomes immediately obvious that the Master Mind principle holds the secret of the *power* wielded by people who surround themselves with other people of brains.

There follows, now, another statement which will lead still nearer to an understanding of the psychic phase of the Master Mind principle: when a group of individual brains is coordinated and functions in harmony, the increased energy created through that alliance becomes available to every individual brain in the group.

Henry Ford began his business career under the handicap of poverty, illiteracy and ignorance. Within the inconceivably short period of 10 years, Mr Ford mastered these three handicaps, and within 25 years made himself one of the richest men in America. Connect with this fact the additional knowledge that Mr Ford's most rapid strides became noticeable from the time he became a personal friend of Thomas A. Edison, and you will begin to understand what the influence of one mind upon another can accomplish. Go a step further, and consider the fact that Mr Ford's most outstanding achievements began from the time he formed the acquaintances of Harvey Firestone, John Burroughs and Luther Burbank (each a man of great brain capacity), and you will have further evidence that *power* may be produced through friendly alliance of minds.

There is little if any doubt that Henry Ford was one of the best-informed men in the business and industrial world. The question of his wealth needs no discussion. Analyse Mr Ford's intimate personal friends, some of whom have already been mentioned, and you will be prepared to understand the following statement: *People take on the nature and the habits and the POWER OF THOUGHT of those with whom they associate in a spirit of sympathy and harmony*.

Henry Ford whipped poverty, illiteracy and ignorance by allying himself with great minds, whose vibrations of thought he absorbed into his own mind. Through his association with Edison, Burbank, Burroughs and Firestone, Mr Ford added to his own brain power the sum and substance of the intelligence, experience, knowledge and spiritual forces of these four men. Moreover, he appropriated and made use of the Master Mind principle through the methods described in this book.

This principle is available to you!

President Franklin Roosevelt brought the best minds of the country to Washington to form a Master Mind group he called his 'brain trust'. During and after World War II, Master Mind groups called 'think tanks' were frequently called upon by leaders of government and industry to help deal with critical problems.

We have already mentioned Mahatma Gandhi. Perhaps the majority of those who have heard of Gandhi look upon him as merely an eccentric little man who went around without formal clothes, and made trouble for the British Government.

In reality, Gandhi was not eccentric but *he was the most powerful man of his generation* (estimated by the number of his followers and their faith in their leader). Moreover, he was probably the most powerful man who ever lived. His power was passive, but it was real.

Let us study the method by which he attained his stupendous *power*. It may be explained in a few words. He came by power through inducing over 200 million people to coordinate, with mind and body, in a spirit of *harmony* for a *definite purpose*.

In brief, Gandhi accomplished a *miracle*, for it is a miracle when 200 million people can be induced – not forced – to cooperate in a spirit of harmony, for a limitless time. If you doubt that this is a miracle, try to induce *any two people* to cooperate in a spirit of harmony for any length of time. Every person who manages a business knows what a difficult matter it is to get employees to work together in a spirit even remotely resembling harmony.

The list of the chief sources from which *power* may be attained is, as you have seen, headed by *Infinite Intelligence*. When two or more people coordinate in a spirit of *harmony*, and work towards a definite objective, they place themselves in position, through that alliance, to absorb power directly from the great universal storehouse of Infinite Intelligence. This is the greatest of all sources of power. It is the source to which the genius turns. It is the source to which every great leader turns (whether conscious of the fact or not).

The other two major sources from which the knowledge necessary for the accumulation of power may be obtained are no more reliable than our five senses. The senses are not always reliable. Infinite Intelligence *does not err*.

In subsequent chapters, the methods by which Infinite Intelligence may be most readily contacted will be adequately described.

This is not a course on religion. No fundamental principle described in this book should be interpreted as being intended to interfere either directly or indirectly with anyone's religious habits. This book has been confined, exclusively, to instructing the reader how to transmute the *definite purpose of desire for money* into its monetary equivalent.

Read, *think* and meditate as you read. Soon, the entire subject will unfold, and you will see it in perspective. You are now seeing the detail of the individual chapters.

Money is shy and elusive. It must be wooed and won by methods not unlike those used by a determined lover in pursuit of a mate. And, coincidental as it is, the power used in the 'wooing' of money is not greatly different from that used in wooing a lover. That power, when successfully used in the pursuit of money, must be mixed with *faith*. It must be mixed with *desire*. It must be mixed with *persistence*. It must be applied through a plan, and that plan must be set into *action*.

Some of the best sources for creating your own Master Mind group are your employees. Andrew Grove, the extremely successful CEO of Intel Corporation, did this. Grove works with a team of technical, marketing, financial and administrative men and women in an informal environment. There are no private offices, special parking spaces or other privileges for executives. Employees have a generous stock option plan so they can share in the gains if the company makes money and the stock rises.

Although the team may appear casual, they follow Grove's lead of being very demanding on themselves. When Intel faced a crisis in 1976, the team willingly put in extra effort, more work hours and did everything was necessary to solve the problems. On another occasion, it was discovered that the Intel Pentium chip had a minor defect that would affect only an insignificant number of operations. Grove's decision to *replace the chips at a cost of $475 million rather than deliver a product that was not perfect was fully endorsed by his colleagues.*

Grove encourages his people to work in small, autonomous work units in which everyone understands the system and their role in it. Each person contributes their knowledge, expertise and creativity. Team members are trained and motivated to produce to the best of their capacity. When crises arise, the team willingly puts in the extra time, energy and brain power to meet and beat the problems faced.

When money comes in quantities known as 'the big money' it flows to the one who accumulates it as easily as water flows downhill. There exists a great unseen stream of *power*, which may be compared to a river, except that it flows in two directions. One side carries all who get into that side of the stream onwards and upwards to *wealth* – and the other side flows in the opposite direction, carrying all who are unfortunate enough to get into it (and not able to extricate themselves from it) downwards to misery and *poverty*.

Every person who has accumulated a great fortune has recognised the existence of this stream of life. It consists of one's *thinking process*. The positive emotions of thought form the side of the stream that carries one to fortune. The negative emotions form the side that carries one down to poverty.

This carries a thought of stupendous importance to the person who is following this book with the object of accumulating a fortune.

If you are in the side of the stream of power that leads to poverty, this may serve as an oar by which you may propel yourself over into the other side of the stream. It can serve you *only* through application and use. Merely reading, and passing judgment on it, either one way or another, will in no way benefit you.

Some people undergo the experience of alternating between the positive and negative sides of the stream, being at times on the positive side, and at times on the negative side. The Wall Street crash of '29 swept millions of people from the positive to the negative side of the stream. Those millions struggled – some of them in desperation and fear – to get back to the positive side of the stream. This book was written especially for those millions.

Poverty and riches often change places. Poverty may, and generally does, voluntarily take the place of riches. When riches take the place of poverty, the change is usually brought about through well-conceived and carefully executed *plans*. Poverty needs no plan. It needs no one to aid it, because it is bold and ruthless. Riches are shy and timid. They have to be 'attracted'.

Anybody can *wish* for riches, and most people do, but only a few know that a definite plan plus a *burning desire* for wealth are the only dependable means of accumulating it.

Ross Perot's attitude exemplifies the power of tough-minded commitment – not only his own but also that of the Master Mind with which he surrounded himself. He had a burning desire for wealth and he achieved it.

Before he started Electronic Data Systems (EDS), he had been the top sales person at IBM. He was cautioned that leaving IBM to start a company from scratch was a mistake. This did not faze Perot. He was inspired by a vision of what could be. His success clearly demonstrates that by sticking to your dream, and transmitting that dream to a team of experts – a Master Mind – who have the know-how to help make it a realisation, leads to success and wealth.

Perot firmly believes that commitment can accomplish miracles. This was exemplified when EDS competed for one of the largest contracts in the computer industry. Two companies, IBM and EDS, were the contestants. IBM was far richer, and had in their staff a more experienced and knowledgeable group of specialists. EDS had a small but dedicated team.

Perot recalls, 'About 30 days into the competition, I walked into the room and our 15 guys were saying, "Gee, we probably can't win but it will be great experience." I didn't jump up and down and chew people out. I just walked to the blackboard and wrote down the seven criteria by which we would be judged. And in a nice low voice said, "We are going to beat them seven to zero." That's the day we won.'

Perot commented that the raises, the bonuses, the stock options and thousands of new jobs created by winning this project were, of course, the tangible rewards of achieving this coup. However, he believes that more important was the immense satisfaction of knowing that by their hard work and creativity, they beat the best in the world. That's what makes a company great — a team working together as a Master Mind to beat the opposition.

CHAPTER 11

THE MYSTERY OF SEX TRANS- MUTATION

(The Tenth Step to Riches)

The meaning of the word 'transmute' is, in simple language, 'the changing or transferring of one element, or form of energy, into another'.

The emotion of sex brings into being a state of mind.

Because of ignorance on the subject, this state of mind is generally associated with the physical. Because of improper influences, to which most people have been subjected in acquiring knowledge of sex, things essentially physical have highly biased the mind.

The emotion of sex has behind it the possibility of three constructive potentialities:

1. The perpetuation of humankind.
2. The maintenance of health (as a therapeutic agency it has no equal).
3. The transformation of mediocrity into genius through transmutation.

Sex transmutation is simple and easily explained. It means the switching of the mind from thoughts of physical expression to thoughts of some other nature.

Sex desire is the most powerful of human desires. When driven by this desire, people develop keenness of imagination, courage, willpower, persistence and creative ability unknown to them at other times. So strong and impelling is the desire for sexual contact that people freely run the risk of life and reputation to indulge it. When harnessed and redirected along other lines, the positive attributes of this motivating force may be used as powerful creative forces in literature, art or in any other profession or calling, including, of course, the accumulation of riches.

The transmutation of sex energy calls for the exercise of willpower, to be sure, but the reward is worth the effort. The desire for sexual expression is inborn and natural. The desire cannot and should not be submerged or eliminated. But it should be given an outlet through forms of expression that enrich the body, mind and spirit. If not given this form of outlet, through transmutation, it will seek outlets through purely physical channels.

A river may be dammed and its water controlled for a time, but eventually it will force an outlet. The same is true of the emotion of sex. It may be submerged and controlled for a time, but its very nature causes it to be ever seeking means of expression. If it is not transmuted into some creative effort it will find a less worthy outlet.

Fortunate, indeed, are those who have discovered how to give sex emotion an outlet through some form of creative effort, for they have, by that discovery, lifted themselves to the status of genius.

Scientific research on the backgrounds of high-achieving men (unfortunately, no similar studies have been made about highly successful women) has disclosed these significant facts:

1. The men of greatest achievement are those with highly developed sex natures; men who have learned the art of sex transmutation.
2. The men who have accumulated great fortunes and achieved outstanding recognition in literature, art, industry, architecture and the professions were motivated by the influence of a woman.

The research from which these astounding discoveries were made went back through the pages of biography and history for more than 2,000 years. Wherever there was evidence available in connection with the lives of men of great achievement, it indicated most convincingly that they possessed highly developed sex natures.

The emotion of sex is an 'irresistible force', against which there can be no such opposition as an 'immovable body'. When driven by this emotion, men become gifted with a super power for action. Understand this truth and you will catch the significance of the statement that sex transmutation will lift one to the status of a genius.

The emotion of sex contains the secret of creative ability.

Destroy the sex glands, whether in man or beast, and you have removed the major source of action. For proof of this, observe what happens to any animal after it has been castrated. A bull becomes as docile as a cow after it has been altered sexually. Sex alteration takes out of the male, whether man or beast, all the *fight* that was in him. Sex alteration of the female has the same effect.

The 10 Mind Stimuli

The human mind responds to stimuli through which it may be 'keyed up' to high rates of vibration, known as enthusiasm, creative imagination, intense desire, etc. The stimuli to which the mind responds most freely are:

1. The desire for sex expression
2. Love
3. A burning desire for fame, power, financial gain, *money*
4. Music
5. Friendship between either those of the same sex or those of the opposite sex
6. A Master Mind alliance based upon the harmony of two or more people who ally themselves for spiritual or temporal advancement
7. Mutual suffering, such as that experienced by people who are persecuted
8. Autosuggestion
9. Fear
10. Narcotics and alcohol

The desire for sex expression comes at the head of the list of stimuli that most effectively 'step up' the vibrations of the mind and start the 'wheels' of physical action. Eight of these stimuli are natural and constructive. Two are destructive. The list is here presented to enable you to make a comparative study of the major sources of mind stimulation. From this study, it will be readily seen that the emotion of sex is, by great odds, the most intense and powerful of all mind stimuli.

This comparison is necessary as a foundation for proof of the statement that transmutation of sex energy may lift one to the status of a genius. Let us find out what constitutes a genius.

A good definition of a genius is 'a person who has discovered how to increase the vibrations of thought to the point where they can freely communicate with sources of knowledge not available through the ordinary rate of vibration of thought'.

The person who thinks will want to ask some questions concerning this definition of genius. The first question will be, 'How may one communicate with sources of knowledge which are not available through the *ordinary* rate of vibration of thought?'

The next question will be, 'Are there known sources of knowledge which are available only to geniuses, and if so, *what are these sources*, and exactly how may they be reached?'

We shall offer proof of the soundness of some of the more important statements made in this book – or at least we shall offer evidence through which you may secure your own proof through experimentation. In doing so, we shall answer both of these questions.

'Genius' is Developed Through the Sixth Sense

The reality of a 'sixth sense' has been fairly well established. This sixth sense is 'creative imagination'. The faculty of creative imagination is one that the majority of people never use during an entire lifetime, and if used at all, it usually happens by mere accident. A relatively small number of people use, *with deliberation and purpose aforethought*, the faculty of creative imagination. Those who use this faculty voluntarily, and with understanding of its functions, are *geniuses*. The faculty of creative imagination is the direct link between the finite mind of humans and Infinite

Intelligence. All so-called revelations, referred to in the realm of religion, and all discoveries of basic or new principles in the field of invention, take place through the faculty of creative imagination. When ideas or concepts flash into one's mind, through what is popularly called a 'hunch', they come from one or more of the following sources:

1. Infinite Intelligence
2. The subconscious mind, in which is stored every sense impression and thought impulse that ever reached the brain through any of the five senses
3. The mind of some other person who has just released the thought, or picture of the idea or concept, through conscious thought
4. The other person's subconscious storehouse

There are no other *known* sources from which 'inspired' ideas or 'hunches' may be received.

The creative imagination functions best when the mind is vibrating (due to some form of mind stimulation) at an exceedingly high rate. That is, when the mind is functioning at a rate of vibration higher than that of ordinary, normal thought.

When brain action has been stimulated, through one or more of the 10 mind stimulants, it has the effect of lifting the individual far above the horizon of ordinary thought, and permits them to envision distance, scope and quality of *thoughts* not available on the lower plane, such as that occupied while engaged in solving the problems of business and professional routine.

When lifted to this higher level of thought, through any form of mind stimulation, an individual occupies, relatively, the same position as someone who has ascended in a plane. While still on the ground, they may see over and beyond the horizon line which limits their vision. Moreover, while on this higher level of thought, the individual is not hampered or bound by any of the stimuli that circumscribe and limit their vision while wrestling with the problems of gaining the three basic necessities of food, clothing and shelter. They are in a world of thought in which the *ordinary*, work-a-day thoughts have been as effectively removed as are the hills, valleys and other limitations of physical vision when rising in an aeroplane.

While on this exalted plane of thought, the creative faculty of the mind is given freedom for action. The way has been cleared for the sixth sense to function; it becomes receptive to ideas that could not reach the individual under any other circumstances. The 'sixth sense' is the faculty that marks the difference between a genius and an ordinary individual.

The more this faculty is used, the more alert and receptive the creative faculty becomes to vibrations originating outside the individual's subconscious mind, and the more the individual relies upon it and makes demands upon it for thought impulses. This faculty can be cultivated and developed only through use.

That which is known as one's 'conscience' operates entirely through the faculty of the sixth sense.

The great artists, writers, musicians and poets become great because they acquire the habit of relying upon the 'still small voice' which speaks from within, through the faculty of creative imagination. It is a fact well known to people who have 'keen' imaginations that their best ideas come through so-called 'hunches'.

There is a great orator who does not attain greatness until he closes his eyes and begins to rely entirely upon the faculty of creative imagination. When asked why he closed his eyes just before the climaxes of his oratory, he replied, 'I do it because then I speak through ideas which come to me from within.'

One of America's most successful and best-known financiers followed the habit of closing his eyes for two or three minutes before making a decision. When asked why he did this, he replied, 'With my eyes closed, I am able to draw upon a source of superior intelligence.'

Dr Elmer R. Gates, of Chevy Chase, Maryland, created more than 200 useful patents, many of them basic, through the process of cultivating and using the creative faculty. His method is significant to anyone interested in attaining the status of genius, in which category Dr Gates unquestionably belonged. Dr Gates was one of the really great, though less publicised, scientists of the world.

In his laboratory, he had what he called his 'personal communication room'. It was practically soundproof, and so arranged that all light could be shut out. It was equipped with a small table on which he kept a pad of writing paper. In front of the table, on the wall, was an electric pushbutton, which controlled the lights. When Dr Gates desired to draw upon the forces available to him through his creative imagination, he would go into this room, seat himself at the table, shut off the lights and *concentrate* upon the *known* factors of the invention on which he was working, remaining in that position until ideas began to 'flash' into his mind in connection with the *unknown* factors of the invention.

On one occasion, ideas came through so fast that he was forced to write for almost three hours. When the thoughts stopped flowing and he examined his notes, he found they contained a minute description of principles that had no parallel among the known data of the scientific world. Moreover, the answer to his problem was intelligently presented in those notes. In this manner Dr Gates completed over 200 patents, which had been begun, but not completed, by 'half-baked' brains. Evidence of the truth of this statement is in the United States Patent Office.

Dr Gates earned his living by 'sitting for ideas' for individuals and corporations. Some of the largest corporations in America paid him substantial fees, by the hour, for 'sitting for ideas'.

The reasoning faculty is often faulty because it is largely guided by our accumulated experience. Not all knowledge that we accumulate through 'experience' is accurate. Ideas received through the creative faculty are much more reliable because they come from sources more reliable than any available to the reasoning faculty of the mind.

The major difference between the genius and the ordinary 'crank' inventor may be found in the fact that the genius works through his faculty of creative imagination while the 'crank' knows nothing of this faculty. The scientific inventor (such as Mr Edison and Dr Gates) makes use of both the synthetic and the creative faculties of imagination.

For example, scientific inventors or 'geniuses' begin an invention by organising and combining the known ideas, or principles accumulated through experience, through the synthetic faculty (the reasoning faculty). If they find this accumulated knowledge to be insufficient for the completion of the invention, they then draw upon the sources of knowledge available to them through their creative faculty. The method by which this is done varies with the individual, but this is the sum and substance of the procedure:

1. **THEY STIMULATE THEIR MINDS SO THAT THEY VIBRATE ON A HIGHER-THAN-AVERAGE PLANE,** using one or more of the 10 mind stimulants or some other stimulant of their choice.
2. **THEY CONCENTRATE** upon the known factors (the finished part) of the invention, and create in their minds a perfect picture of unknown factors (the unfinished part) of the invention. They hold this picture in mind until it has been taken over by the subconscious mind, and then relax by clearing their minds of *all* thought, and wait for the answer to pop up.

Sometimes the results are both definite and immediate. At other times, the results are negative, depending upon the state of development of the 'sixth sense' or creative faculty.

Mr Edison tried out more than 10,000 different combinations of ideas through the synthetic faculty of his imagination before he 'tuned in' through the creative faculty, and got the answer that perfected the incandescent light. His experience was similar when he produced the talking machine.

There is plenty of reliable evidence that the faculty of creative imagination exists. This evidence is available through accurate analysis of people who have become leaders in their respective callings, without having had extensive educations. Lincoln was a notable example of a leader who achieved greatness through the discovery and use of his faculty of creative imagination. He discovered and began to use this faculty as the result of the stimulation of love, which he experienced after he met Anne Rutledge.

The pages of history are filled with records of great leaders whose achievements may be traced directly to the influence of women who aroused the creative faculties of their minds, through the stimulation of sex desire. Napoleon Bonaparte was one of these. When inspired by his first wife, Josephine, he was irresistible and invincible. When his 'better judgment' or reasoning faculty prompted him to put Josephine aside, he began to decline. His defeat and St Helena were not far distant.

If good taste would permit, we might easily mention scores of well-known men who climbed to great heights of achievement under the stimulating influence of their wives, only to drop back to destruction *after* money and power went to their heads, and they put aside the old wife for a new one. Napoleon was not the only man to discover that sex influence, from the right source, is more powerful than any substitute of expediency which may be created by mere reason.

The human mind responds to stimulation!

Among the greatest and most powerful of these stimuli is the urge of sex. When harnessed and transmuted, this driving force is capable of lifting people into that higher sphere of thought that enables them to master the sources of worry and petty annoyance that beset their pathway on the lower plane.

Unfortunately, only the geniuses have made the discovery. Others have accepted the experience of sex urge without discovering one of its major potentialities – a fact that accounts for the great number of 'others' as compared to the limited number of geniuses.

Sex energy is the creative energy of all geniuses. There never has been, and never will be, a great leader, builder or artist lacking in this driving force of sex.

Surely no one will misunderstand these statements to mean that *all* who are highly sexed are geniuses! One attains to the status of a genius *only* when, and *if*, one's mind is stimulated so that it draws upon the forces available, through the creative faculty of the imagination. Chief among the stimuli with which this 'stepping up' of the vibrations may be produced is sex energy. The mere possession of this energy is not sufficient to produce a genius. The energy must be transmuted from desire for physical contact into some other form of desire and action before it will lift one to the status of a genius.

Far from becoming geniuses because of great sex desires, all too many people lower themselves, through misunderstanding and misuse of this great force, to the status of the lower animals.

Why People Seldom Succeed Before 40

I discovered, from the analysis of over 25,000 people, that those who succeed in an outstanding way seldom do so before the age of 40. More often, they do not strike their real pace until they are well beyond the age of 50. This fact was so astounding that it prompted me to go into the study of its cause most carefully, carrying the investigation over a period of more than 12 years.

This study disclosed that the major reason why the majority of people who succeed do not begin to do so before the age of 40 to 50 is their tendency to *dissipate* their energies through overindulgence in physical expression of the emotion of sex. Most people never learn that the urge of sex has other possibilities, which far transcend in importance that of mere physical expression. The majority of those who make this discovery do so after having wasted many years when the sex energy is at its height, prior to the age of 45 to 50. This is usually followed by noteworthy achievement.

The lives of many people up to, and sometimes well past, the age of 40 reflect a continued dissipation of energies, which could have been more profitably channelled. Their finer and more powerful emotions are sown wildly to the four winds. Out of this habit grew the term 'sowing one's wild oats'.

The desire for sexual expression is by far the strongest and most impelling of all the human emotions. For this very reason this desire, when harnessed and transmuted into action other than that of physical expression, may raise one to the status of a genius.

One of America's most able businessmen frankly admitted that his attractive secretary was responsible for most of the plans he created. He confessed that her presence lifted him to heights of creative imagination, such as he could experience under no other stimulus.

History is not lacking in examples of people who attained the status of geniuses as the result of using artificial mind stimulants in the form of alcohol and narcotics. Edgar Allen Poe wrote *The Raven* while under the influence of alcohol, 'dreaming dreams that mortal never dared to dream before'. James Whitcomb Riley did his best writing while under the influence of alcohol. Perhaps it was thus he saw 'the ordered intermingling of the real and the dream, the mill above the river, and the mist above the stream'. Robert Burns wrote best when intoxicated: 'For Auld Lang Syne, my dear, we'll take a cup of kindness yet, for Auld Lang Syne.'

But let it be remembered that many such people have destroyed themselves in the end. Nature has prepared her own potions with which people may safely stimulate their minds so they vibrate on a plane that enables them to tune in to fine and rare thoughts from 'the great unknown'! No satisfactory substitute for Nature's stimulants has ever been found.

Psychologists recognise that there is a very close relationship between sex desires and spiritual urges – a fact which accounts for the peculiar behaviour of people who participate in the orgies known as religious 'revivals', common among the primitive types.

The world is ruled, and the destiny of civilisation is established, by the human emotions. People are influenced in their actions not by reason so much as by 'feelings'. The creative faculty of the mind is set into action entirely by emotions, and not by cold reason. The most powerful of all human emotions is that of sex. There are other mind stimulants, some of which have been listed, but no one of them, nor all of them combined, can equal the driving power of sex.

A mind stimulant is any influence that will either temporarily, or permanently, increase the vibrations of thought. The 10 major stimulants described are those most commonly resorted to. Through these sources one may commune with Infinite Intelligence or enter, at will, the storehouse of the subconscious mind – either one's own or that of another person.

A teacher who has trained and directed the efforts of more than 30,000 sales people made the astounding discovery that highly sexed people are the most efficient sales reps. The explanation is that the factor of personality known as 'personal magnetism' is nothing more nor less than sex energy. Highly sexed people always have a plentiful supply of magnetism. Through cultivation and understanding, this vital force may be drawn upon and used to great advantage in the relationships between people. This energy may be communicated to others through the following media:

1. The handshake. The touch of the hand indicates, instantly, the presence of magnetism, or the lack of it.

2. The tone of voice. Magnetism, or sex energy, is the factor with which the voice may be coloured, or made musical and charming.

3. Posture and carriage of the body. Highly sexed people move briskly, and with grace and ease.

4. The vibrations of thought. Highly sexed people mix the emotion of sex with their thoughts, or may do so at will, and in that way may influence those around them.

5. Body adornment. People who are highly sexed are usually very careful about their personal appearance. They usually select clothing of a style becoming to their personality, physique, complexion, etc.

When employing salespeople, the more capable sales manager looks for the quality of personal magnetism as the first require-ment for the job. People who lack sex energy will never become enthusiastic nor inspire others with enthusiasm, and enthusiasm is one of the most important requisites in salesmanship, no matter what one is selling. The public speaker, orator, preacher, lawyer or salesperson who is lacking in sex energy is a 'flop' as far as being able to influence others is concerned. Couple with this the fact that most people can be influenced only through an appeal to their emotions, and you will understand the impor-tance of sex energy as a part of the salesperson's natural ability. Master sales reps attain the status of mastery in selling because they, either consciously or unconsciously, transmute the energy of sex into *sales enthusiasm*! In this statement may be found a very practical suggestion as to the actual meaning of sex trans-mutation.

Salespeople who know how to take their minds off the subject of sex and direct it in sales effort with as much enthusiasm and determination as they would apply to its original purpose have acquired the art of sex transmutation, whether they know it or not. The majority of salespeople who transmute their sex energy do so without being in the least aware of what they are doing, or how they are doing it.

Transmutation of sex energy calls for more willpower than the average person cares to use for this purpose. Those who find it difficult to summon willpower sufficient for transmutation may gradually acquire this ability. The reward for the practice is more than worth the effort.

The entire subject of sex is one of which the majority of people appear to be unpardonably ignorant. The urge of sex has been grossly misunderstood, slandered and burlesqued by the ignorant and the evil minded for so long that the very word sex is seldom used in polite society. Men and women who are known to be blessed – yes, *blessed* – with highly sexed natures are usually looked upon with suspicion. Instead of being called blessed, they are usually called cursed.

Millions of people, even in this age of enlightenment, have developed inferiority complexes because of this false belief that a highly sexed nature is a curse. These statements of the virtue of sex energy should not be construed as justification for the libertine. The emotion of sex is a virtue *only* when used intelligently and with discrimination. It may often be misused to such an extent that it debases, instead of enriches, both body and mind. The better use of this power is the burden of this chapter.

It seemed quite significant to the author when he made the discovery that practically every great male leader, whom he had the privilege of analysing, was a man whose achievements were largely inspired by a woman. In many instances, the 'woman in the case' was a modest, self-denying wife, of whom the public had heard little or nothing. In a few instances, the source of inspiration has been traced to the 'other woman'. Perhaps such cases may not be entirely unknown to you.

Intemperance in sex habits is just as detrimental as intemperance in habits of drinking and eating. In this age in which we live, an age that began with World War I, intemperance in habits of sex is common. This orgy of indulgence may account for the shortage of great leaders. No one can avail of the forces of creative imagination while dissipating them. Humans are the only creatures on earth that violate Nature's purpose in this connection. Every other animal indulges its sex nature in moderation, and with purpose that harmonises with the laws of Nature. Every other animal responds to the call of sex only in 'season'. The human inclination is to declare 'open season'.

Every intelligent person knows that stimulation in excess, through alcoholic drink and narcotics, is a form of intemperance that destroys the vital organs of the body, including the brain. Not every person knows, however, that overindulgence in sex expression may become a habit as destructive and as detrimental to creative effort as narcotics or alcohol.

A sex-mad person is not essentially different to a dope-mad person! Both have lost control over their faculties of reason and willpower. Sexual overindulgence may not only destroy reason and willpower, but it may also lead to either temporary or permanent insanity. Many cases of hypochondria (imaginary illness) grow out of habits developed in ignorance of the true function of sex.

From these brief references to the subject, it may be readily seen that ignorance on the subject of sex transmutation forces stupendous penalties on the one hand, and withholds equally stupendous benefits on the other.

Widespread ignorance about sex is due to the fact that the subject has been surrounded with mystery and beclouded by dark silence. The conspiracy of mystery and silence has increased curiosity and desire to acquire more knowledge on this 'verboten' subject. To the shame of all law-makers, and most physicians – by training best qualified to educate youth on that subject – such information has not been easily available.

Seldom does an individual embark upon highly creative effort in any field of endeavour before the age of 40. For the average person, the greatest capacity to create is between 40 and 60. These statements are based upon careful analysis of thousands of men and women. They should be encouraging to those who fail to arrive before the age of 40, and to those who become frightened at the approach of 'old age', around the 40-year mark. The years between 40 and 50 are, as a rule, the most fruitful. One should approach this age not with fear and trembling, but with hope and eager anticipation.

If you want evidence that most people do not begin to do their best work before the age of 40, study the records of successful people and you will find it. Henry Ford had not 'hit his pace' of achievement until he had passed the age of 40. Andrew Carnegie was well past 40 before he began to reap the reward of his efforts. James J. Hill was still running a telegraph key at the age of 40. His stupendous achievements took place after that age. Biographies of industrialists and financiers are filled with evidence that the period from 40 to 60 is the most productive age.

Between the ages of 30 and 40, one begins to learn (if one

ever learns) the art of sex transmutation. This discovery is generally accidental, and more often than otherwise, the people who make it are totally unconscious of this discovery. They may observe that their powers of achievement have increased around the age of 35 to 40, but in most cases they are not familiar with the cause of this change; that Nature begins to harmonise the emotions of love and sex in the individual between the ages of 30 and 40, so that they may draw upon these great forces and apply them jointly as stimuli to action.

Sex, alone, is a mighty urge to action, but its forces are like a cyclone – they are often uncontrollable. When the emotion of love begins to mix itself with the emotion of sex, the result is calmness of purpose, poise, accuracy of judgment and balance. What person who has reached the age of 40 is so unfortunate as to be unable to analyse these statements, and to corroborate them by personal experience?

Love, romance and sex are all emotions capable of driving people to heights of super achievement. Love is the emotion that serves as a safety valve, and ensures balance, poise and constructive effort. When combined, these three emotions may lift one to the altitude of a genius. There are geniuses, however, who know little of the emotion of love. Most of them may be found engaged in some form of action which is destructive, or at least not based upon justice and fairness towards others. If good taste would permit, a dozen geniuses could be named in the field of industry and finance who ride ruthlessly over the rights of others. They seem totally lacking in conscience.

The emotions are states of mind. Nature has provided us with a 'chemistry of the mind' which operates in a manner similar to the principles of chemistry of matter. A chemist may create a deadly poison by mixing certain elements, none of which are –

in themselves – harmful in the right proportions. The emotions may, likewise, be combined to create a deadly poison. The emotions of sex and jealousy, when mixed, may turn a person into an insane beast.

The presence of any one or more of the destructive emotions in the human mind, through the chemistry of the mind, sets up a poison that may destroy one's sense of justice and fairness. In extreme cases, the presence of any combination of these emotions in the mind may destroy one's reason.

The road to genius consists of the development, control and use of sex, love and romance. Briefly, the process may be stated as follows:

Encourage the presence of these emotions as the dominating thoughts in your mind, and discourage the presence of all the destructive emotions. The mind is a creature of habit. It thrives upon the dominating thoughts fed it. Through the faculty of willpower, you may discourage the presence of any emotion, and encourage the presence of any other. Control of the mind, through the power of will, is not difficult. Control comes from persistence and habit. The secret of control lies in understanding the process of transmutation. When any negative emotion presents itself in your mind, it can be transmuted into a positive, or constructive, emotion by the simple procedure of changing your thoughts.

THERE IS NO OTHER ROAD TO GENIUS THAN THROUGH VOLUNTARY SELF-EFFORT! People may attain great heights of financial or business achievement, solely by the driving force of sex energy, but history is filled with evidence that they may, and usually do, carry with them certain character traits which rob them of the ability to either hold, or enjoy, their good fortune. This is worthy of analysis, thought and meditation, for it states a truth, the knowledge of which may be helpful to all people. Ignorance of this has cost thousands of people their privilege of *happiness*, even though they possessed riches.

The emotions of love and sex leave their unmistakable marks upon the features. Moreover, these signs are so visible that all who wish may read them. People who are driven by the storm of passion, based upon sex desires alone, plainly advertise that fact to the entire world by the expression of their eyes and the lines of their faces. The emotion of love, when mixed with the emotion of sex, softens, modifies and beautifies the facial expression. No character analyst is needed to tell you this. You may observe it for yourself.

The emotion of love brings out and develops the artistic and aesthetic nature of a person. It leaves its impress upon one's very soul, even after the fire has been subdued by time and circumstance.

Memories of love never pass. They linger, guide and influence long after the source of stimulation has faded. There is nothing new in this. Every person who has been moved by *genuine love* knows that it leaves enduring traces upon the human heart. The effect of love endures because love is spiritual in nature. Those who cannot be stimulated to great heights of achievement by love are hopeless – they are dead, though they may seem to live.

Even the memories of love are sufficient to lift one to a higher plane of creative effort. The major force of love may spend itself and pass away, like a fire that has burned itself out, but it leaves behind indelible marks as evidence that it passed that way. Its departure often prepares the human heart for a still greater love.

Go back into your yesterdays, at times, and bathe your mind in the beautiful memories of past love. It will soften the influence of the present worries and annoyances. It will give you a source of escape from the unpleasant realities of life, and maybe – who knows? – your mind will yield to you, during this temporary retreat into the world of fantasy, ideas or plans which may change the entire financial or spiritual status of your life.

If you believe yourself unfortunate because you have 'loved and lost', perish the thought. One who has loved truly can never lose entirely. Love is whimsical and temperamental. Its nature is ephemeral and transitory. It comes when it pleases and goes away without warning. Accept and enjoy it while it remains, but spend no time worrying about its departure. Worry will never bring it back.

Dismiss, also, the thought that love never comes but once. Love may come and go, times without number, but there are no two love experiences that affect you in just the same way. There may be, and there usually is, one love experience that leaves a deeper imprint on the heart than all the others, but all love experiences are beneficial, except to the person who becomes resentful and cynical when love makes its departure.

There should be no disappointment over love, and there would be none if people understood the difference between the emotions of love and sex. The major difference is that love is spiritual, while sex is biological. No experience that touches the human heart with a spiritual force can possibly be harmful, except through ignorance or jealousy.

Love is, without question, life's greatest experience. It brings us into communion with Infinite Intelligence. When mixed with the emotions of romance and sex, it may lead us far up the ladder of creative effort. The emotions of love, sex and romance are sides of the eternal triangle of achievement-building genius. Nature creates geniuses through no other force.

Love is an emotion with many sides, shades and colours. The love one feels for parents or children is quite different from that which one feels for one's sweetheart. One is mixed with the emotion of sex while the other is not.

The love one feels in true friendship is not the same as that felt for one's sweetheart, parents or children, but it, too, is a form of love.

Then there is the emotion of love for things inanimate, such as the love of Nature's handiwork. But the most intense and burning of all these various kinds of love is that experienced in the blending of the emotions of love and sex. Marriages not blessed with the eternal affinity of love, properly balanced and proportioned with sex, cannot be happy ones and seldom endure. Love, alone, will not bring happiness in marriage, nor will sex alone. When these two beautiful emotions are blended, marriage may bring about a state of mind closest to the spiritual that one may ever know on this earthly plane.

When the emotion of romance is added to those of love and sex, the obstructions between the finite mind of man and Infinite Intelligence are removed. Then a genius has been born!

What a different story is this to those usually associated with the emotion of sex. Here is an interpretation of the emotion that lifts it out of the commonplace, and makes of it potter's clay in the hands of God, from which He fashions all that is beautiful and inspiring. It is an interpretation that would, when properly understood, bring harmony out of the chaos that exists in too many marriages. The disharmonies often expressed in the form of nagging may usually be traced to lack of knowledge on the subject of sex. Where love, romance and the proper understanding of the emotion and function of sex abide, there is no disharmony between married people.

CHAPTER 12

THE SUBCONSCIOUS MIND:

the Connecting Link

(The Eleventh Step to Riches)

The subconscious mind consists of a field of consciousness in which every impulse of thought that reaches the objective mind through any of the five senses is classified and recorded. From here, thoughts may be recalled or withdrawn as letters may be taken from a filing cabinet.

It receives and files sense impressions or thoughts, regardless of their nature. You may *voluntarily* plant in your subconscious mind any plan, thought or purpose which you desire to translate into its physical or monetary equivalent. The subconscious acts first on the dominating desires that have been mixed with emotional feeling, such as faith.

Consider this in connection with the instructions in Chapter 2 on desire, for taking the six steps there outlined, and the instructions in Chapter 7 on planning, and you will understand the importance of the thought conveyed.

THE SUBCONSCIOUS MIND WORKS DAY AND NIGHT. It draws upon the forces of Infinite Intelligence for the power with which it voluntarily transmutes desires into their physical equivalent. To accomplish this it always makes use of the most practical media.

You cannot entirely control your subconscious mind, but you can voluntarily hand over to it any plan, desire or purpose you wish to be transformed into concrete form. Read, again, the instructions for using the subconscious mind in Chapter 4.

There is plenty of evidence to support the belief that the subconscious mind is the connecting link between the finite mind and Infinite Intelligence. It is the intermediary through which one may draw upon the forces of Infinite Intelligence at will. It, alone, contains the secret process by which mental impulses are modified and changed into their spiritual equivalent. It, alone, is the medium through which prayer may be transmitted to the source capable of answering prayer.

The possibilities of creative effort connected with the subconscious mind are stupendous and imponderable. They inspire one with awe.

I never approach the discussion of the subconscious mind without a feeling of littleness and inferiority due, perhaps, to the fact that the entire stock of knowledge on this subject is so pitifully limited. The very fact that the subconscious mind is the medium of communication between the thinking mind and Infinite Intelligence is, of itself, a thought that almost paralyses one's reason.

After you have accepted, as a reality, the existence of the subconscious mind – and understand its possibilities as a medium for transmuting your *desires* into their physical or monetary equivalent – you will comprehend the full significance of the instructions given in Chapter 2. You will also understand why you have been repeatedly admonished to *make your desires clear and to put them in writing*. The necessity of *persistence* in carrying out instructions will also become clear.

The 13 principles are the stimuli with which you acquire the ability to reach and to influence your subconscious mind. Do not become discouraged if you cannot do this upon the first attempt. Remember that the subconscious mind may be voluntarily directed only through habit, under the directions given in Chapter 3 on faith. You have not yet had time to master faith. Be patient. Be persistent.

A good many statements in the chapters on faith and auto-suggestion will be repeated here for the benefit of your subconscious mind. Remember, your subconscious mind functions voluntarily, whether you make any effort to influence it or not. This naturally suggests to you that thoughts of fear and poverty, and all negative thoughts, serve as stimuli to your subconscious mind, unless you master these impulses and give it more desirable food upon which it may feed.

The subconscious mind will not remain idle! If you fail to plant *desires* in your subconscious mind, it will feed upon the thoughts that reach it as the result of your neglect. We have already explained that thought impulses, both negative and positive, are reaching the subconscious mind continuously from the four sources mentioned in Chapter 11 on Sex Transmutation.

For the present, it is sufficient to remember that you are living daily in the midst of all manner of thought impulses that are reaching your subconscious mind, without your knowledge. Some of these impulses are negative, some are positive. You are now engaged in trying to help shut off the flow of negative impulses, and to aid in voluntarily influencing your subconscious mind through positive impulses of *desire*.

When you achieve this, you will possess the key that unlocks the door to your subconscious mind. Moreover, you will control that door so completely that no undesirable thought may influence your subconscious mind.

Everything that is created *begins* in the form of a thought impulse. Nothing can be created that is not first conceived in *thought*. Through the aid of the imagination, thought impulses may be assembled into plans. The imagination, when under control, may be used for the creation of plans or purposes that lead to success in one's chosen occupation.

All thought impulses intended for transmutation into their physical equivalent and voluntarily planted in the subconscious mind must pass through the imagination and be mixed with faith. The 'mixing' of faith with a plan, or purpose, intended for submission to the subconscious mind may be done *only* through the imagination.

From these statements, you will readily observe that voluntary use of the subconscious mind calls for coordination and application of all the principles.

Ella Wheeler Wilcox, a famous poet and journalist of the late 19th and early 20th century, gave evidence of her understanding of the power of the subconscious mind when she wrote:

> You never can tell what a thought will do
>   In bringing you hate or love –
> For thoughts are things, and their airy wings
>   Are swifter than carrier doves.
> They follow the law of the universe –
>   Each thing creates its kind,

> And they speed o'er the track to bring you back
> Whatever went out from your mind.

Ms Wilcox understood the truth that thoughts which go out from one's mind also imbed themselves deeply in one's subconscious, where they serve as a magnet, pattern or blueprint by which the subconscious mind is influenced while translating them into their physical equivalent. Thoughts are truly things, for the reason that every material thing begins in the form of thought-energy.

The subconscious mind is more susceptible to influence by impulses of thought mixed with 'feeling' or emotion than by those originating solely in the reasoning portion of the mind. In fact, there is much evidence to support the theory that *only* emotionalised thoughts have any *action* influence upon the subconscious mind. It is a well-known fact that emotion or feeling rules the majority of people. If it is true that the subconscious mind responds more quickly to, and is influenced more readily by, thought impulses well mixed with emotion, it is essential to become familiar with the more important of the emotions.

There are seven major positive emotions and seven major negative emotions. The negatives voluntarily inject themselves into the thought impulses, ensuring their passage into the subconscious mind. The positives must be injected, through the principle of autosuggestion, into the thought impulses that an individual wishes to pass on to the subconscious mind. (Instructions have been given in Chapter 4 on autosuggestion.)

These emotions, or feeling impulses, may be likened to yeast in a loaf of bread because they constitute the *action* element, which transforms thought impulses from the passive to the active state. Thus may one understand why thought impulses which have been well mixed with emotion are acted upon more readily than thought impulses originating in 'cold reason'.

You are preparing yourself to influence and control the 'inner audience' of your subconscious mind in order to hand over to it the *desire* for money, which you wish transmuted into its monetary equivalent. It is essential, therefore, that you understand the method of approach to this 'inner audience'. You must speak its language or it will not heed your call. It understands best the language of emotion or feeling. Let us, therefore, describe here the seven major positive emotions and the seven major negative emotions, so that you may draw upon the positives and avoid the negatives when giving instructions to your subconscious mind.

The Seven Major Positive Emotions

The emotion of DESIRE
The emotion of FAITH
The emotion of LOVE
The emotion of SEX
The emotion of ENTHUSIASM
The emotion of ROMANCE
The emotion of HOPE

There are other positive emotions, but these are the seven most powerful, and the ones most commonly used in creative effort. Master these seven emotions (they can be mastered only by *use*), and the other positive emotions will be at your command when you need them. Remember, in this connection, that you are studying a book intended to help you develop a 'money consciousness' by filling your mind with positive emotions. You do not become money conscious by filling your mind with negative emotions.

The Seven Major Negative Emotions
(to be avoided)

> The emotion of FEAR
> The emotion of JEALOUSY
> The emotion of HATRED
> The emotion of REVENGE
> The emotion of GREED
> The emotion of SUPERSTITION
> The emotion of ANGER

Positive and negative emotions cannot occupy the mind at the same time. One or the other must dominate. It is your responsibility to make sure that positive emotions constitute the dominating influence of your mind. Here the law of *habit* will come to your aid. *Form the habit* of applying and using the positive emotions! Eventually, they will dominate your mind so completely that the negatives *cannot enter it.*

Only by following these instructions literally, and continuously, can you gain control over your subconscious mind. The presence of a single negative in your conscious mind is sufficient to destroy all chances of constructive aid from your subconscious mind.

If you are an observant person, you must have noticed that most people resort to prayer *only* after everything else has *failed*! Or else they pray by a ritual of meaningless words. And, because it is a fact that most people who pray do so *only after everything else has failed*, they go to prayer with their minds filled with *fear* and *doubt*, which are the emotions the subconscious mind acts upon and passes on to Infinite Intelligence. Likewise, that is the emotion Infinite Intelligence receives and *acts upon*.

If you pray for a thing, but have fear as you pray that you may not receive it, or that your prayer will not be acted upon by Infinite Intelligence, your prayer *will have been in vain*.

Prayer does, sometimes, result in the realisation of that for which one prays. If you have ever had the experience of receiving something for which you prayed, go back in your memory and recall your actual *state of mind* while you were praying, and you will know for sure that the theory here described is more than a theory.

The time will come when schools and educational institutions will teach the 'science of prayer'. Moreover, prayer may then be reduced to a science. When that time comes (it will come as soon as humankind is ready for it and demands it), no one will approach the Universal Mind in a state of fear, for the very good reason that there will be no such emotion as fear. Ignorance, superstition and false teaching will have disappeared, and we will have attained our true status as children of Infinite Intelligence. A few have already attained this blessing.

If you believe this prophecy is far-fetched, take a look at the human race in retrospect. Less than 200 years ago, it was commonly believed that lightning was evidence of the wrath of God, and people feared it. Now, thanks to the power of *faith*, we have harnessed lightning and made it turn the wheels of industry. Until relatively recent times, it was believed that the space between the planets was nothing but a great void, a stretch of dead nothingness. Now, thanks to this same power of *faith*, we know that far from being either dead or a void, the space between the planets is very much alive, that it is the highest form of vibration known, excepting, perhaps, the vibration of *thought*. Moreover, we know that this living, pulsating, vibratory energy that permeates every atom of matter and fills every niche of space connects every human brain with every other human brain.

What reason do we have to believe that this same energy does not connect every human brain with Infinite Intelligence?

There are no tollgates between the finite mind of humans and Infinite Intelligence. The communication costs nothing except patience, faith, persistence, understanding and a *sincere desire* to communicate. Moreover, the approach can be made only by each of us ourselves. Paid prayers are worthless. Infinite Intelligence does no business by proxy. You either go direct or you do not communicate.

You may buy prayer books and repeat them until the day of your doom, without avail. Thoughts that you wish to communicate to Infinite Intelligence must undergo transformation, such as can be given only through your own subconscious mind.

The method by which you may communicate with Infinite Intelligence is very similar to that through which the vibration of sound is communicated by wireless communication If you understand the working principle of radio, TV and cellular phones, you know that audio and video cannot be communicated through the ether until it has been 'stepped up', or changed into a rate of vibration which the human ear or eye cannot detect. The sending station picks up the audio and video, and 'scrambles' or modifies it by stepping up the vibration millions of times. Only in this way can the vibrations be communicated through the ether. After this transformation has taken place, the ether 'picks up' the energy and carries that energy to receiving stations, and these receiving sets 'step' that energy back down to its original rate of vibration so it can be seen and heard.

The subconscious mind is the intermediary that translates one's prayers into terms that Infinite Intelligence can recognise, presents the message and brings back the answer in the form of a definite plan or idea for procuring the object of the prayer. Understand this principle and you will know why mere words read from a prayer book cannot, and will never, serve as an agency of communication between the human mind and Infinite Intelligence.

Before your prayer will reach Infinite Intelligence (a statement of the author's theory only), it is probably transformed from its original thought vibration into terms of spiritual vibration. Faith is the only known agency that will give your thoughts a spiritual nature. *Faith* and *fear* make poor bedfellows. Where one is found, the other cannot exist.

CHAPTER 13

THE BRAIN:
a Broadcasting and Receiving Station for Thought

(The Twelfth Step to Riches)

In a study by the author with Dr Alexander Graham Bell and Dr Elmer R. Gates, it was concluded that every human brain is both a broadcasting and receiving station for the vibration of thought.

Through the medium of the ether, in a fashion similar to that employed by the basic principle of radio and other wireless communication, every human brain is capable of picking up vibrations of thought released by other brains.

In connection with the above statement, compare and consider the description of the creative imagination, as outlined in Chapter 6 on imagination. The creative imagination is the 'receiving set' of the brain, which receives thoughts released by the brains of others. It is the agency of communication between one's conscious, or reasoning, mind and the four sources from which one may receive thought stimuli.

When stimulated or 'stepped up' to a high rate of vibration, the mind becomes more receptive to the vibration of thought that reaches it through the ether from outside sources. This 'stepping up' process takes place through the positive emotions or the negative emotions. Through the emotions, the vibrations of thought may be increased.

Vibrations of an exceedingly high rate are the only vibrations picked up and carried, by the ether, from one brain to another. Thought is energy travelling at an exceedingly high rate of vibration. Thought which has been modified or 'stepped up' by any of the major emotions vibrates at a much higher rate than ordinary thought. It is this type of thought that passes from one brain to another, through the broadcasting machinery of the human brain.

As far as intensity and driving force are concerned, the emotion of sex stands at the head of the list of human emotions. A brain stimulated by the emotion of sex vibrates at a much more rapid rate than it does when that emotion is quiescent or absent.

The result of sex transmutation is the increase of the rate of vibration of thoughts to such a pitch that the creative imagination becomes highly receptive to ideas it picks up from the ether. When the brain is vibrating at a rapid rate, it not only attracts thoughts and ideas released by other brains, it also gives one's own thoughts that 'feeling' which is essential for those thoughts to be picked up and acted upon by the subconscious mind.

Thus, you will see that the broadcasting principle is the factor through which you mix feeling or emotion with your thoughts and pass them on to your subconscious mind.

The subconscious mind is the 'sending station' of the brain, through which vibrations of thought are broadcast. The creative iImagination is the 'receiving set', through which the vibrations of thought are picked up from the ether.

Along with these important factors of the subconscious mind and the creative imagination, consider now the principle of autosuggestion, the medium by which you may put into operation your 'broadcasting' station.

Through the instructions described in Chapter 4, you were definitely informed of the method by which *desire* may be transmuted into its monetary equivalent.

Operation of your mental 'broadcasting' station is a comparatively simple procedure. You have but three principles to bear in mind, and to apply, when you wish to use your broadcasting station – the SUBCONSCIOUS MIND, CREATIVE IMAGINATION and AUTOSUGGESTION. The stimuli through which you put these three principles into action have been described – the procedure begins with *desire*.

The Greatest Forces are 'Intangible'

The Depression of the 1930s brought the world to the very borderline of understanding intangible and unseen forces. Through the ages that have passed, people have depended too much upon their physical senses, and have limited their knowledge to physical things that they could see, touch, weigh and measure.

We are now entering the most marvellous of all ages – an age that will teach us something of the intangible forces of the world about us. Perhaps we shall learn, as we pass through this age, that the 'other self' is more powerful than the physical self we see when we look into a mirror.

Sometimes we speak lightly of the intangibles – the things we cannot perceive through any of our five senses – but we should never forget that we are all controlled by unseen and intangible forces.

The whole of humankind has not the power to cope with nor control the intangible force wrapped up in the rolling waves of the oceans. The human mind does not have the capacity to understand the intangible force of gravity – which keeps this little earth suspended in mid-air and keeps us from falling from it – much less the power to control that force. All of us are entirely subservient to the intangible force which comes with a thunderstorm, and we are just as helpless in the presence of the intangible force of electricity. Indeed, many of us do not even know what electricity is, where it comes from, or what is its purpose!

Nor is this by any means the end of our ignorance in connection with things unseen and intangible. We do not understand the intangible force (and intelligence) wrapped up in the soil of the earth – the force which provides us with every morsel of food we eat, every article of clothing we wear and every coin we carry in our pockets.

The Dramatic Story of the Brain

Last, but not least, with all our boasted culture and education, we understand little or nothing of the intangible force (the greatest of all the intangibles) of thought. We know but little concerning the physical brain and its vast network of intricate machinery through which the power of thought is translated into its material equivalent. However, we are now entering an age which shall yield enlightenment on the subject. Already scientists have begun to turn their attention to the study of this stupendous thing called a brain. While they are still in the kindergarten stage of their studies, they have uncovered enough to know that the central switchboard of the human brain, the number of lines which connect each brain cell with another, equals the figure one followed by 15 million zeros.

'The figure is so stupendous,' said Dr C. Judson Herrick of the University of Chicago, 'that astronomical figures dealing with hundreds of millions of light years become insignificant by comparison. It has been determined that there are from 10,000,000,000 to 14,000,000,000 nerve cells in the human cerebral cortex, and we know that these are arranged in definite patterns. These arrangements are not haphazard. They are orderly. Recently developed methods of electro-physiology draw off action currents from very precisely located cells, or fibres with micro-electrodes, amplify them, and record potential differences to a millionth of a volt.'

It is inconceivable that such a network of intricate machinery should be in existence for the sole purpose of carrying on the physical functions incidental to growth and maintenance of the physical body. Is it not likely that the same system, which gives billions of brain cells the media for communication one with another, provides also the means of communication with other intangible forces?

In the late 1930s, the *New York Times* published an editorial showing that at least one great university, and one intelligent investigator in the field of mental phenomena, were carrying out organised research through which conclusions had been reached that parallel many of those described in this and the following chapter. The editorial briefly analysed the work carried out by Dr Rhine and his associates at Duke University as follows:

'What is "Telepathy"?'

'A month ago we cited on this page some of the remarkable results achieved by Professor Rhine and his associates in Duke University from more than a hundred thousand tests to determine the existence of "telepathy" and "clairvoyance". These results were summarised in the first two articles in *Harpers Magazine*. In the second that has now appeared, the author, E.H. Wright, attempts to summarise what has been learned, or what it seems reasonable to infer, regarding the exact nature of these "extra-sensory" modes of perception.

'The actual existence of telepathy and clairvoyance now seems to some scientists enormously probable as the result of Rhine's experiments. Various percipients were asked to name as many cards in a special pack as they could without looking at them and without other sensory access to them. About a score of men and women were discovered who could regularly name so many of the cards correctly that "there was not one chance in many a million million of their having done their feats by luck or accident".

'But how did they do them? These powers, assuming that they exist, do not seem to be sensory. There is no known organ for them. The experiments worked just as well at distances of several hundred miles as they did in the same room. These facts also dispose, in Mr Wright's opinion, of the attempt to explain telepathy or clairvoyance through any physical theory of radiation. All known forms of radiant energy decline inversely as the square of the distance traversed. Telepathy and clairvoyance do not. But they do vary through physical causes as our other mental powers do. Contrary to widespread opinion, they do not improve when the percipient is asleep or half-asleep, but, on the contrary, when he is most wide-awake and alert. Rhine discovered that a narcotic will invariably lower a percipient's score, while a stimulant will always send it higher. The most reliable performer apparently cannot make a good score unless he tries to do his best.

'One conclusion that Wright draws with some confidence is that telepathy and clairvoyance are really one and the same gift. That is, the faculty that "sees" a card face down on a table seems to be exactly the same one that "reads" a thought residing only in another mind. There are several grounds for believing this. So far, for example, the two gifts have been found in every person who enjoys either of them. In every one so far the two have been of equal vigour, almost exactly. Screens, walls, distances, have no effect at all on either. Wright advances from this conclusion to express what he puts forward as no more than the mere "hunch" that other extra-sensory experiences, prophetic dreams, premonitions of disaster and the like, may also prove to be part of the same faculty. The reader is not asked to accept any of these conclusions unless he finds it necessary, but the evidence that Rhine has piled up must remain impressive.'

In view of Dr Rhine's announcement in connection with the conditions under which the mind responds to what he terms 'extra-sensory' modes of perception, I now feel privileged to add to his testimony. My associates and I have discovered what we believe to be the ideal conditions under which the mind can be stimulated so that the sixth sense described in the next chapter can be made to function in a practical way.

The conditions to which I refer consist of a close working alliance between myself and two members of my staff. Through experimentation and practice, we have discovered how to stimulate our minds (by applying the principle used in connection with the 'Invisible Counsellors' described in the next chapter). In doing so we can, by a process of blending our three minds into one, find the solution to a great variety of personal problems submitted by my clients.

The procedure is very simple. We sit down at a conference table, clearly state the nature of the problem under consideration, and then begin discussing it. Each contributes whatever thoughts may occur. The strange thing about this method of mind stimulation is that it places each participant in communication with unknown sources of knowledge definitely outside his own experience.

If you understand the principle described in Chapter 10 on the Master Mind, you of course recognise the round-table procedure described here as being a practical application of the Master Mind.

This method of mind stimulation, through harmonious discussion of definite subjects between three people, illustrates the simplest and most practical use of the Master Mind.

By adopting and following a similar plan, any student of this philosophy may come into possession of the famous Carnegie formula briefly described in the Author's Preface. If it means nothing to you at this time, mark this page and read it again after you have finished the last chapter.

CHAPTER 14

THE SIXTH SENSE:
the Door to the Temple of Wisdom

(The Thirteenth Step to Riches)

The 'thirteenth' principle is known as the *sixth sense*. Infinite Intelligence may, and will, communicate voluntarily through the sixth sense without any effort from, or demands by, the individual.

This principle is the apex of the philosophy. It can be assimilated, understood and applied *only* by first mastering the other 12 principles.

The *sixth sense* is the portion of the subconscious mind that has been referred to as the 'creative imagination'. It has also been referred to as the 'receiving set' through which ideas, plans, and thoughts flash into the mind. The 'flashes' are sometimes called 'hunches' or 'inspirations'.

The sixth sense defies description! It cannot be described to a person who has not mastered the other principles of this philosophy because such a person has no knowledge or experience with which the sixth sense may be compared. Understanding of the sixth sense comes only by meditation through mind development from within. The sixth sense is probably the medium of contact between the finite mind of individuals and Infinite Intelligence. For this reason, it is a mixture of both the mental and the spiritual. It is believed to be the point at which the mind of an individual contacts the Universal Mind.

After you have mastered the principles described in this book, you will be prepared to accept as truth a statement that may, otherwise, be incredible to you, namely: through the aid of the sixth sense, you will be warned of impending dangers in time to avoid them, and notified of opportunities in time to embrace them.

With the development of the sixth sense there comes to your aid, and to do your bidding, a 'guardian angel' who will open to you at all times the door to the Temple of Wisdom.

You will never know whether or not this is a statement of truth, except by following the instructions described in the pages of this book, or some similar procedure.

The author is not a believer in, nor an advocate of, 'miracles'. He has enough knowledge of Nature to understand that Nature never deviates from her established laws. Some of her laws are so incomprehensible that they produce what appear to be 'miracles'. The sixth sense comes as near to being a miracle as anything I have ever experienced, and it appears so only because I do not understand the method by which this principle is operated.

This much the author does know – that there is a power, or a First Cause, or an Intelligence, which permeates every atom of matter and embraces every unit of perceptible energy; that this

Infinite Intelligence converts acorns into oak trees, causes water to flow downhill in response to the law of gravity, follows night with day and winter with summer, each maintaining its proper place and relationship to the other. This Intelligence may, through the principles of this philosophy, be induced to aid in transmuting *desires* into concrete, or material, form. The author has this knowledge, because he has experimented with it and has *experienced it.*

Step by step, through the preceding chapters, you have been led to this, the last principle. If you have mastered each of the preceding principles, you are now prepared to accept, without being sceptical, the stupendous claims made here. If you have not mastered the other principles, you must do so before you may determine, definitely, whether or not the claims made in this chapter are fact or fiction.

While I was passing through the age of 'hero worship' I found myself trying to imitate those whom I most admired. Moreover, I discovered that the element of *faith*, with which I endeavoured to imitate my idols, gave me great capacity to do so quite successfully.

I have never entirely divested myself of this habit of hero worship, although I have passed the age commonly given over to such. My experience has taught me that the next best thing to being truly great is to emulate the great, by feeling and action, as closely as possible.

Long before I had ever written a line for publication, or endeavoured to deliver a speech in public, I followed the habit of reshaping my own character by trying to imitate the nine men whose lives and life works had been most impressive to me. These nine men were Emerson, Paine, Edison, Darwin, Lincoln, Burbank, Napoleon, Ford and Carnegie. Every night, over a long period of years, I held an imaginary council meeting with this group whom I called my 'Invisible Counsellors'.

The procedure was this. Just before going to sleep at night, I would shut my eyes and see, in my imagination, this group of men seated with me around my council table. Here I had not only an opportunity to sit among those whom I considered to be great, but I actually dominated the group by serving as the Chairman.

I had a very *definite purpose* in indulging my imagination through these nightly meetings. My purpose was to rebuild my own character so it would represent a composite of the characters of my imaginary counsellors. Realising, as I did early in life, that I had to overcome the handicap of my birth into an environment of ignorance and superstition, I deliberately assigned myself the task of voluntary rebirth through the method here described.

Building Character Through Autosuggestion

Being an earnest student of psychology, I knew that all people have become what they are because of their *dominating thoughts and desires*. I knew that every deeply seated desire seeks outward expression through which it may be transmuted into reality. I knew that self-suggestion is a powerful factor in building character, that it is, in fact, the sole principle through which character is built.

With this knowledge of the principles of mind operation, I was fairly well armed with the equipment needed to rebuild my character. In these imaginary council meetings I called on my cabinet members for the knowledge I wished each to contribute, addressing myself to each member in audible words, as follows:

'Mr Emerson, I desire to acquire from you the marvellous understanding of Nature which distinguished your life. I ask that you make an impress upon my subconscious mind of whatever qualities you possessed that enabled you to understand and adapt yourself to the laws of Nature. I ask that you assist me in reaching and drawing upon whatever sources of knowledge are available to this end.

'Mr Burbank, I request that you pass on to me the knowledge which enabled you to so harmonise the laws of Nature that you caused the cactus to shed its thorns and become an edible food. Give me access to the knowledge which enabled you to make two blades of grass grow where but one grew before, and helped you to blend the colouring of the flowers with more splendour and harmony, for you, alone, have successfully gilded the lily.

'Napoleon, I desire to acquire from you, by emulation, the marvellous ability you possessed to inspire people, and to arouse them to greater and more determined spirit of action. Also to acquire the spirit of enduring *faith*, which enabled you to turn defeat into victory, and to surmount staggering obstacles. Emperor of Fate, King of Chance, Man of Destiny, I salute you!

'Mr Paine, I desire to acquire from you the freedom of thought and the courage and clarity with which to express convictions that so distinguished you!

'Mr Darwin, I wish to acquire from you the marvellous patience and ability to study cause and effect without bias or prejudice so exemplified by you in the field of natural science.

'Mr Lincoln, I desire to build into my own character the keen sense of justice, the untiring spirit of patience, the sense of humour, the human understanding and the tolerance that were your distinguishing characteristics.

'Mr Carnegie, I am already indebted to you for my choice of

a life work, which has brought me great happiness and peace of mind. I wish to acquire a thorough understanding of the principles of organised effort, which you used so effectively in the building of a great industrial enterprise.

'Mr Ford, you have been among the most helpful of the men who have supplied much of the material essential to my work. I wish to acquire your spirit of persistence, the determination, poise and self-confidence that have enabled you to master poverty, organise, unify and simplify human effort, so I may help others to follow in your footsteps.

'Mr Edison, I have seated you nearest to me, at my right, because of the personal cooperation you have given me during my research into the causes of success and failure. I wish to acquire from you the marvellous spirit of *faith*, with which you have uncovered so many of Nature's secrets, the spirit of unremitting toil with which you have so often wrested victory from defeat.'

My method of addressing the members of the imaginary cabinet would vary according to the traits of character in which I was most interested in acquiring at the time. I studied the records of their lives with painstaking care. After some months of this nightly procedure, I was astounded by the discovery that these imaginary figures became, apparently, real.

Each of these nine men developed individual characteristics, which surprised me. For example, Lincoln developed the habit of always being late then walking around in solemn parade. When he came, he walked very slowly, with his hands clasped behind him. Once in a while, he would stop as he passed and rest his hand, momentarily, upon my shoulder. He always wore an expression of seriousness upon his face. Rarely did I see him smile. The cares of a sundered nation made him grave.

That was not true of the others. Burbank and Paine often indulged in witty repartee that seemed, at times, to shock the other members of the cabinet. One night Paine suggested that I prepare a lecture on 'The Age of Reason', and deliver it from the pulpit of a church that I formerly attended. Many around the table laughed heartily at the suggestion. Not Napoleon! He drew his mouth down at the corners and groaned so loudly that all turned and looked at him with amazement. To him the church was but a pawn of the State, not to be reformed, but to be used as a convenient inciter to mass activity by the people.

On one occasion Burbank was late. When he came, he was excited with enthusiasm, and explained that he had been late because of an experiment he was making through which he hoped to be able to grow apples on any sort of tree. Paine chided him by reminding him that it was an apple that started all the trouble between man and woman. Darwin chuckled heartily as he suggested that Burbank should watch out for little serpents when he went into the forest to gather apples, as they had the habit of growing into big snakes. Emerson observed, 'No serpents, no apples,' and Napoleon remarked, 'No apples, no state!'

Lincoln developed the habit of always being the last one to leave the table after each meeting. On one occasion, he leaned across the end of the table, his arms folded, and remained in that position for many minutes. I made no attempt to disturb him. Finally, he lifted his head slowly, got up and walked to the door. Then he turned around, came back, laid his hand on my shoulder and said, 'My boy, you will need much courage if you remain steadfast in carrying out your purpose in life. But remember, when difficulties overtake you, the common people have common sense. Adversity will develop it.'

One evening Edison arrived ahead of all the others. He walked over and seated himself at my left, where Emerson was accustomed to sit, and said, 'You are destined to witness the discovery of the secret of life. When the time comes, you will observe that life consists of great swarms of energy, or entities, each as intelligent as human beings think themselves to be. These units of life group together like hives of bees, and remain together until they disintegrate, through lack of harmony. These units have differences of opinion, the same as human beings, and often fight among themselves. These meetings which you are conducting will be very helpful to you. They will bring to your rescue some of the same units of life that served the members of your cabinet, during their lives. These units are eternal. THEY NEVER DIE! Your own thoughts and *desires* serve as the magnet that attracts units of life, from the great ocean of life out there. Only the friendly units are attracted – the ones that harmonise with the nature of your *desires*.'

The other members of the cabinet began to enter the room. Edison got up and slowly walked around to his own seat. Edison was still living when this happened. It impressed me so greatly that I went to see him and told him about the experience. He smiled broadly and said, 'Your dream was more a reality than you may imagine it to have been.' He added no further explanation to his statement.

These meetings became so realistic that I started to be fearful of their consequences, and discontinued them for several months. The experiences were so uncanny, I was afraid if I continued them I would lose sight of the fact that the meetings were purely experiences of my imagination.

Some six months after I had discontinued the practice I was awakened one night, or thought I was, and saw Lincoln standing at my bedside. He said, 'The world will soon need your services. It is about to undergo a period of chaos that will cause men and women to lose faith and become panic stricken. Go ahead with your work and complete your philosophy. That is your mission in life. If you neglect it, for any cause whatsoever, you will be reduced to a primal state, and be compelled to retrace the cycles through which you have passed during thousands of years.

The following morning I was unable to tell whether I had dreamed this or had actually been awake. I have never since found out which it was, but I do know that the dream, if it were a dream, was so vivid in my mind the next day that I resumed my meetings that night.

At our next meeting, the members of my cabinet all filed into the room together, and stood at their accustomed places at the council table. Lincoln raised a glass and said, 'Gentlemen, let us drink a toast to a friend who has returned to the fold.'

After that, I began to add new members to my cabinet. Now it consists of more than 50, among them Christ, St Paul, Galileo, Copernicus, Aristotle, Plato, Socrates, Homer, Voltaire, Bruno, Spinoza, Drummond, Kant, Schopenhauer, Newton, Confucius, Elbert Hubbard, Brann, Ingersol, Wilson and William James.

This is the first time I have had the courage to mention this. Previously I have remained quiet on the subject because I knew, from my own attitude in connection with such matters, that I would be misunderstood if I described my unusual experience. I have been emboldened now to reduce my experience to the printed page because I am now less concerned about what 'they say' than I was in the years that have passed. One of the blessings of maturity is that it sometimes brings one greater courage to be truthful, regardless of what those who do not understand may think or say.

Lest I be misunderstood, I wish here to state most emphatically that I still regard my cabinet meetings as purely imaginary, but I feel entitled to suggest that they have led me into glorious paths of adventure, rekindled an appreciation of true greatness, encouraged creative endeavour, and emboldened the expression of honest thought.

Somewhere in the cell structure of the brain is located an organ which receives vibrations of thought ordinarily called 'hunches'. So far, science has not discovered where this organ of the sixth sense is located, but this is not important. The fact remains that human beings do receive accurate knowledge through sources other than the physical senses. Such knowledge, generally, is received when the mind is under the influence of extraordinary stimulation. Any emergency that arouses the emotions and causes the heart to beat more rapidly than normal may, and generally does, bring the sixth sense into action. Anyone who has experienced a near accident while driving knows that on such occasions the sixth sense often comes to one's rescue, and aids, by split seconds, in avoiding the accident.

These facts are mentioned preliminary to a statement of fact I shall now make, namely that during my meetings with the 'Invisible Counsellors' I find my mind most receptive to ideas, thoughts and knowledge that reach me through the sixth sense. I can truthfully say that I owe my counsellors full credit for such ideas, facts or knowledge I receive through 'inspiration'.

On scores of occasions when I have faced emergencies – some of them so grave that my life was in jeopardy – I have been miraculously guided past these difficulties through the influence of my counsellors.

My original purpose in conducting council meetings with imaginary beings was solely that of impressing my own subconscious mind – through the principle of autosuggestion – with certain characteristics I desired to acquire. In more recent years, my experimentation has taken on an entirely different trend. I now go to my imaginary counsellors with every difficult problem that confronts my clients and me. The results are often astonishing, although I do not depend entirely on this form of counsel.

You, of course, have recognised that this chapter covers a subject with which the majority of people are unfamiliar. The sixth sense will be of great interest and benefit to the person whose aim is to accumulate vast wealth, but it need not claim the attention of those whose desires are more modest.

Henry Ford undoubtedly understood and made practical use of the sixth sense. His vast business and financial operations made it necessary for him to understand and use this principle. Thomas A. Edison understood and used the sixth sense in connection with the development of inventions, especially those involving basic patents where he had no human experience or accumulated knowledge to guide him. This was the case while he was working on the talking machine and the moving picture machine.

Nearly all great leaders – such as Napoleon, Joan of Arc, Christ, Buddha, Confucius and Mohammed – understood and probably made use of the sixth sense almost continuously. The major portion of their greatness consisted of their knowledge of this principle.

The sixth sense is not something one can take off and put on at will. Ability to use this great power comes slowly, through application of the other principles outlined in this book. Seldom does any individual come into workable knowledge of the sixth sense before the age of 40. More often the knowledge is not available until one is well past 50. This is because the spiritual forces with which the sixth sense is so closely related only mature and become usable through years of meditation, self-examination and serious thought.

No matter who you are, or what may have been your purpose in reading this book, you can profit by it without understanding the principle described in this chapter. This is especially true if your major purpose is that of accumulation of money or other material things.

This chapter on the sixth sense was included because the book was designed to present a complete philosophy by which individuals may unerringly guide themselves in attaining whatever they ask of life. The starting point of all achievement is *desire*. The finishing point is that brand of *knowledge* that leads to understanding – understanding of self, understanding of others, understanding of the laws of Nature, recognition and understanding of *happiness*.

This sort of understanding comes in its fullness only through familiarity with, and use of, the principle of the sixth sense. Therefore that principle had to be included as a part of this philosophy, for the benefit of those who demand more than money.

You must have observed that while reading the chapter you were lifted to a high level of mental stimulation. Splendid! Come back to this again a month from now, read it once more and observe that your mind will soar to a still higher level of stimulation. Repeat this experience from time to time, without being concerned as to how much or how little you learn at the time. Eventually you will find yourself in possession of a power that will enable you to throw off discouragement, master fear, overcome procrastination and draw freely upon your imagination.

Then you will have felt the touch of that unknown 'something' which has been the moving spirit of every truly great thinker, leader, artist, musician, writer, statesman. Then you will be in a position to transmute your *desires* into their physical or financial counterpart as easily as you may lie down and quit at the first sign of opposition.

CHAPTER 15

HOW TO OUTWIT THE SIX GHOSTS OF FEAR

(Clearing the Brain for Riches)

Before you can put any portion of this philosophy into successful use, your mind must be prepared to receive it. The preparation is not difficult. It begins with study, analysis and understanding of three enemies you shall have to clear out. These are *indecision*, *doubt* and *fear*!

The sixth sense will never function while these three negatives, or any of them, remain in your mind. The members of this unholy trio are closely related; where one is found, the other two are close at hand.

Indecision is the seedling of *fear*! Remember this, as you read. Indecision crystallises into *doubt*, the two blend and become *fear*! The 'blending' process is often slow. This is one reason why these three enemies are so dangerous. They germinate and grow without their presence being observed.

The remainder of this chapter describes an end that must be attained before the philosophy, as a whole, can be put into practical use. It also analyses a condition that has reduced huge numbers of people to poverty, and it states a truth that must be understood by all who accumulate riches, whether measured in terms of money or a state of mind of far greater value.

The purpose of this chapter is to turn the spotlight upon the cause and the cure of the six basic fears. Before we can master an enemy, we must know its name, its habits and its place of abode. As you read, analyse yourself carefully, and determine which, if any, of the six common fears have attached themselves to you.

Do not be deceived by the habits of these subtle enemies. Sometimes they remain hidden in the subconscious mind where they are difficult to locate, and still more difficult to eliminate.

The Six Basic Fears

There are six basic fears. Every human suffers from some combination of them at one time or another. Most people are fortunate if they do not suffer from the entire six. Named in the order of their most common appearance, they are:

The fear of POVERTY
The fear of CRITICISM
The fear of ILL HEALTH
The fear of LOSS OF LOVE OF SOMEONE
The fear of OLD AGE
The fear of DEATH

All other fears are of minor importance and can be grouped under these six headings.

The prevalence of these fears, as a curse to the world, runs in cycles. For almost six years, while the Depression was on, we floundered in the cycle of *fear of poverty*. During the periods when we were at war or faced with terror, we were in the cycle of *fear of death*. Even in periods of prosperity and peace, we are in the cycle of *fear of ill health*, as evidenced by the epidemic of various diseases which spread themselves all over the world.

Fears are nothing more than states of mind. One's state of mind is subject to control and direction. Doctors, as everyone knows, are less subject to attack by disease than ordinary laymen for the reason that doctors *do not fear disease*. Doctors have been known to treat hundreds of people suffering from such contagious diseases as smallpox in a day, without becoming infected. Their immunity against the disease consisted largely, if not solely, in their absolute lack of *fear*.

We can create nothing that is not first conceived in the form of an impulse of thought. Following this statement comes another of still greater importance, namely, THOUGHT IMPULSES BEGIN IMMEDIATELY TO TRANSLATE THEMSELVES INTO THEIR PHYSICAL EQUIVALENT, WHETHER THOSE THOUGHTS ARE VOLUNTARY OR INVOLUNTARY. Thought impulses picked up through the ether by mere chance (thoughts released by other minds) may determine one's financial, business, professional or social destiny just as surely as the thought impulses one creates by intent and design.

We are here laying the foundation for the presentation of a fact of great importance to the person who does not understand why some people appear to be 'lucky' while others of equal or greater ability, training, experience and brain capacity seem destined to ride with misfortune. This may be explained by the statement that human beings have the ability to control their own minds completely. With this control, they may open their minds to the thought impulses released by other brains, or close the doors tightly and admit only thought impulses of their own choice.

Nature has endowed us with absolute control over but one thing, and that is *thought*. This fact, coupled with the additional fact that everything people create begins in the form of a thought, leads one very near to the principle by which *fear* may be mastered.

If it is true that *all thought has a tendency to clothe itself in its physical equivalent* (and this is true beyond any reasonable room for doubt), it is equally true that thought impulses of fear and poverty cannot be translated into terms of courage and financial gain.

Following the Wall Street crash of 1929, the people of America were compelled to think of poverty. Slowly but surely that mass thought was crystallised into its physical equivalent, which was known as a 'depression'. This had to happen. It is in conformity with the laws of Nature.

The Fear of Poverty

There can be no compromise between *poverty* and *riches*! The two roads that lead to poverty and riches travel in opposite directions. If you want riches, you must refuse to accept any circumstance that leads towards poverty. (The word 'riches' is here used in its broadest sense, meaning financial, spiritual, mental and material estates.) The starting point of the path that leads to riches is *desire*. In Chapters 1 and 2, you received full instructions for the proper use of desire. In this chapter on *fear* you have complete instructions for preparing your mind to make practical use of desire.

Here, then, is the place to give yourself a challenge that will definitely determine how much of this philosophy you have absorbed. Here is the point at which you can turn prophet and foretell, accurately, what the future holds in store for you. If, after reading this chapter, you are willing to accept poverty, you may as well make up your mind to receive poverty. This is one decision you cannot avoid.

If you demand riches, determine what form and how much will be required to satisfy you. You know the road that leads to riches. You have been given a road map, which, if followed, will keep you on that road. If you neglect to make the start, or stop before you arrive, no one will be to blame but *you*. This responsibility is yours. No alibi will save you from accepting the responsibility if you now fail or refuse to demand riches of life. The acceptance calls for but one thing – the only thing you can control – and that is a *state of mind*. A state of mind is something that one assumes. It cannot be purchased; it must be created.

Fear of poverty is a state of mind, nothing else! But it is sufficient to destroy one's chances of achievement in any undertaking. This fear paralyses the faculty of reason, destroys the faculty of imagination, kills off self-reliance, undermines enthusiasm, discourages initiative, leads to uncertainty of purpose, encourages procrastination, wipes out enthusiasm and makes self-control an impossibility. It takes the charm from one's personality, destroys the possibility of accurate thinking, diverts concentration of effort; it masters persistence, turns the willpower into nothingness, destroys ambition, beclouds the memory and invites failure in every conceivable form; it kills love and assassinates the finer emotions of the heart, discourages friendship and invites disaster in a hundred forms, leads to sleeplessness, misery and unhappiness – and all this despite the obvious truth that we live in a society of overabundance of everything the heart could desire, with nothing standing between us and our desires, except lack of a definite purpose.

The Fear of Poverty is, without doubt, the most destructive of the six basic fears. It has been placed at the head of the list because it is the most difficult to master. Considerable courage is required to state the truth about the origin of this fear, and still greater courage to accept the truth after it has been stated. The fear of poverty grew out of the human tendency to *prey upon others economically*. Nearly all animals lower than humans are motivated by instinct, but as their capacity to 'think' is limited, they prey upon one another physically. Humans, with their superior sense of intuition, with the capacity to think and to reason, do not eat other humans bodily; they get more satisfaction out of 'eating' them *financially*.

The age in which we live seems to be consumed by money-madness. People are considered less than the dust of the earth unless they can display a fat bank account; but if they have money – *never mind how acquired* – they are too often idolised and treated as being above the law. They rule in politics, dominate in business and the whole world about them bows in respect when they pass by.

Nothing brings so much suffering and humility as *poverty*! Only those who have experienced poverty understand the full meaning of this. It is no wonder that we fear poverty. Through a long line of inherited experiences we have learned, for sure, that some people cannot be trusted where matters of money and earthly possessions are concerned. This is a rather stinging indictment, the worst part of it being that it is *true*.

Many marriages are motivated by the wealth possessed by one or both of the contracting parties. It is no wonder, therefore, that the divorce courts are busy. So eager are people to possess wealth that they will acquire it in any feasible manner – through legal methods if possible, but through other methods if necessary or expedient.

Self-analysis may disclose weaknesses that one does not like to acknowledge. This form of examination is essential to all who demand of life more than mediocrity and poverty. Remember, as you check yourself point by point, that you are the court and the jury, the prosecution and the defence, the plaintiff and the defendant. Face the facts squarely. Ask yourself definite questions and demand direct replies. When the examination is over, you will know more about yourself. If you do not feel that you can be an impartial judge in this self-examination, call upon someone who knows you well to serve as judge while you cross-examine yourself. You are after the truth. Get it, no matter at what cost, even though it may temporarily embarrass you!

The majority of people, if asked what they fear most, would reply, 'I fear nothing.' The reply would be inaccurate because few people realise that they are bound, handicapped, whipped spiritually and physically through some form of fear. So subtle and deeply seated is the emotion of fear that one may go through life burdened with it, never recognising its presence. Only a courageous analysis will disclose the presence of this universal enemy. When you begin such an analysis, search deeply into your character. Here is a list of the symptoms you should look for:

Symptoms of the Fear of Poverty

INDIFFERENCE. Commonly expressed through lack of ambition; willingness to tolerate poverty; acceptance of whatever compensation life may offer without protest; mental and physical laziness; lack of initiative, imagination, enthusiasm and self-control.

INDECISION. The habit of permitting others to do one's thinking; staying 'on the fence'.

DOUBT. Generally expressed through alibis and excuses designed to cover up, explain away or apologise for one's failures; sometimes expressed in the form of envy of those who are successful, or by criticising them.

WORRY. Usually expressed by finding fault with others; a tendency to spend beyond one's income; neglect of personal appearance; scowling and frowning; intemperance in the use of alcoholic drink; sometimes through the use of narcotics; nervousness; lack of poise; self-consciousness and lack of self-reliance.

OVERCAUTION. The habit of looking for the negative side of every circumstance, thinking and talking of possible failure instead of concentrating upon the means of succeeding; knowing all the roads to disaster but never searching for the plans to avoid failure; waiting for 'the right time' to begin putting ideas and plans into action, until the waiting becomes a permanent habit; remembering those who have failed, and forgetting those who have succeeded; seeing the hole in the doughnut but overlooking the doughnut.

PROCRASTINATION. The habit of putting off until tomorrow matters that should have been done last year; spending enough time in creating alibis and excuses to have done the job. This symptom is closely related to overcaution, doubt and worry; refusal to accept responsibility when it can be avoided; willingness to compromise rather than put up a stiff fight; compromising with difficulties instead of harnessing and using them as stepping stones to advancement; bargaining with life for a penny instead of demanding prosperity, opulence, riches, contentment and happiness; and planning what to do *if and when overtaken by failure instead of burning all bridges and making retreat impossible*. This is manifested further by weakness of, and often total lack of, self-confidence, definiteness of purpose, self-control, initiative, enthusiasm, ambition, thrift and sound reasoning ability; *expecting poverty instead of demanding riches*, and association with those who accept poverty instead of seeking the company of those who demand and receive riches.

The Fear of Criticism

Most people are at the least very uncomfortable when criticised. In some cases they may become depressed and despondent when others censure them. The fear of criticism robs people of their initiative, destroys their power of imagination, limits their individuality, takes away their self-reliance, and does them damage in a hundred other ways. Parents often do their children irreparable injury by criticising them. The mother of one of my boyhood chums used to punish him with a switch almost daily, always completing the job with the statement, 'You'll end up in prison before you are twenty.' He was sent to a reform school at the age of 17.

Criticism is the one form of service of which everyone has too much. Everyone has a stock of it that is handed out, gratis, whether called for or not. One's nearest relatives are often the worst offenders. It should be recognised as a crime (in reality it is a crime of the worst nature) for any parent to build inferiority complexes in the mind of a child through unnecessary criticism. Employers who understand human nature get the best there is out of people not by criticism but by constructive suggestion.

Parents may accomplish the same results with their children. Criticism will plant *fear* or resentment in the human heart but it will not build love or affection.

The Fear of Ill Health

This fear may be traced to both physical and social heredity. It is closely associated in origin with the causes of fear of old age and death because it leads one closely to the border of 'terrible worlds' of which nothing is really known, but concerning which some discomforting stories have been told. Certain unethical people engaged in the business of 'selling health' have had not a little to do with keeping alive the fear of ill health.

In the main, ill health is feared because of the suffering it causes and the fear and uncertainty of what may happen when death comes. In addition, there is the fear of the economic toll it may claim.

A reputable doctor estimated that 75 per cent of all people who visit doctors for professional service are suffering with hypochondria (imaginary illness). It has been shown most convincingly that the fear of disease, even where there is not the slightest cause for fear, often produces the physical symptoms of the disease feared. Powerful and mighty is the human mind! It builds or it destroys.

Through a series of experiments conducted some years ago, it was proved that people might be made ill by suggestion. We conducted this experiment by causing three acquaintances to visit the 'victims', each of whom asked the question, 'What ails you? You look terribly ill.' The first questioner usually provoked a grin, and a nonchalant 'Oh, nothing, I'm all right,' from the victim. The second questioner was usually answered with the statement, 'I don't know exactly, but I do feel bad.' The third questioner was usually met with the frank admission that the victim was actually feeling ill.

Try this on an acquaintance if you doubt that it will make them uncomfortable, but do not carry the experiment too far. In some primitive cultures, people take vengeance upon their enemies by placing a 'spell' on the victim. Because they believe the spell is real, victims do become sick and often die.

There is overwhelming evidence that disease sometimes begins in the form of a negative thought impulse. Such an impulse may be passed from one mind to another by suggestion, or created by an individual in their own mind.

Doctors sometimes send patients into new climates for their health because a change of 'mental attitude' is necessary. The seed of fear of ill health lives in every human mind. Worry, fear, discouragement, disappointment in love and business affairs cause this seed to germinate and grow.

The Fear of Loss of Love

The original source of this inherent fear needs little description. It obviously grew out of ancient man's polygamous habit of stealing his fellow man's mate and taking liberties with her whenever he could.

The fear of the loss of love of someone is the most painful of all the six basic fears. It probably plays more havoc with the body and mind than any of the others.

One of the distinguishing symptoms of this fear is *jealousy*: being suspicious of friends and loved ones without any reasonable evidence. Another is the habit of accusing one's partner of infidelity without grounds. Further symptoms are a general suspicion of everyone, absolute faith in no one, and finding fault with friends, relatives, business associates and loved ones upon the slightest provocation, or without any cause whatsoever.

The Fear of Old Age

The possibility of ill health, which is more common as people grow older, is a major cause of this common fear. Eroticism also enters into the cause of the fear of old age, as no one cherishes the thought of diminishing sexual attraction.

Another contributing cause of the fear of old age is the possibility of loss of freedom and independence, as old age may bring with it the loss of both physical and economic freedom.

Some people show a tendency to slow down and develop an inferiority complex when they get older, falsely believing themselves to be 'slipping' because of age. (The truth is that some of our most useful years, mentally and spiritually, are those in later life.) Unfortunately, there are older men and women who lose their initiative, imagination and self-reliance by falsely believing themselves too old to exercise these qualities.

The Fear of Death

To some this is the cruellest of all the basic fears. The reason is obvious. We know not what to expect after death. As Shakespeare stated so well in *Hamlet*, it is 'The undiscovered country from whose bourne no traveller returns'.

The fear of death is not as common now as it was during the age when there were no great colleges and universities. Scientists have turned the spotlight of truth upon the world, and this truth is rapidly freeing people from this terrible fear of death. Through the aid of biology, astronomy, geology and other related sciences, the fears of the dark ages that gripped the minds of people and destroyed their reason have been dispelled.

This fear is useless. Death will come, no matter what anyone may think about it. Accept it as a necessity and pass the thought out of your mind. It must be a necessity or it would not come to all.

The entire world is made up of only two things, *energy* and *matter*. In elementary physics we learn that neither matter nor energy (the only two known realities) can be created or destroyed. Both matter and energy can be transformed.

Life is energy, if it is anything. If neither energy nor matter can be destroyed, of course life cannot be destroyed. Life, like other forms of energy, may be passed through various processes of transition or change, but it cannot be destroyed. Death is mere transition.

If death is not mere change or transition, then nothing comes after death except a long, eternal peaceful sleep, and sleep is nothing to be feared. Thus you may wipe out, forever, the fear of death.

Worry

Worry is a state of mind based upon fear. It works slowly but persistently. It is insidious and subtle. Step by step it 'digs itself in' until it paralyses one's reasoning faculty and destroys self-confidence and initiative. Worry is a form of sustained fear caused by indecision, therefore it is a state of mind which can be controlled.

An unsettled mind is helpless. Indecision makes an unsettled mind. Most individuals lack the willpower to reach decisions promptly and to stand by them after they have been made, even during normal business conditions. During periods of economic unrest, people are handicapped not only by their inherent tendency to be slow at reaching decisions, but also by the indecision of others around them who have created a state of 'mass indecision'.

The six basic fears become translated into a state of worry through indecision. Relieve yourself forever of the fear of death by reaching a decision to accept death as an inescapable event. Whip the fear of poverty by reaching a decision to get along with whatever wealth you can accumulate *without worry*. Put your foot upon the neck of the fear of criticism by reaching a decision *not to worry* about what other people think, do or say. Eliminate the fear of old age by reaching a decision to accept it, not as a handicap, but as a great blessing which carries with it wisdom, self-control and understanding not known to youth.

Acquit yourself of the fear of ill health by the decision to forget symptoms. Master the fear of loss of love by reaching a decision to get along without love, if that is necessary.

Kill the habit of worry, in all its forms, by reaching a general, blanket decision that nothing life has to offer is worth the price of worry. With this decision will come poise, peace of mind and calmness of thought that will bring happiness.

A person whose mind is filled with fear not only destroys their own chances of intelligent action, but transmits these destructive vibrations to the minds of other people and destroys their chances as well.

Even a dog or a horse knows when its master lacks courage; moreover, a dog or horse will pick up the vibrations of fear thrown off by its master, and behave accordingly. One finds this same capacity to pick up the vibrations of fear lower down the line of intelligence in the animal kingdom. A honeybee immediately senses fear in the mind of a person. For reasons unknown, a bee will sting the person whose mind is releasing vibrations of fear much more readily than it will molest the person whose mind registers no fear.

The vibrations of fear pass from one mind to another just as quickly and as surely as the sound of the human voice passes from the broadcasting station to the receiving station and *by the self-same medium*.

Mental telepathy is a reality. Thoughts pass from one mind to another voluntarily, whether or not this fact is recognised by either the person releasing the thoughts or the person who picks up those thoughts.

The person who gives expression, by word of mouth, to negative or destructive thoughts is practically certain to experience the results of those words in the form of a destructive 'kickback'. The release of destructive thought impulses alone, without the aid of words, also produces a 'kickback' in more ways than one. First of all, and perhaps most important to be remembered, the person who releases thoughts of a destructive nature must suffer damage through the breaking down of the faculty of creative imagination. Secondly, the presence in the mind of any destructive emotion develops a negative personality that repels people, and often converts them into antagonists. The third source of damage to the person who entertains or releases negative thoughts lies in this significant fact – these thought impulses are not only damaging to others but they *imbed themselves in the subconscious mind of the person releasing them*, and there become a part of their character.

One is never through with a thought merely by releasing it.

When a thought is released, it spreads in every direction through the medium of the ether, but it also plants itself permanently in the subconscious mind of the person releasing it.

Your business in life is, presumably, to achieve success. To be successful, you must find peace of mind, acquire the material needs of life and, above all, attain *happiness*. All of these evidences of success begin in the form of thought impulses.

You may control your own mind; you have the power to feed it whatever thought impulses you choose. With this privilege goes also the responsibility of using it constructively. You are the master of your own earthly destiny just as surely as you have the power to control your own thoughts. You may influence, direct and eventually control your own environment, making your life what you want it to be. On the other hand, you may neglect to exercise the privilege that is yours – to make your life to order, thus casting yourself upon the broad sea of 'circumstance' where you will be tossed hither and yon, like a chip on the waves of the ocean.

CHAPTER 16

THE DEVIL'S WORKSHOP

(The Seventh Basic Evil)

In addition to the six basic fears, there is another evil by which people suffer. It constitutes a rich soil in which the seeds of failure grow abundantly. It is so subtle that its presence is often not detected. This affliction cannot properly be classed as a fear. IT IS MORE DEEPLY SEATED AND MORE OFTEN FATAL THAN ALL OF THE SIX FEARS. For want of a better name, let us call this evil *susceptibility to negative influences*.

People who accumulate great riches always protect themselves against this evil. The poverty stricken never do. Those who succeed in any calling must prepare their minds to resist the evil. If you are reading this philosophy for the purpose of accumulating riches, you should examine yourself very carefully to determine whether you are susceptible to negative influences. If you neglect this self-analysis, you will forfeit your right to attain the object of your desires.

Make the analysis searching. After you read the questions prepared for this self-analysis, hold yourself to strict account in your answers. Go at the task as carefully as you would search for any other enemy you knew to be waiting to ambush you and deal with your own faults as you would a more tangible enemy.

You can easily protect yourself against highway robbers, because the law provides organised cooperation for your benefit, but the 'seventh basic evil' is more difficult to master. It strikes when you are not aware of its presence, when you are asleep and while you are awake. Moreover, its weapon is intangible because it consists of merely a *state of mind*. This evil is also dangerous because it strikes in as many different forms as there are human experiences. Sometimes it enters the mind through the well-meant words of one's own relatives. At other times it bores from within, through one's own mental attitude. Always it is as deadly as poison, even though it may not kill as quickly.

How to Protect Yourself against Negative Influences

To protect yourself against negative influences, whether of your own making or the result of the activities of negative people around you, recognise that you have a *willpower*. Put it into constant use until it builds a wall of immunity against negative influences in your own mind. Recognise the fact that you and every other human being are, by nature, lazy, indifferent and susceptible to all suggestions that harmonise with your weaknesses.

Recognise that you are, by nature, susceptible to all six basic fears. Set up habits for the purpose of counteracting all these fears.

Recognise that negative influences often work on you through your subconscious mind and are therefore difficult to detect. Keep your mind closed against all people who depress or discourage you in any way.

Deliberately seek the company of people who influence you to *think and act for yourself.*

Do not *expect* troubles as they have a tendency not to disappoint.

Without doubt, the most common weakness of all human beings is the habit of leaving their minds open to the negative influence of other people. This weakness is all the more damaging because most people do not recognise that they are cursed by it, and many who acknowledge it neglect or refuse to correct the evil until it becomes an uncontrollable part of their daily habits.

To aid those who wish to see themselves as they really are, the following list of questions has been prepared. Read the questions and state your answers aloud, so you can hear your own voice. This will make it easier for you to be truthful with yourself.

Self-analysis Test Questions

Do you often complain often of 'feeling bad'. If so, what is the cause?

Do you find fault with other people at the slightest provocation?

Do you frequently make mistakes in your work? If so, why?

Are you sarcastic and offensive in your conversation?

Do you deliberately avoid the association of anyone? If so, why?

Do you suffer frequently with indigestion? If so, what is the cause?

Does life seem futile and the future hopeless to you? If so, why?

Do you like your occupation? If not, why?

Do you often feel self-pity? If so why?

Are you envious of those who excel you?

To which do you devote most time: thinking of success or of failure?

Are you gaining or losing self-confidence, as you grow older?

Do you learn something of value from all mistakes?

Are you permitting some relative or acquaintance to worry you? If so, why?

Are you sometimes 'in the clouds' and at other times in the depths of despondency?

Who has the most inspiring influence upon you? 'What is the cause?

Do you tolerate negative or discouraging influences that you can avoid?

Are you careless of your personal appearance? If so, when and why?

Have you learned how to 'drown your troubles' by being too busy to be annoyed by them?

Would you call yourself a 'spineless weakling' if you permitted others to do your thinking for you?

Do you neglect internal bathing until autointoxication makes you ill tempered and irritable?

How many preventable disturbances annoy you, and why do you tolerate them?

Do you resort to liquor, narcotics or cigarettes to 'quiet your nerves'? If so, why do you not try willpower instead?

Does anyone 'nag' you, and if so, for what reason?

Do you have a DEFINITE MAJOR PURPOSE, and if so, what is it, and what plan have you for achieving it?

Do you suffer from any of the Six Basic Fears? If so, which ones?

Have you a method by which you can shield yourself against the negative influence of others?

Do you make deliberate use of autosuggestion to make your mind positive?

Which do you value most, your material possessions or your privilege of controlling your own thoughts?

Do others easily influence you, against your own judgment?

Has today added anything of value to your stock of knowledge or state of mind?

Do you face squarely the circumstances that make you unhappy, or sidestep the responsibility?

Do you analyse all mistakes and failures and try to profit by them, or do you take the attitude that this is not your duty?

Can you name three of your most damaging weaknesses? What are you doing to correct them?

Do you encourage other people to bring their worries to you for sympathy?

Do you choose, from your daily experiences, lessons or influences that aid in your personal advancement?

Does your presence have a negative influence on other people as a rule?

What habits of other people annoy you most?

Do you form your own opinions or permit yourself to be influenced by other people?

Have you learned how to create a mental state of mind with which you can shield yourself against all discouraging influences?

Does your occupation inspire you with faith and hope?

Are you conscious of possessing spiritual forces of sufficient power to enable you to keep your mind free from all forms of FEAR?

Does your religion help you to keep your own mind positive?

Do you feel it your duty to share other people's worries? If so, why?

If you believe that 'birds of a feather flock together', what have you learned about yourself by studying the friends you attract?

What connection, if any, do you see between the people with whom you associate most closely, and any unhappiness you may experience?

Could it be possible that some person you consider to be a friend is, in reality, your worst enemy because of their negative influence on your mind?

By what rules do you judge who is helpful and who is damaging to you?

Are your intimate associates mentally superior or inferior to you?

How much time out of every 24 hours do you devote to:
  a. your occupation
  b. sleep
  c. play and relaxation
  d. acquiring useful knowledge
  e. plain waste?

Who among your acquaintances
  a. encourages you most
  b. cautions you most
  c. discourages you most
  d. helps you most in other ways?

What is your greatest worry? Why do you tolerate it?

When others offer you free, unsolicited advice, do you accept it without question or analyse their motive?

What, above all else, do you most *desire*? Do you intend to acquire it? Are you willing to subordinate all other desires for this one? How much time daily do you devote to acquiring it?

Do you change your mind often? If so, why?

Do you usually finish everything you begin?

Are you easily impressed by other people's business or professional titles, university degrees or wealth?

Are you easily influenced by what other people think or say of you?

Do you cater to people because of their social or financial status?

Whom do you believe to be the greatest person living? In what respect is this person superior to you?

How much time have you devoted to studying and answering these questions? (At least one day is necessary for analysing and answering the entire list.)

If you have answered all these questions truthfully, you know more about yourself than the majority of people. Study the questions carefully. Come back to them once each week for several months. You will be astounded at the amount of valuable additional knowledge you will have gained by the simple method of answering the questions truthfully. If you are not certain of the answers to some of the questions, seek the counsel of those who know you well – especially those who have no motive in flattering you – and see yourself through their eyes. The experience will be astonishing.

You have *absolute control* over but one thing, and that is your thoughts. This is the most significant and inspiring of all known facts! It reflects our divine nature. This divine prerogative is the sole means by which you may control your own destiny. If you fail to control your own mind, you may be sure you will control nothing else.

If you must be careless with your possessions, let it be in connection with material things. Your mind is your spiritual estate! Protect and use it with the care to which divine royalty is entitled. You were given a *willpower* for this purpose.

Unfortunately, there is no legal protection against those who, either by design or ignorance, poison the minds of others by negative suggestion. This form of destruction should be punishable by heavy legal penalties because it may and often does destroy one's chances of acquiring material things that are protected by law.

People with negative minds tried to convince Thomas A. Edison that he could not build a machine that would record and reproduce the human voice, 'Because,' they said, 'no one else has ever produced such a machine.' Edison did not believe them. He knew that the mind could produce *anything the mind could conceive and believe*, and that knowledge was the thing that lifted him above the common herd.

Men with negative minds told F.W. Woolworth he would go 'broke' trying to run a store on five and ten cent sales. He did not believe them. He knew he could do anything, within reason, if he backed his plans with faith. Exercising his right to keep other men's negative suggestions out of his mind, he piled up a fortune of more than a hundred million dollars.

Men with negative minds told George Washington he could not hope to win against the vastly superior forces of the British, but he exercised his divine right to *believe*.

Doubting Thomases scoffed scornfully when Henry Ford tried out his first crudely built automobile on the streets of Detroit. Some said the thing would never become practical. Others said no one would pay money for such a contraption. Ford said, 'I'll belt the earth with dependable motor cars,' and he did! His decision to trust his own judgment piled up a fortune far greater than the next five generations of his descendants could squander. Henry Ford has been repeatedly mentioned, because he is an astounding example of what someone with a mind of their own and a will to control it can accomplish. His record knocks the foundation from under that timeworn alibi, 'I never had a chance.' Ford never had a chance either, but he *created an opportunity and backed it with persistence until it made him richer than Croesus.*

Mind control is the result of self-discipline and habit. You either control your mind or it controls you. There is no halfway compromise. The most practical of all methods for controlling the mind is the habit of keeping it busy with a definite purpose, backed by a definite plan. Study the record of people who have achieved noteworthy success and you will observe that they have control over their own minds; moreover, that they exercise that control and direct it towards the attainment of definite objectives. Without this control, success is not possible.

55 Famous Alibis

People who do not succeed have one distinguishing trait in common. They know all the reasons for failure, and have what they believe to be airtight alibis to explain away their own lack of achievement.

Some of these alibis are clever, and a few of them are justifiable by the facts. But alibis cannot be used for money. The world wants to know only one thing – *have you achieved success?*

A character analyst compiled a list of the most commonly used alibis. As you read the list, examine yourself carefully and determine how many of these alibis, if any, are your own property. Remember, too, the philosophy presented in this book makes every one of these alibis obsolete:

1. IF only I didn't have a wife and family . . .
2. IF only I had enough 'pull' . . .
3. IF only I had money . . .

4. IF only I had a good education . . .

5. IF only I could get a job . . .

6. IF only I had good health . . .

7. IF only I had time . . .

8. IF only times were better . . .

9. IF only other people understood me . . .

10. IF only conditions around me were different . . .

11. IF only I could live my life over again . . .

12. IF only I did not fear what 'they' would say . . .

13. IF only I had been given a chance . . .

14. IF only I now had a chance . . .

15. IF only other people didn't 'have it in for me' . . .

16. IF only nothing happened to stop me . . .

17. IF only I were younger . . .

18. IF only I could do what I want . . .

19. IF only I had been born rich . . .

20. IF only I could meet 'the right people' . . .

21. IF only I had the talent some people have . . .

22. IF only I dared assert myself . . .

23. IF only I had embraced past opportunities . . .

24. IF only people didn't get on my nerves . . .

25. IF only I didn't have to keep house and look after the children . . .

26. IF only I could save some money . . .

27. IF only the boss appreciated me . . .

28. IF only I had somebody to help me . . .

29. IF only my family understood me . . .

30. IF only I lived in a big city . . .

31. IF only I could just get started . . .

32. IF only I were free . . .

33. IF only I had the personality of some people . . .

34. IF only I were not so fat . . .

35. IF only my talents were known . . .

36. IF only I could just get a 'break' . . .

37. IF only I could get out of debt . . .

38. IF only I hadn't failed . . .

39. IF only I knew how . . .

40. IF only everybody didn't oppose me . . .

41. IF only I didn't have so many worries . . .

42. IF only I could marry the right person . . .

43. IF only people weren't so dumb . . .

44. IF only my family were not so extravagant . . .

45. IF only I were sure of myself . . .

46. IF only luck were not against me . . .

47. IF only I had not been born under the wrong star . . .

48. IF only it were not true that 'what is to be will be' . . .

49. IF only I did not have to work so hard . . .

50. IF only I hadn't lost my money . . .

51. IF only I lived in a different neighbourhood . . .

52. IF only I didn't have a 'past' . . .

53. IF only I had a business of my own . . .

54. IF only other people would listen to me . . .

55. IF only – and this is the greatest of them all – I had the courage to see myself as I really am, I would find out what is wrong with me and correct it. Then I might have a chance to profit by my mistakes and learn something from the experience of others. I know there is something *wrong* with me or I would now be where *I would have been if* I had spent more time analysing my weaknesses, and less time building alibis to cover them.

Building alibis with which to explain away failure is a habit as old as the human race, and is fatal to success! Why do people cling to their pet alibis? The answer is obvious. They defend their alibis because *they create* them!

An alibi is the child of one's own imagination. It is human nature to defend one's own brainchild.

Building alibis is a deeply rooted habit. Habits are difficult to break, especially when they provide justification for something we do. Plato had this truth in mind when he said, 'The first and best victory is to conquer self. To be conquered by self is, of all things, the most shameful and vile.'

Another philosopher had the same thought in mind when he said, 'It was a great surprise to me when I discovered that most of the ugliness I saw in others was but a reflection of my own nature.'

'It has always been a mystery to me,' said Elbert Hubbard, 'why people spend so much time deliberately fooling themselves by creating alibis to cover their weaknesses. If used differently, this same time would be sufficient to cure the weakness, then no alibis would be needed.'

In parting, I would remind you that life is a draughts board, and the player opposite you is *time*. If you hesitate before moving, or neglect to move promptly, your draughts will be wiped off the board by time. You are playing against a partner who will not tolerate *indecision*!

Previously you may have had a logical excuse for not having forced life to come through with whatever you asked. However, that alibi is now obsolete because you are in possession of the master key that unlocks the door to life's bountiful riches.

The master key is intangible but it is powerful! It is the privilege of creating, in your own mind, a *burning desire* for a definite form of riches. There is no penalty for the use of the key, but there is a price you must pay if you do not use it. The price is *failure*. There is a reward of stupendous proportions if you put the key to use. It is the satisfaction that comes to all who conquer self and force life to pay whatever is asked.

The reward is worthy of your effort. Will you make the start and be convinced?

'If we are related,' said the immortal Emerson, 'we shall meet.' In closing, may I borrow his thought, and say, 'If we are related, we have, through these pages, met.'

INDEX